THE OFF

EASTERN SHORE OF 13 VIRGINIA GUIDEBOOK

OAK GROVE METHODIST CHURCH

by KIRK MARINER

Illustrations by Dolores Tyler

Miona Publications
Onancock, Virginia
23417

TABLE OF CONTENTS

INTRODUCING THE EASTERN SHORE OF VIRGINIA   **1**
    Where Is It?
    Demythologizing the Eastern Shore
    Why Visit It?
    How to Use This Book

1   ROUTE 13   **15**
    The Main Drag
    Where to Get Off It
    and Why

The Islands:
2   CHINCOTEAGUE AND ASSATEAGUE   **41**
    Vacation Resort on Ocean and Bay

3   TANGIER ISLAND   **58**
    Life in the Center of the Chesapeake

4   THE BARRIER ISLANDS   **67**
    Nature Untamed

The Towns:
5   ACCOMAC   **74**
    Historical Jewel of the Eastern Shore

6   CAPE CHARLES   **81**
    The Railroad's Once-and-Future "City"

7   EASTVILLE   **88**
    History Lives Just Off the Highway

8   ONANCOCK   **95**
    Port Town for Three Centuries

9   PARKSLEY   **105**
    Victoriana on the Railroad

10 WACHAPREAGUE   **110**
    The Fisherman's Enduring Resort

TABLE OF CONTENTS

Up the Seaside:

11 THE LOWER SEASIDE   **116**

    (Kiptopeake to Accomac)
        Blood on the doorstep,
        the oldest Sunday School,
        and sights and smells of the sea

12 THE UPPER SEASIDE   **130**

    (Accomac to Franklin City)
        A boy in an iron coffin,
        a rocket base to outer space,
        and the Eastern Shore's favorite ghost town

Down the Bayside:

13 THE UPPER ACCOMACK BAYSIDE   **142**

    (Maryland to Onancock)
        In the footsteps of a Presbyterian,
        a White Rabbit and a root cellar,
        and the ghost of villages past

14 THE LOWER ACCOMACK BAYSIDE   **155**

    (Onancock to Belle Haven)
        First drama, oldest church,
        steamboat wharves and scenic creeks,
        and a trip through Little Hell

15 THE NORTHAMPTON BAYSIDE   **169**

    (Belle Haven to Shadyside)
        Silver Beach and Crystal Palace,
        Anglican church and ancient inn,
        and the Shore's only cabinet officer

Helps for the Traveler:

16 WHERE TO STAY, WHERE TO EAT   **178**

    MAPS   **200**

    INDEX   **202**

INTRODUCING THE EASTERN SHORE

A guidebook to the Eastern Shore of Virginia?!?

Most people have never heard of the place. The great majority of those who have are not really certain where it is. Many of those who do know where it is are always planning to visit it someday, but most of them never get around to doing so. And most of those who do visit it find that it is somehow not quite what they anticipated.

But—funny thing!—among those who have heard of the Eastern Shore of Virginia, and found out where it is, and paid a visit to see what it has to offer, there is a surprisingly high proportion of people who have fallen in love with the place.

This guidebook is your invitation to join the ranks of those who know and love this unique little peninsula.

Where Is It?

To find the Eastern Shore of Virginia you will need a good map, better than the one you carry in your head, or the map the TV weatherman uses, or the maps those restaurants put on their placemats. Too many such maps, including some that should know better, simply ignore the Eastern Shore of Virginia, or—worse!—consign it altogether to Maryland.

The Eastern Shore of Virginia should not be confused with any one of the several peninsulas separated by the great rivers of Tidewater Virginia. It is not the "Northern Neck" or "The Peninsula" and is nowhere near the rivers York, Rappahannock, or Potomac. The Eastern Shore of Virginia means something different from just the eastern coastline of Virginia. The Eastern Shore of Virginia is a very specific and distinct place that lies twenty or more miles across the Chesapeake Bay from the rest of Virginia. It is the southernmost portion of the Delmarva Peninsula, which is comprised of parts of Delaware, Maryland, and Virginia (hence its name "Del-Mar-Va"), that peninsula without which there would be no Chesapeake Bay and the waves of the Atlantic Ocean would crash into the very heart of Virginia and lash up against the harbor at Baltimore.

Because it is not connected to the rest of Virginia and joined by land only to Maryland, the Eastern Shore of Virginia looks on a map like a logical extension of Maryland. But in fact it has been a part of Virginia since before Maryland came into being. Despite some cultural affinities to the Eastern Shore of Maryland just above it, the Virginia Eastern Shore has always been both officially and emotionally Virginian to the core—though only since 1964 has it been joined to the rest of the state by highway across a 17-mile bridge-tunnel complex.

The Eastern Shore consists of two entire Virginia counties, Accomack and Northampton, with a combined population of about 45,000. Shore folk grow up scrutinizing maps to make sure that they include their Eastern Shore correctly in Virginia, not in Maryland. It says

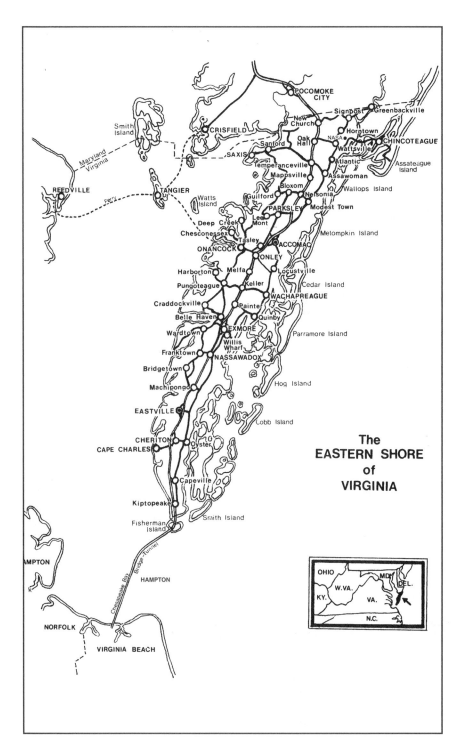

The
EASTERN SHORE
of
VIRGINIA

something about the pace of life on the Shore that although such mis-drawn maps are frequently found, rarely is offense taken at them. Such mistakes are only to be expected in that hurried world west of Chesapeake Bay known as the "Western Shore."

Demythologizing the Eastern Shore

Much of what some people think they know about the Eastern Shore of Virginia is simply not true, so we begin with an attempt to dispel some of the more tenacious misconceptions.

(1) *The Eastern Shore of Virginia is a sandbar or beach, and everything there is on the water.* Not so. You might guess from looking at a map that you can drive up the main highway and get views of the Chesapeake Bay and the Atlantic Ocean in turn, but you cannot. Though it is almost completely surrounded by water, the Eastern Shore is primarily agricultural. Though all of its inhabitants live within a few miles of either ocean or bay, more of them make their living from the land than from the sea. Though the Shore is rightly renowned for its seafood, its fishing, its access to the water, the traveler will find that once he leaves the Bridge-Tunnel heading north up the Shore he will never again see navigable water from the main highway. This is good solid *terra firma*, not an "outer bank."

(2) *The Eastern Shore is backward.* Not so. Geography may decree that the Eastern Shore of Virginia be isolated, but isolated does not necessarily mean "backward." The myth that the Shore is primitive is hard to dispel because there are some pockets of an earlier and simpler day still to be found here, but although its pace of life is slower than in some other places, the Shore is well abreast of the rest of the country. Popular images notwithstanding, local inhabitants wear shoes (except on the beach or while clamming) and have access to the latest styles in clothing and hairdos. People drive automobiles (except on Tangier Island) and worry about the price of gasoline. Owning a pony is not *de rigeur* (except, perhaps, in Chincoteague), and nowhere do the locals carry a six-shooter. Only among a few in a few villages are the local dialects pronounced, and nowhere are visitors shunned or expelled. People on the Eastern Shore send their children away to college (even the Ivy League), jog and play tennis, commute to work, use DSL lines, and talk current politics. Travelers to the Eastern Shore can expect to replenish their supplies of deodorant, the latest in headache remedies, and contact lens solution right from the local store shelves. There are motels with swimming pools and restaurants with salad bars. Time may march slowly here, but it has hardly ceased to march.

(3) *The Eastern Shore is a place of great poverty.* Not so—at least, not exactly. Many people expect to find pronounced and visible poverty on the Eastern Shore of Virginia, as in the stark landscapes of the nation's urban ghettos, or the impoverished mountain communities of Appalachia. In fact, the Eastern Shore itself is a fertile and prosperous land, and most of its people live accordingly: modestly prosperous and comfortable, dwellers in adequate homes, eaters of adequate

food, wearers of up-to-date clothing.

That said, it must also be said that Northampton has, in recent years, too often enjoyed the dubious distinction of having the lowest per capita income among the counties of Virginia, and that neighboring Accomack has not always been that much higher up the list. It will be obvious to even the most casual observer that most African American citizens of the Shore, who constitute between a third and a half of the population, are generally less affluent than their white neighbors, and that there are pockets of real poverty, both black and white. On the very flat and relatively small Eastern Shore the juxtaposition of the haves and the have-nots will often seem startling, simply because they live in such close proximity.

In addition, each summer brings to the Shore a number of this nation's truly poor: migrant farm workers. No doubt the plight of the migrant worker in particular has to some extent contributed to the image of the Eastern Shore in general among those who view the place from a distance. Up close you will probably discover that while its citizens do not evenly share the land's productivity, the Eastern Shore is far from "third-world."

(4) *The Eastern Shore is spectacularly beautiful.* Well, not so—not exactly. The Eastern Shore has a subtle, not a spectacular beauty. In all fairness it must be conceded that there are other parts of the country, and of Virginia, with more scenery, more beautiful vistas, more picture-postcard views awaiting your camera. Breath-taking scenery does not, as some anticipate, lie waiting just around every corner. But there are many beautiful places on the peninsula, and this guidebook will seek them out for you.

Why Visit It?

There is a great deal to see and to sample on the Eastern Shore of Virginia, far more than most people realize. And what it has to offer, it offers in healthy doses.

The Water

The Eastern Shore of Virginia is almost completely surrounded by water. And for those who like fishing, crabbing, hunting, boating, sailing, clamming, water-skiing, swimming, bathing, and just plain looking, the Shore's location is its primary asset.

Ironically the water is not so ever-present on the Shore as most people expect. A century ago that was not the case, for in those days people traveled by water, traded by water, and communicated by water. But when the railroad came to the Shore in 1884, the tracks were laid squarely down the center of the peninsula, and the commerce of the Shore turned its back to the water. Today the automobile has replaced the railroad, but the result is the same: as often as not you have to seek out the water. Today most of the old landings and wharves are quiet and isolated, and chances are that when you come to the water's edge you will find yourself alone with just the sea and the sky and the creatures to which they are home. The water is often hidden away behind a final row of trees or on the other side of a field or down an increasingly narrowing road. But it is never far distant, and it can be found and enjoyed.

On the Chesapeake Bay side of the Shore — "Bayside," in the local terminology—the peninsula is deeply indented by creeks. A "creek" by Eastern Shore standards is not a trickling stream but a wide, shallow tidal estuary. Several of them are half a mile wide or more, able to accommodate large vessels. The creeks of the Bayside are quiet and beautiful, their docks and landings almost too many to number.

On the Atlantic Ocean side of the Shore — "Seaside," as it is called—the ocean itself is for the most part inaccessible. A series of Barrier Islands, uninhabited and isolated, protect the Seaside from the ocean's waves. Only at Assateague Island can the ocean be reached easily for bathing, surfing, fishing, and the like. Fishing boats, both charter and commercial, venture regularly into the Atlantic from Chincoteague, Wachapreague, Willis Wharf, Oyster, and Cape Charles. But except for scattered spots like these, a Seaside landing is likely to find you on one of the small shallow bays that separate the mainland from the Barrier Islands.

Those with their own boats will find the Shore's waters accessible to them on almost every hand. There are publicly maintained landing docks and ramps up and down the Shore, and numerous smaller places from which to launch into the water.

Swimmers will find that only at Assateague will they be able to reach the ocean without a boat. Swimming in the Chesapeake, without the crashing surf, is less exciting but more accessible; the prime spots for it are Guard Shore, Silver Beach, Smith's Beach, and Cape Charles.

There is a scenic quality to the waters around the Shore, even for those who are content simply to observe from the safety of dry ground. For every quiet and isolated dock there is another landing over which looms a significant plantation house from a former century. Here one will find only a dilapidated pier, there the fleet of an entire community of watermen. At one spot only the birds and the lapping waves make a sound, at another the silence will be broken by two men repairing a motor or bringing in a day's catch.

And wherever there is water, this guidebook will help to sniff it out—more than enough of it to please for whatever purpose.

Historic Architecture

A second great drawing-card for the Eastern Shore of Virginia is its historic architecture. For the admirer of old homes and churches and historic buildings, this part of Virginia is nothing less than a treasure trove, for the most part still undiscovered by the thousands who pass through it every year.

There are, in the two counties of the Shore, more than 400 buildings that have been in use since before 1865—approximately one for every 1.7 square miles of land. One may find himself miles from the water on the Shore, but it is a rare spot where some old building is not visible. Historic structures are everywhere to be found: lined up next to each other in villages like Accomac and Eastville, looming magnificently over wide and beautiful creeks, hiding behind barns and tucked away in backyards, even rotting away gradually in the middle of cornfields. Churches, lighthouses, courthouses, schools, even out-buildings are among the landmarks, but the bulk of the Shore's best historic architecture consists of country houses of the 18th and early 19th centuries. Of the hundreds of historic buildings on the Shore, about two dozen are officially designated Virginia Historic Landmarks and included in the National Register of Historic Places.

Unfortunately not all of the Shore's admirable architecture is accessible to the visitor. Although scores of old homes have been preserved, many are off-limits simply because they are private homes. A great number of the finest homes, dating from an age when water transportation had not yet given way to land transportation, stand at the end of long, lonely, sometimes very private lanes, not visible from the public roads and guarded by signs intended to protect the owners' privacy.

Even so, all is not lost for the visitor. Most occupants of the most important examples of historic architecture are aware of the public's interest, so that at least once a year a number of old homes are opened to the public. That once a year is Garden Week, usually observed on the last Saturday in April. On this occasion a few dollars will get you a block ticket that will enable you to amble in and out of some of the finest old homes on the Eastern Shore, or even on the East Coast. Although only about six or eight homes are likely to be open for Garden Week in any given year, a total of about 80 such places have been examined by the public in recent years. If your trip to the Shore is for the purpose of admiring its fine architecture, it should by all means be timed to coincide with the annual Garden Week tour. That time of year is, also, the season when the Shore is at its loveliest.

(Garden Week: Historic Garden Week headquarters are at 12 East Franklin Street, Richmond, Virginia 23219, telephone 804-644-7776. Local headquarters on the Shore changes from year to year, but information about Garden Week can be obtained easily. Inquire at the Eastern Shore Public Library in Accomac, 757-787-3400; the Eastern Shore of Virginia Historical Society in Onancock, 757-787-8012; or the Eastern Shore of Virginia Chamber of Commerce, 757-787-2460. Clerk's offices adjacent to the courthouses in Accomac and Eastville can suggest individuals who may provide information concerning access to specific homes and sites. *The Eastern Shore News*, published twice a week, gives wide publicity to the homes and landmarks opened each Garden Week.)

This guidebook has adopted a conservative approach to viewing the Shore's historic buildings. We tell you what you can see from the public roadway. We lead you to the front gate, but stop there, encouraging you not to violate any resident's right to privacy. This means, of course, that many an important and beautiful building goes unmentioned in this guidebook. But don't be discouraged—there is more than enough to see and admire, even without an invitation to come inside.

A Brief Lesson in the Historic Architecture of the Eastern Shore

The earliest residents of the Eastern Shore brought their architectural styles from England; not for them the rustic log cabin, but the clapboard and brick houses they had known in the mother country.

A law of 1660 required any who would lay claim to a plot of ground to build upon it a house at least 12 feet square. Undoubtedly many of the houses built to meet this requirement looked like "Pear Valley" (see illustration): a single-room clapboard house with large outside chimney and upstairs loft. Soon two other variations on this same design emerged. One was the basic one-room house doubled, two downstairs rooms, each with its own front door, and chimneys at either end. The other, more grand variation was the "story-and-a-half" house, like the "Arbuckle House" in Assawoman (see illustration), in which the upstairs loft has become a full-fledged room with

PEAR VALLEY

dormer windows. Today the peninsula boasts only three homes that can definitely be dated to the 1600s, but in the centuries that followed these three basic designs were repeated many times.

ARBUCKLE HOUSE

About the middle of the 1700s homeowners became more prosperous, and began to add to their basic one-room and two-room
structures. As new sections were added to the house, the old house
often became the "quarter kitchen" of a much larger home, and the
old and the new sections were connected with an enclosed passage-
way, or "colonnade," as the Eastern Shore has always called it. In
this development lay the seeds of the distinctive architectural styles
of the Eastern Shore of Virginia, for as Shore folk built their houses one section at a time, stringing them out in long rows as the family grew or as money became available, they found an almost end-
less variety of ways in which to connect the main house to the older
kitchen. The most simple was to connect the two with a simple
colonnade, as at "Mt. Wharton" near Assawoman (see illustration).
Somewhat grander in design was the "step" or "telescope" house,

MT. WHARTON, ASSAWOMAN

three sections each of which was larger than the one before it, as at
"Drummond's Mill Farm" (see illustration). A third variation, especially popular after 1800, was the "double house," in which a colonnade joined two iden-
tical or near-equal
sections, as in the
"Little House" in
Accomac (see illustra-
tion).

DRUMMOND'S MILL POND

But the most
grand and important
of these variations
was the four-part
arrangement known
as the "big house, lit-
tle house, colonnade,
kitchen," the Eastern Shore of Virginia's own distinctive and most
celebrated style (see illustration of "Seymour House"). Frequent by
the end of the 1700s, the "big house, little house, colonnade,
kitchen" became almost commonplace on the Shore in the early
1800s. There are many variations on the theme, for residents
turned one of the four sections of the house this way or that, or

LITTLE HOUSE, ACCOMAC

strung them out in different ways, or grouped them in an L-shape. The style has never really died out, for even today Eastern Shore people build a new home by stringing together older houses collect-

SEYMOUR HOUSE
"BIG HOUSE, LITTLE HOUSE, COLONNADE AND KITCHEN"

ed from various parts of the peninsula, the "big house" from here, the "little house" from there.

Towards the middle of the 1800s a new style emerged across the Shore: the "ship's carpenter" house. It had two rooms on the first floor, two rooms above on the second floor, and, most characteristically, a gable on the third floor facing front over a central door. By this time bricks were of better quality than in former years, and chimneys could be placed in the center of the house, not simply on the ends. From the "ship's carpenter" house it was only a step to the kind of house that became most common in farm and village across the shore by the beginning of the 20th century: the "T house," in which a back section of two stories was added perpendicular to the basic front "ship's carpenter" section.

Victorian styles entered the Eastern Shore with the coming of the railroad in the 1880s but made only a limited inroad into the predominating native styles. Although a number of admirable Victorian homes can be seen on the Shore—especially in such towns as Accomac, Eastville, Onley, Parksley, and Cape Charles—the Shore's use of bow windows, gabled roofs, turrets, spires, and gingerbread porches was restrained. But because many an older home was "modernized" by Victorian Gothic additions, it sometimes takes a practiced eye to see the native design beneath the added details.

The several architectural styles used on the Eastern Shore of Virginia do not fall into neat chronological periods but were used simultaneously for decades, even centuries. With a little practice, however, the visitor can become adept at dating the many old homes and buildings that dot the Shore's landscape. For those who might enjoy the house-dating game, here are some helpful rules of thumb:

A **gambrel roof** usually indicates a house with considerable age. On the Eastern Shore this feature was most frequently used from 1730 to the 1770s.

A **semi-outside chimney**, sunk halfway into the brick end of a house, is usually later than a chimney that stands completely free of the building. The semi-outside chimney was the "rage" among Eastern Shore buildings from 1770 to 1850.

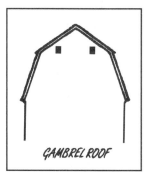

GAMBREL ROOF

Double front doorways usually indicate an older house. This was an 18th-century style usually found in the "two-room" house, the doors being an important source of ventilation.

Porches are _not_ a reliable method of dating old homes on the Eastern Shore. Local builders have always added porches where desired regardless of purity of style, with the result that the style of a porch or the presence of a porch is rarely a sure indication of the date of a house.

By far the best means for dating most old houses on the Eastern Shore of Virginia is the arrangement of the **window panes.** With the coming of the railroad in 1884 it became possible to import window glass cut in larger sections than previously available, with the very happy result that today many a house on the Shore can be dated, regardless of its style, by the size of its window panes. Prior to 1884, the window panes were smaller, often grouped in a "six-over-six" or a "nine-over-six" arrangement. After 1884 the

WINDOW PANES
BEFORE   AFTER
1884   1884

panes were larger, usually grouped "two-over-two." Thus unless a
house or a portion of a house has been "done over" and its windows
deliberately changed, the size and grouping of the window panes
provide one of the most valuable clues to its age.

A Slower Pace

Those who enjoy the country will find that the Eastern Shore of
Virginia is rural in quite a remarkable way. Rarely does one find a place
where villages are so numerous, or so small.

The total population of the Eastern Shore of Virginia is equal
approximately to that of the university city of Charlottesville. Yet there
are no fewer than one hundred and eleven separate and distinct villages
on the Shore, half of which are "official" enough to have a U.S. post
office. Travelers passing through the Shore on Route 13 slow down
(they are at least *supposed* to slow down) every three or four miles for
a small hamlet. Chances are, three or four miles in either direction off
the highway there lies yet another village, another roadside, another
speed zone.

Such tiny towns are so integral a part of the Eastern Shore landscape that few people have ever taken notice of the fact that the number, the size, and the proximity of them is unusual. Of this ancient part
of the country it is safe to say that almost *every* corner or intersection
has its own distinct identity. On the Eastern Shore a few houses constitute a settlement, a hundred residents a sizable town, a thousand people a metropolis. The largest community on the Shore is Chincoteague,
population about 3,500. Only three other towns—Cape Charles,
Exmore, and Onancock—can boast more than 1,000 inhabitants.
There are no cities, not even small ones. But of incorporated towns
(communities of 300 or more with an elected town government), of
which most Virginia counties have two or three, the Eastern Shore has
no fewer than 19.

The village life of the Shore is surely one of its unheralded assets,
and admirers of country stores, post offices, and churches will find more
than enough to explore. The country store is still the center of community life in a number of places, the spot where the local news is dis-
pensed with the soft drinks and the sandwich meat. Many country
stores on the Shore look like scenes out of a simpler era; not a few of
them are the best and only place in town to get a meal-size sandwich.
The local post office may well be located in a building about the size of
your dining room, or or even in a private home. And down the street
will stand the local church, usually Methodist, which shares its preacher
with at least one and maybe two or more other churches every Sunday.

The Shore's towns are as varied and as distinctive as their names:
Oyster, Hacks Neck, Modest Town, Birdsnest, Horsey, Horntown,
Temperanceville. And for every "place" you can distinguish from the
surrounding countryside, the local residents can tell you about another
place just down the road that was, in former years, equally as alive. In
some places, like Marsh Market, Wiseville, Bobtown, and Wagram, the

village is gone and the name alone survives. But wherever there is a corner there is likely to be a name, and if a name also a story. This land has been settled for centuries, time enough for many a community to rise and fall, and leave its mark.

Some of the towns of the Shore cluster near the water, some along the railroad. Others are historic sites, boasting a lovely old church or a handsome mansion house. Not always are they picturesque, nor even identified by a road sign; sometimes you can pass through a "place" without even knowing it. But look closely: Eastern Shore people have always lived like this. It is definitely a part of the charm of the place.

A Modern Place

. . . And many people will find the Eastern Shore of Virginia to their liking not because it is historic, or rural, or isolated, but because it touches their particular interests.

Horse lovers nationwide have heard of Chincoteague's Pony Penning, held every year in late July. Subject of book and magazine article, television program and even Hollywood movie, Pony Penning draws tens of thousands of people every year—without a doubt the primary attraction on the Eastern Shore of Virginia (see page 56).

Space buffs make their way to Wallops Island, just a few miles from Chincoteague, where since 1945 an important part of the nation's space program has taken place. Nineteen of the manmade satellites that have orbited the earth blasted off from this corner of the Eastern Shore of Virginia.

For some people the chief reason for passing through the Eastern Shore is the chance to cross the Chesapeake Bay Bridge-Tunnel, the 17-mile system of bridges and tunnels that links the peninsula to the rest of the state. And the Bridge-Tunnel is definitely something to see, a brief journey out into the world's shipping lanes from the safety of the car.

Bird-watchers, nature-lovers, and naturalists are discovering the Eastern Shore of Virginia, just as the Shore is discovering its own assets in that field of interest. Migrating birds flying south stop on the Shore to build up strength prior to crossing Chesapeake Bay, and flying north stop on the Shore to recuperate from the crossing—and as a result the Shore is a haven for bird-watchers. There are national wildlife refuges at opposite ends of the peninsula, Assateague and Cape Charles, and they offer several events for "birders." The Waterfowl Open House at Assateague each November is described in Chapter 2 (see page 57). The International Migratory Bird Celebration is held annually in May at both refuges: Cape Charles (call 331-2760) and Chincoteague (call 336-6122). The Eastern Shore Birding Festival, sponsored by the Eastern Shore of Virginia Chamber of Commerce annually since 1993, takes place in September at Sunset Beach Inn at the Bridge-Tunnel and in Onancock (757-787-2460, www.esvachamber.org/festivals/birding/). In addition, the Virginia Coast Reserve offers a wide variety of wildlife tours of the Barrier Islands (see Chapter 4).

The Eastern Shore becomes more and more a focus of interest as wooden decoys continue to soar in popularity. Eastern Shore of Virginia decoys rank high among the "classics" so sought by collectors; carved waterfowl by native Eastern Shore carvers have sold for tens of thousands of dollars. In Chincoteague there is a handsome decoy museum and an annual Decoy Festival that brings aficionados to the island in increasing numbers every year.

Even genealogists find their way to the Eastern Shore of Virginia in disproportionate numbers. Not surprisingly, for the records of Northampton County are the oldest continuous court records in the country, dating from 1632, and those of Accomack County are the second oldest, dating from 1663. Many an ancestor has been tracked down in the courthouses in Eastville and Accomac, where these invaluable antique treasures are made accessible to the general public.

Not all the events that bring people to the Eastern Shore are held on Chincoteague Island. Quite apart from the island's famous events (see Chapter 2) the Shore also offers:

Harvest Festival: Held annually in October at the Sunset Beach Resort, sponsored by the Eastern Shore Chamber of Commerce. A celebration of local foods, with music, art exhibits, etc. Tickets available to Chamber members in December, to the public in May (Eastern Shore Chamber of Commerce, P. O. Box 460, Melfa; 757-787-2460; www.esvatourism@esva.net; esvachamber.org).

Between the Waters Bike Tour: Sponsored annually in October by Citizens for a Better Eastern Shore (CBES). Four cycling routes range from 25 to 100 miles; rest stops with refreshments. Reservations required. (Citizens for a Better Eastern Shore, PO Box 882, Eastville; 678-7157; www.biketour@cbes.org).

Small Garden Tour: Annually on the Sunday following Mother's Day, sponsored by the local affiliate of Habitat for Humanity. Self-guided tour of at least five private gardens from colonial to modern, all unique. (Eastern Shore of Virginia Habitat for Humanity, 12143 Bank Avenue, Exmore VA, 442-4687; www.easternshorehabitat.org).

Community Events: A number of Eastern Shore communities hold annual festivals and events celebrating and promoting their heritage and lifestyle. Among them are:

Cape Charles Tomato Festival in September (331-4884, www.esvaccfallfestival. com).

Chincoteague Blueberry Festival in July on the weekend prior to Pony Penning (824-3868, www.chincoteagueblueberryfestival.com).

Onancock Harborfest in September (787-3363; www.onancock.org).

Parksley: Spring Festival (June), Motorcycle Rally (August).

In addition, there are annual fireman's carnivals at Chincoteague and Wachapreague in July. The Chamber of Commerce (757-787-2460) maintains up-to-date information on these and many other such events.

Why visit the Eastern Shore of Virginia? From all appearances, increasing numbers of people are finding their reasons. New inns are cropping up, new shops appearing, more traffic than ever is crossing the Bridge-Tunnel—all in all the signs suggest that the Eastern Shore of Virginia, located within an easy drive of some of the nation's most populous urban centers, is on the verge of being discovered.

So whether you've chosen the Eastern Shore in order to walk its beaches, to photograph the wildlife or the architecture, to indulge in a slower pace for a while, or to seek out an ancestor, you got here just in time.

Welcome. Enjoy.

How to Use This Book

There's nothing complex about this guidebook, but a few pointers may be in order.

All the information you will need about the Shore's commercial establishments is gathered into Chapter 16, "Where to Stay, Where to Eat." The emphasis in the other chapters is on scenic and historical, not commercial, sites.

Chapter 1, on Route 13, is the longest in the book because its material is given twice: once for travelers heading north, once for travelers heading south. Thereafter there are chapters on the islands, and then six chapters devoted to towns. The rest of the Shore is covered by tours that move *up* the Seaside, starting in the south, and *down* the Bayside, starting in the north.

The Eastern Shore of Virginia is relatively small and contained, and the distance across it is nowhere great. It should be easy, referring to the maps on page 2 and at the back of the book, to zip back and forth across the peninsula, or up and down it, as you wish. In fact, we encourage you to do so.

The Shore has one public transportation system, Star Transit (789-8322). Regular routes covering the entire Shore operate 5:45 a.m. - 5:00 p.m. Monday-Friday, and there is also a Demand Response Route in operation 5:45 a.m. - 4:00 p.m.

Places and landmarks marked in this book with an asterisk (*) may be omitted if time is tight. The asterisk does not mean that they are of lesser interest or importance, but only that they may be more distant, or difficult to get to, or less visible from the public roads. On the maps, such tours are indicated by broken lines.

The telephone Area code for the entire Eastern Shore of Virginia is 757.

HOLLY BROOK PLANTATION

1   ROUTE 13

The Main Drag
Where to Get Off It and Why

Unless you plan to arrive by boat or plane, you will undoubtedly enter the Eastern Shore of Virginia via U.S. Route 13, the main artery of the peninsula that connects it with all points south and most points north.

Do not judge the Eastern Shore by Route 13!

Like too many other places in the world, the Shore turns it least attractive face to its main thoroughfare. Once a pleasant drive through flat fertile farmland, Route 13 is fast becoming a continuous stretch of unplanned rural blight. Open fields are giving way to chicken factories, car washes, billboards, and roadside gift shops. Quaint little turn-of-the-century villages are emptying their inhabitants into same-faced new homes lining the highway. If all you want from the Eastern Shore of Virginia is to get through it on your way to somewhere else, Route 13 is for you. If, however, you want to see what the Shore is really like, get off Route 13 as quickly as possible, and as much as possible stay off it.

It is out of evil necessity, not because the highway has so much to offer, that this chapter on Route 13 comes so early. Sooner or later you will have to orient yourself to this backbone and spinal column of the peninsula where most of the services you will need—motels, restaurants, service stations, stores and shops—are to be found. But the real purpose of this chapter is to entice you away from the highway to see some of the Shore's more inviting places.

This chapter reads, first, from north to south, beginning at the Maryland boundary and ending at the Chesapeake Bay Bridge-Tunnel. Then it turns around and repeats itself reading from the opposite direction. So if you're entering the Shore from the north, read on. If you're entering the Shore from the south, across the Bridge-Tunnel, skip to page 27 and start reading there. You will encounter exactly the same information.

And if and when you get the urge to wander aside from the highway, by all means follow that urge. Unless you do, you won't really see the Eastern Shore of Virginia.

ROUTE 13, NORTH TO SOUTH

Begin at the Maryland-Virginia border, 6 miles below Pocomoke City, 35 miles below Salisbury, Maryland. The tour of the UPPER ACCOMACK BAYSIDE also begins at this point (see Chapter 13).

On the right one mile below the state line is the **Virginia Information Center**. This is a state facility; rest rooms and information are free.

NEW CHURCH *(1.7 miles below Maryland)*, the first village on your route, has been settled since the late 1700s, but has little to show for its age. One block off the highway to the right stands **The Garden and the Sea Inn** *(4188 Nelson Road)*, housed in old Bloxom's Tavern. The back part of this building was erected in 1802, the front part, with its lovely Victorian gingerbread porch, about 1900.
Turn in New Church to see:
FRANKLIN CITY, a "ghost town" on the marshes of Chincoteague Bay, see page 139 *(Turn left on Horntown Road #708 to Horntown, then left on Fleming Road #679 to its end, a total distance of 10 miles).*

T'S CORNER *(Traffic signal at Route 175, 4 miles below Maryland)* was known as Logg Town in the 1770s; its present name dates from 1936, when T. Edward Mears opened his service station here.
Turn at T's Corner to see:
CHINCOTEAGUE ISLAND, with **ASSATEAGUE ISLAND** the Shore's most famous and visited community, described in detail in

Chapter 2 *(Turn left on Route #175 and travel 10.5 miles)*.
WALLOPS ISLAND, NASA installation, see page 135 *(On Route #175 after 4.5 miles)*.

OAK HALL *(1 mile below T's Corner)*. **Downings United Methodist Church** on the left is the oldest of its faith on the Shore, established 1772, erected 1854; this building was used by the Union army as a stable for horses during the Civil War. The original **Oak Hall** was an old plantation house that stood on the southern edge of the village; it burned in the 1940s, and today the site is occupied by a large southern-style house on the left *(7465 Lankford Highway)*. **Arcadia High School** preserves the name given to this area by Florentine explorer Giovanni da Verrazzano in 1524.

TEMPERANCEVILLE *(3.5 miles below T's Corner)* is so named because the four men who gave the land for the original town center agreed never to sell whiskey on their lands or to permit a barroom. Just off the highway to the left stands the **Lyric Theatre** *(30182 Temperanceville Road)*, the oldest surviving movie theatre on the Shore (1913), silent since the early 1930s.
Just over a mile below town stands old **Conquest Chapel** on the right, still identifiable as a church although since 1930 it has served as store, shop, home, service station, and just about everything else.
Turn in Temperanceville to see:
SAXIS, isolated, authentic fishing village, see page 146 *(Turn right on Saxis Road #695 and travel 10 miles)*.

MAPPSVILLE *(7 miles below T's Corner)* offers nothing pretty to look at, but two things that may be of interest: local produce stands, and one of the several migrant labor camps which house seasonal farm laborers while they are on the Shore.

NELSONIA *(Traffic signal at Route #187, 9.5 miles below T's Corner)* was once known as Helltown, then renamed for S. R. Nelson, its first postmaster.
Turn in Nelsonia to see:
MODEST TOWN, tiny 19th-century hamlet, see page 133 *(Turn left on Route #187 and travel 1.75 miles)*.
Guard Shore, swimming area with wide view of Chesapeake Bay, see page 149 *(Turn right on Route #187; at Bloxom town line turn right on Bethel Church Road #687 and left immediately on Mitchell Road #684 which becomes Guard Shore Road; follow #684 to water, a total distance of 5 miles)*.

Zion Baptist Church *(4.2 miles below Nelsonia)* juxtaposes two church buildings, a new brick one built in 1917 and, across the road from it, an older frame building of 1852. A quarter mile further south on the left stands **Metompkin Baptist Church**, founded in 1877 as

"Colored Zion Mission."
Turn at Zion Church to see:
UPPER ACCOMACK SEASIDE, tour heading north paralleling Route 13 (see Chapter 12).

FISHER'S CORNER *(Traffic signal at Route #176, 4.5 miles below Nelsonia),* the intersection for Parksley, was known in the 1780s as "Poorhouse Corner."
Turn at Fisher's Corner to see:
PARKSLEY, quiet Victorian residential town with a railroad museum, described in detail in Chapter 9 *(Turn right on Route #176 and travel 2.5 miles).*

ACCOMAC *(Turn left on Front Street 2 miles below the Parksley traffic signal, or left on Courthouse Avenue another 2 miles beyond; Business Route 13 through town parallels Route 13).* The seat of Accomack County is one of the jewels of the Eastern Shore, a small town laden with fascinating architecture and history. It is described in detail in Chapter 5.

TASLEY *(6 miles below Parksley traffic signal),* arguably the least attractive town on the peninsula, does boast one distinction: Its highway overpass above the old railroad is the highest point on the Eastern Shore of Virginia, a whopping 70 feet or so above sea level.

ONLEY *(Traffic signal at Route #179, 7 miles below Parksley light).* Pronounced like the ordinary household word "only," this town was established in 1884 and named for the nearby home of Gov. Henry A. Wise. Its commercial shopping center area is the largest on the Virginia Shore. The handsome **Eastern Shore of Virginia Produce Exchange Building** *(Turn left on Route #179 at the second light and follow 1 block past railroad tracks)* is all that is left of Virginia's first, the nation's second farmers' marketing cooperative; chartered in 1900, it handled a quarter of a billion dollars worth of local produce before dissolving in 1955. **Nandua High School** preserves the name of an Indian village located near here in the 1600s.
Turn in Onley to see:
ONANCOCK, lovely 300-year-old town situated on the water, described in Chapter 8 *(Turn right on Route #179 and travel 1 mile).*
TANGIER, the Shore's most isolated community, an island in the middle of Chesapeake Bay reached by passenger ferry (in season); see Chapter 3 *(Follow Route #179 to ferry dock at Onancock Wharf).*
LOWER ACCOMACK BAYSIDE, tour heading south from Onancock, see Chapter 14.
LOCUSTVILLE, tiny early-19th century village on old stage route, see page 127 *(Turn left on Route #179 and follow through Onley 3 miles, then left on Drummondtown Road #605; total distance of 3.5 miles).*

MELFA *(3.5 miles below Onley)* lies east of the highway and is largely of 20th-century vintage. Visible on the left is the old **Railroad Station**, now a private home. **Eastern Shore Community College** offers a two-year Associate Degree in several fields. The **Eastern Shore Chamber of Commerce** on the right below the college, offers information about events and sites on the peninsula, both Accomack and Northampton Counties.

Turn in Melfa to see:

Oak Grove United Methodist Church, pretty country church with the nation's oldest Sunday school, see page 126 *(Turn left on Main Street #626; at street's end turn left on Phillips Drive #639, then right immediately on Mapp Road #624; after 1 mile turn right on Seaside Road #600; total distance of 1.7 miles).*

KELLER *(6 miles below Onley)* was established in 1884 and named for a railroad contractor. In its prime it had 3 general stores, 5 grocery stores, 2 clothes shops, 2 barber shops, a barrel factory, a feed store, a blacksmith, and 2 hotels, each of which had a barroom. It is now well past its prime. Two short blocks off the highway on Second Street stands lovely little **Mears Memorial United Methodist Church** (1908). *****Hollies Baptist Church** *(Turn right on Route #180, then right on Hollies Church Road #620; total distance of 1 mile)*, erected 1792, is the third oldest church building on the Eastern Shore of Virginia, and architecturally unlike any other.

Turn in Keller to see:

WACHAPREAGUE, quiet fishing resort described in Chapter 10 *(Turn left on Route #180 at northern edge of town and travel 4 miles).*

PUNGOTEAGUE, historic village with Shore's oldest church, site of America's first drama, see page 159 *(Turn right on Route #180 and travel 3 miles).*

HARBORTON, attractive waterfront village of late 1800s, see page 162 *(3 miles beyond Pungoteague on Route #180).*

PAINTER *(Traffic signal at Route 182, 9.75 miles below Onley)*, another railroad town, lies largely to your left. **Garrisons United Methodist Church** *(.25 mile off highway to the left)* is actually two church buildings joined back-to-back; the older front portion was erected in 1855 and moved here in 1927; the newer back portion was erected here in 1905.

Turn in Painter to see:

QUINBY, seaside village with handsome old home Warwick, see page 124 *(Turn left on Route #182 and travel 3 miles).*

EXMORE *(2.75 miles below Painter)* is the fourth largest community on the Virginia Eastern Shore. Established by the railroad in 1884, its name allegedly comes from the fact that it was the 10th station south of Delaware, thus when trains pulled in here there were "X more" stations still to go. Actually the town's name is simply that of a section of Devon in England.

Downtown Exmore *(Turn left on Business Route 13 at first traffic signal)* has in recent years lost most of its businesses to the highway; the visitors most likely to find it attractive are antiquers. Among its more noteworthy structures are the old **Telegraph Office** *(12138 Bank Street)*, dating from about 1910, the 1940s **Duer Building** *(3328 Commercial Street)*, and the abandoned **Department Store** at the corner of Main and Willis Wharf. The commercial building at the corner of Main and Westfield began life in 1938 as the **Cameo Theatre**; the last film shown here was "The Red Pony" in 1957. Crowded by newer structures but still holding its ground is the **John W. Chandler House** *(3342 Main Street)*, built in the Queen Anne style about 1890.

The **Exmore Railroad Museum** *(On the railroad at end of Bank Street)* is housed in a station (c. 1900) moved to this site from Belle Haven; its exhibits include a caboose. Further south on Main Street the tiny **Cobbs Railroad Station**, also moved to town, awaits restoration. Still further south is the **Exmore Diner** *(4264 Main Street),* which began life in New Jersey in 1940 and was brought to this site by railroad in 1953.

When Exmore was founded, the small village of **Hadlock** lay just to the south; what's left of it clusters just off Route 13 where it rejoins the railroad south of Exmore *(Turn right on Bayside Road)*. Nearby, actually on Route 13 in the vacant lot between two businesses just south of the traffic signal, is an old burial ground where the tombstone of Robert Hadlock [1758-1831] bears a handsome but worn family crest.

Turn in Exmore to see:

WILLIS WHARF, fishing village, see page 122 *(From center of town turn left on Willis Wharf Road #603; 1.5 miles)*.

NORTHAMPTON BAYSIDE, tour heading south paralleling Route 13, described in Chapter 15 *(Turn right on Route #183 at traffic signal)*.

NASSAWADOX *(Traffic signal 5 miles below Exmore)*. This relatively new town, founded 1884, bears an old Indian name. **Shore Memorial Hospital**, on the right, is the only hospital on the Eastern Shore of Virginia. The oldest part of town lies to your left. (For more of Nassawadox see page 122.)

Turn in Nassawadox to see:

Brownsville, headquarters of Virginia Coast Reserve, see page 122 *(At traffic light turn left on Rogers Drive, then left on Seaside Road #600 and right on Brownsville Road #608, 2.5 miles)*.

BARRIER ISLANDS, headquarters of Virginia Coast Reserve at Brownsville, see Chapter 4.

FRANKTOWN, tiny country village of 19th-century homes, see page 172 *(Turn right on Franktown Road #609 and travel 1 mile)*.

Hungars Episcopal Church, handsome colonial church of 1742, see page 175 *(Turn right on Rogers Drive #606, then left on Bayside Road #618 and through Franktown 2 miles to church on left. Upon leaving church, turn left on Bayside Road #622 and rejoin Route 13 after 3 miles at Shadyside. This detour past Hungars Church is 9 miles long, compared to the 6 miles of Route 13 that it parallels).*

WEIRWOOD *(1.5 miles south of Nassawadox)* consists of a small cluster of homes, and on the right the old **Machipongo Railroad Station**, now abandoned.
Turn in Weirwood to see:
BAYFORD, attractive waterfront village, see page 174 *(Turn right on Bayford Road #617 and travel 4.2 miles).*
Red Bank Landing, quiet waterfront scene, see page 122 *(Turn left on Red Bank Road #617 and travel 2 miles).*

BIRDSNEST *(3 miles south of Nassawadox)* was established in 1884 and named for old **Birdsnest Tavern** nearby *(see page 122).*

MACHIPONGO *(4.5 miles below Nassawadox)* means "Bad Dust" or "Much Dust" in the Indian language. On the right is the **Barrier Islands Center**, preserving and celebrating the heritage of the islands that line the Shore's seaside. There are interesting exhibits in the stately main building, which is the old Northampton County Almshouse, built in 1803, but two other structures on the site also merit inspection. The smaller single-story frame building was built around 1910 as an annex to the almshouse for the county's African American poor. Even smaller but oldest of all is the old "quarter kitchen," built around 1725 before the farm became the "Poorhouse Farm." *(Open 10:00-4:00 daily except Sundays and holidays; admission charged.)*

SHADYSIDE *(5 miles below Nassawadox)* looks like part of Machipongo, but had its own post office until 1927, and still retains its separate name among some of the older natives.
Turn in Shadyside to see:
Pear Valley, the Shore's oldest house, erected in 1672; see page 177 *(Turn right on Wilsonia Neck Road #628, then left on Pear Valley Lane #689; Pear Valley is the one-room house behind the first farmhouse; .5 mile).*

Holly Brook Plantation *(8 miles below Nassawadox)* stands on the left, not easy to see from this direction, an old Eastern Shore house of four sections built at different times in different places. The oldest portion is the section furthest from the road, dating from the early 1700s; the dormered section adjacent to it dates from about 1840. Both of these sections were moved to this site from Keller, some 17 miles away. The "big house" was built about 1750, and the small section next to it was originally a schoolhouse that stood elsewhere on the property.

EASTVILLE *(Turn right on Courthouse Road 8.7 miles below Exmore, or on Willow Oak Road .8 mile further south; Business Route 13 parallels Route 13 in and through the village).* The tiny village of Eastville, seat of Northampton County, is a showplace—lovely, historic, quiet, and easily accessible. You can detour off Route 13, see the town, and rejoin the highway with no added miles. There is so much to see that the town merits its own Chapter 7.

Eyre Hall *(3 miles south of Eastville turn right on Eyre Hall Lane)* is almost too good to be true. Unquestionably one of the Shore's finest homes, it is so near Route 13 that its entrance gate opens right on the highway. So strong is the tradition of hospitality here that the house is open every year at Garden Week, and its formal gardens are open to the public, free of charge, year round.

Eyre Hall is a Virginia Historic Landmark, "one of the best preserved eighteenth century plantation complexes" in the state. Littleton Eyre built the earliest part of the house in the mid-1700s; his descendants still own the property.

Inside, the house is as impressive as it is outside. The entrance hallway is so large that it constitutes, in effect, a summer parlor, with views of Cherrystone Creek in the distance. Admired architectural details include arched ceilings, carved mantelpieces, and a fine antique wallpaper entitled "The Banks of the Bosphorus," printed in Paris in 1816. Heirlooms abound in every room, including the "Morningstar Bowl," named for a favorite racehorse who so delighted his master that he was given champagne to drink from the family silver. From above the mantels, generations of Eyres look down, painted by the likes of Benjamin West and Thomas Sully.

At the back of the house is the most extensively preserved formal garden on the Eastern Shore of Virginia, a geometrically arranged pattern of magnolia, yew, crepe myrtle, and boxwood. At one side of the garden a brick wall surrounds the family cemetery, where the tombstones are large and horizontal over brick foundations. Adjacent to the cemetery are the ruins of the "orangerie," a substantial brick structure of 1819 which once served as a greenhouse for the estate. During the winters this building housed plants and trees which, during the summers, were moved out into the garden; large windows faced south for sunlight, and two fireplaces, their remains still quite visible, kept the temperature warm enough to protect such tropical trees as oranges and lemons. Vent holes are still visible in the upper walls of the eastern end, facing the garden. The tiny frame structure in the front yard at the picket fence is the "dairy," and opposite towards the garden stands the equally ancient smoke house.

It is half a mile from Route 13 up the tree-shaded lane to this plantation, and well worth the trip for those who are serious about seeing the real Eastern Shore.

*CHESAPEAKE *(Turn left on Cobbs Station Road #636)* is a tiny settlement worthy of note as the *original* place of that name in Virginia. The railroad station established here in 1890 became the nucleus of a little town named Chesapeake, and it still bore that name when, in 1963, a new city on the Western Shore voted to name itself Chesapeake. On June 7, 1963, the village of Chesapeake, population perhaps 50, was required by the U.S. Post Office to relinquish its name to the new City of Chesapeake, and the little village post office was renamed Cobbs. **Tidewater Institute** *(5138 Cobbs Station Road)*, a black private school, operated here from 1907 until 1935, but is no more; an historical marker stands in front of its only remaining building, a dormitory. ***Salem Methodist Church**, described on the historical marker on the left side of Route 13, stood on Cobbs Station Road at its intersection with Seaside Road, a mile to the east; only a few graves mark that site.

CHERITON *(14 miles below Exmore)* is yet another railroad town, larger and more attractive than most of the others, with a tiny but lively downtown business section. It is a town of churches. Baptist and Methodist churches, both erected in 1920, vie prominently for attention from opposite corners at Sunnyside Road. Older than both is **African Baptist Church** *(4224 Sunnyside Road)*, founded in 1869; this building dates from 1892. Still looking churchly, though not always used for that purpose, is the original Baptist building at 21132 North Bayside Road; built in 1898, it has since housed Episcopal and Lutheran congregations. Just south of town stands ***Holmes Presbyterian Church** *(Turn left on Bayview Circle #684, 1 mile below the center of town)*, erected in 1846; still visible on the eastern side of the building is the "slave door"through which African American worshipers entered and climbed to the balcony. From 1943 to 1953 the pastor of this church was John A. Wood, father of author Catherine Marshall, father-in-law of her renowned husband Rev. Peter Marshall, and husband of Leonora W. Wood, who was the subject of her daughter's novel *Christy* in 1967. Leonora Wood was an avid fan of Eastern Shore history, and in 1952 published the first guidebook to the peninsula.

Cherrystone Wharf *(Turn on Cherrystone Road and cross over Route 13, then right immediately on Cherrystone Road #663 and travel 2 miles)* has a view worth turning aside to see. Until the railroad bypassed it, this was the principal landing point for the lower Eastern Shore, with regular ferry service to Norfolk and Hampton. In the 1870s a developer laid out a new town around the wharf, and soon Cherrystone could boast a hotel, a church, several stores, and many homes. **Huntington** *(2598 Cherrystone Road)*, the large house behind the fence as you enter the village, dates from about 1800, but stands where the prominent Col. Obedience Robins lived in the early 1600s. Robins, who lies buried beside the house, was visited here frequently by his good friend the "Laughing King" of the Accomac Indians. **Cherrystone Inn** *(2159 Cherrystone Road)* probably dates back to the 1700s; the cannon in the front yard is a 6-pounder of the 1840s, all that remains of the Civil War defenses of the site. The last house on the right is **Cherry Core** *(2127 Cherrystone Road)*, the central section of which dates from the early 1700s, the largest section of which was moved here from Exmore, 17 miles to the north. Across the street is **Kimberley Cottage** *(2132 Cherrystone Road)*, built in 1880 by the man who attempted to develop Cherrystone, and the last remnants of the **Wharf**, whose ancient pilings are still visible at low tide. South of Cherrystone stood ***The Towne** *(Turn on Townfield Drive)*, the Shore's first community, established in the 1630s and abandoned soon afterwards; the site is now occupied by the Cherrystone Campground. Back on Route 13, not quite visible from the highway, is **Tower Hill**, a handsome brick home c. 1750 *(Turn right on Parsons Circle #641, right into gate of Tower Hill Estates, then take two lefts; .9 mile to Tower Hill)*.

Turn in Cheriton to see:

CAPE CHARLES, the railroad's little resort "city" on the bay, described in Chapter 6 *(Turn right on Route #184 at traffic signal and travel 3 miles)*.

OYSTER, little fishing village, see page 119 *(Take Business Route 13 into center of town, turn left on Sunnyside Road; 1.5 miles)*.

Below the second Cheriton light, look to the right for **Stratton Manor**, sitting well back from the road in the field; this handsome frame house dates from at least as early as 1764. Half a mile beyond it on the left is **Kiptopeake Elementary School** (1993), which boasts, curiously, an obelisk that rises just to the left of its front door. This is a gravestone, for the burial ground of the family who donated the land lies adjacent to the entrance. For a view of ***Old Plantation Creek** turn right on Jacobia Lane #684, 1.1 miles to water. **Lower Northampton Baptist Church** *(1.7 miles below Cheriton light)* is the oldest Baptist congregation on the peninsula, founded by Elijah Baker, who preached his first sermon near here on Easter Sunday 1776. This third building on the site dates from 1913. A mile further south on the left is **First Baptist Church**, founded in 1877; during his years as a seminarian, Martin Luther King preached once in this building of 1913.

Arlington and the Custis Tombs *(3.5 miles below Cheriton turn right on Arlington Road #644; at first intersection keep straight on Custis Tomb Drive. Enter Arlington Plantation and turn right; a small sign points to the tombs adjacent to 2157 Arlington Chase Road, 2.3 miles from Route 13)*

At the edge of a new residential development, in a stately grove of trees overlooking Old Plantation Creek, a brick wall surrounds two ornate old tombstones. This is the burial ground of the Custis family of Arlington, one of the great local dynasties of Eastern Shore gentry. John Custis settled this land and named it Arlington in 1657; John Custis IV inherited the estate in 1714. These are the two men buried here, but the story of Arlington belongs principally to the younger John Custis.

As a wealthy family the Custises maintained a home not only here but also in Williamsburg, and it was there in 1705 that John Custis IV [1679-1750] began wooing the fair Frances Parke [1686-1715]. With elaborate language and courtly letters befitting an 18th-century gentleman he pressed and won his suit, and the two were married, a prominent and handsome couple, in 1706. The marriage proved to be a disaster. Mrs. Custis was a "Tartar, shrewish and curst," while Mr. Custis was easily her equal in eccentric and irascible behavior.

The two grew to dislike each other so much that they would not speak to one another or use each other's name. The faithful butler Pompey was often caught between them. "Pompey, ask your Master if he will have coffee or tea, with cream or sugar," Frances would say. "Tell your mistress, Pompey, that I will take coffee with sugar and cream," John would reply.

One day, quite unexpectedly, John invited Frances to go riding with him in his carriage. She accepted, and they started off in silence towards the bay on what should have been a lovely and leisurely ride. When they reached the shore, however, John Custis did not turn the carriage up the beach but drove straight out into the water. "Where are you going, Mr. Custis?" asked his surprised wife.

"To Hell, Madam," was his reply.

"Drive on, Sir," said she icily. "Anywhere is better than living at Arlington with you."

When the water began to splash around her feet she asked again, and got the same reply, and when the water was almost to the seat of the gig she asked a third time. At this point Custis turned the horse and started back to shore. "If I were to go to Hell and the devil himself were to come out and meet us," said he, never looking at his wife, "I do not believe you would be frightened."

"No, Sir," said she, "I know you well enough not to be afraid of anywhere you may go."

Their marriage reached such an impasse that they finally drew up a long legal document dividing their estate and their daily lives into separate spheres. Mrs. Custis died soon afterwards. John lived in Williamsburg for some years after her death, never remarried, and died in 1750.

The son of this marriage was Daniel Parke Custis, who was the first husband of Martha Washington. The great-grandchildren of John IV and Frances Custis were George Washington Parke Custis and Eleanor "Nelly" Custis, whom George and Martha Washington raised at Mount Vernon. George Washington Parke Custis built a new mansion overlooking the city of Washington on the Potomac, and named it Arlington after this old family land on the Eastern Shore. His daughter married Robert E. Lee, who owned the estate until it was confiscated by the Federal government during the Civil War.

The mansion at Arlington, built about 1670, was in its time one of the finest houses in Virginia, but eventually fell into ruin and disappeared. It was the site of an extensive archaelogical survey (1988-1994), after which the excavation was backfilled in such a manner as to show the size and location of the house; the site is open daily free of charge for self-guided tours. A much later house stands at the end of a long lane as you return to Route 13; this too bears the name Arlington.

There is a tradition that John Custis IV chose to be buried standing up. For certain he carved upon his tomb his insistence that he

> Liv'd but Seven Years
> which was the space of time
> He Kept a Bachelors house
> at Arlington.

His wife Frances lies buried in Williamsburg, apart in death as in life.

THE CAPE. At Capeville *(4 miles below Cheriton)*, Route 13 rejoins the route of an old railroad for its final dash down the cape to the Bridge-Tunnel. The several small villages in this area lie off the highway to the left. The old **Townsend Railroad Station** stands on the right at Townsend Drive #646. ***Pickett's Harbor** (Turn right on Townsend Drive, then right on Arlington Road #645 and left on Pickett's Harbor Drive #646)* offers an isolated view of the bay. **Kiptopeake State Park** *(Turn right on Kiptopeake Drive #704)* occupies the site where the ferries docked from 1950 until 1964, its harbor created by sunken concrete-filled ships resting on the bottom of the bay. Apart from the ships themselves, the view across the Chesapeake here is wide and beautiful. The park offers swimming, fishing, camping, trails, and scenery; fee for parking. Turn left immediately before the Bridge-Tunnel toll booth for the **Eastern Shore of Virginia Welcome Center**, which offers information, local displays, and rest rooms.

Turn at the Bridge-Tunnel to see:

Eastern Shore of Virginia National Wildlife Refuge, with scenic views across the cape, see page 117 *(Turn left on Seaside Road #600 at Sunset Beach Inn and travel .5 mile).*

LOWER SEASIDE, tour heading north paralleling Route 13, described in Chapter 11 *(Turn left on Seaside Road #600 at Sunset Beach Inn).*

(Continue reading through "South Island," although the next paragraphs are also for those traveling Route 13 from south to north.)

ROUTE 13, SOUTH TO NORTH

The Chesapeake Bay Bridge-Tunnel is from either direction a magnificent sight, well worth, at least once, the time, the distance, and the toll ($12) that it takes to see it.

When you approach it from the north, the Bridge-Tunnel turns its many sides to you, laid out like a map for examination. And just off the Shore you climb the trestle to its highest point where, on a good day, you can see the opposite shore, 17 miles away.

When you approach it from the south, heading towards the Shore from Virginia Beach, you're on the Bridge-Tunnel almost before you know it. Your road narrows, you climb a few feet, then suddenly the land stops beneath you and you're headed straight out to sea. The rails on either side converge in the distance, as if you're heading nowhere.

The Chesapeake Bay Bridge-Tunnel, the answer to the Eastern Shore's centuries-old dream of being linked to the rest of the state, opened on April 12, 1964, and has been greeted on every hand with superlatives. One of "Five Future Wonders of the World," said *Reader's Digest*, one of "Seven Engineering Wonders of the World," said others; "World's Longest Bridge-Tunnel System," says the *Guinness Book of World Records*. The Bridge-Tunnel took four years, $200 million, half a million cubic yards of concrete, 55,000 tons of steel, and seven human lives to build. It crosses the mouth of the Chesapeake Bay from Cape Charles on the north to Virginia Beach on the south, 17.5 miles of two-lane highway of which 15.5 are over water and 2 are under water. Before the Bridge-Tunnel, a fleet of car ferries plied between Kiptopeake Beach and Little Creek in Norfolk in 90 minutes; since 1964 the same trip takes only about 20 minutes.

The span had only two lanes until 1999 when the southbound trestle was completed at a cost of $300 million, 50 percent more than the original construction. Still to come will be parallel tunnels, which will necessitate the creation of new "islands" and, therefore, cost even more ($600 million).

The description that follows runs first from north to south for those starting out from the Shore. If you're driving in the opposite direction, skip now and begin reading at "South Island" below, where the same information is given in reverse for those heading up the Shore from Virginia Beach.

Wise Point, the very tip of the Delmarva Peninsula, is named for John S. Wise [1846-1913], congressman and writer, whose home "Kiptopeake" stood just west of the Administration Building and toll booths. The first trestle takes you over Fisherman Inlet to **Fisherman Island**, a wildlife refuge with no stopping or entry permitted. Just to the east is Smith Island, discovered and named by Captain John Smith in 1608; on it stands **Cape Charles Lighthouse**, erected 1895, at

1.2 million candlepower the strongest light in the Chesapeake region.

North Channel Bridge carries the highway to its highest point on the span, 80 feet above the surface of the water. From this bridge you can likely see the other shore, Virginia Beach, on your left. For the most part the Bridge-Tunnel highway is 20 feet above the water, and the water beneath it is from 20 to 40 feet deep. This bridge, however, crosses a channel that is 70 feet deep, and without it fishermen pursuing their catch would have to detour 11 miles out into the bay over the first tunnel to round this point. The bridge is sometimes called "Dunton's Hump" after Ammon G. Dunton, who persuaded the builders to include it in the span in order to accommodate the local fishermen.

Six miles separate Wise Point from the first of the four islands that are the anchor points for the two tunnels that dip beneath the bay. **Chesapeake Channel Tunnel** is a little over a mile long, and is crossed by vessels heading up the bay to Baltimore and points north. It was necessary to tunnel, rather than to bridge, the two main channels at the bay's entrance to insure that the vital harbor at Hampton Roads would not be blocked by fallen trestles in the event of war. The tunnel ends on **West Island**, from which you should be able to see the City of Hampton on your right, with the tall Hotel Chamberlain at Old Point Comfort.

Thimble Shoals Channel Tunnel burrows beneath the channel used by vessels going into Hampton Roads, and is slightly longer than the other tunnel. Many people do not understand that highway tunnels such as this do not rest on the floor of the bay, but are dug into the ground beneath the bottom. When you reach the lowest part of these tunnels, you will be 47 feet beneath not the surface of the bay but the floor of the bay.

South Island is the only part of the Bridge-Tunnel on which you can stop for close examination. It is at the southern end of the Thimble Shoals Channel Tunnel, 3.3 miles from the Virginia Beach shore.

Viewed up close, South Island is all concrete and asphalt—not surprisingly, since all four of the islands in this span are man-made. It took over four million cubic yards of sand and more than a million tons of rock to raise these islands up from the ocean floor. Each island covers 8 acres and is 30 feet above the water.

On South Island there is a public, free fishing pier, for the 2,600 concrete piles on which the highway rests attract great schools of fish. The view from South Island, aided by coin-operated telescopes, includes three lighthouses, two at Cape Henry and one at Cape Charles, which from this distance seems to float on the waves. On the Virginia Beach shore can be seen the highway bridge over Lynnhaven Inlet (left of Route 13), Ocean View (right of Route 13), Hampton, and—if you're lucky—large ocean-going vessels headed into or out of Hampton Roads. There is also a restaurant, with gift and souvenir shop.

Historical panels on the northern side of South Island include a small bronze plaque commemrating the **Battle of the Chesapeake**

Capes, a decisive naval engagement of the American Revolution fought in these waters on September 5, 1781. A French fleet of 28 ships, allies of the Americans and commanded by Admiral Francois Joseph Paul Comte de Grasse, lay at anchor near the Virginia Beach shore just east of South Island, effectively bottling up Britain's land forces at Yorktown under General Cornwallis. On the morning of September 5 an equally large British fleet under Admirals Graves and Hood bore down upon them from the Atlantic, intent upon breaking through to relieve Cornwallis. Admiral de Grasse quickly put his ships to sea and about 5 miles from Cape Henry, at 4:15 in the afternoon, engaged the British line in battle. No ships were lost on either side, but because the British could not break through to relieve Cornwallis, an American victory at Yorktown was insured, ending the Revolution. Had you been able to stand here in 1781, you could have seen many of the maneuvers of this very important battle.

Also on South Island is another plaque honoring the man chiefly responsible for the building of the Bridge-Tunnel and for whom it is officially named: Lucius J. Kellam Jr. [1911-1995] of Belle Haven on the Eastern Shore.

(This ends the tour of Route 13 from north to south. What follows is the same information from south to north.)

Thimble Shoals Channel Tunnel burrows beneath the channel used by vessels going into Hampton Roads, and is slightly longer than the other tunnel. It was necessary to tunnel, rather than to bridge, the two main channels at the bay's entrance to insure that the vital harbor at Hampton Roads would not be blocked by fallen trestles in the event of war. Emerging from the tunnel, heading for **West Island**, you should be able to see the City of Hampton on your left, with the tall Hotel Chamberlain at Old Point Comfort.

Chesapeake Channel Tunnel is a little over a mile long, and dips beneath the channel used by vessels heading up the bay to Baltimore and points north. Many people do not understand that highway tunnels such as this do not rest on the floor of the bay, but are dug into the ground beneath the bottom. When you reach the lowest part of these two tunnels, you will be 47 feet beneath not the surface of the bay but the floor of the bay.

Six miles separate the second tunnel from land, and as you approach the Eastern Shore the highway rises to **North Channel Bridge**, the highest point on the span, 80 feet above the surface of the water. From here you can likely see the other shore, Virginia Beach, on your right. For the most part the Bridge-Tunnel highway is 20 feet above the water, and the water beneath it is from 20 to 40 feet deep. This bridge, however, crosses a channel that is 70 feet deep, and without it fishermen pursuing their catch would have to detour 11 miles out into the bay over the first tunnel to round this point. The bridge is sometimes called "Dunton's Hump" after Ammon G. Dunton, who persuaded the builders to include it in the span in order to accommodate the local fishermen.

At the end of North Channel Bridge you land on **Fisherman Island**, a wildlife refuge with no stopping or entry permitted. Just to the east, straight ahead, is Smith Island, discovered and named by Captain John Smith in 1608; on it is **Cape Charles Lighthouse**, erected in 1895, at 1.2 candlepower the strongest light in the Chesapeake region. The final span takes you over Fisherman Inlet to **Wise Point**, the very tip of the Delmarva Peninsula. This is named for John S. Wise [1846-1913], congressman and writer, whose home "Kiptopeake" stood just west of the Administration Building and toll booths. The **Eastern Shore of Virginia Welcome Center** *(First right turn, opposite the toll booth)* offers information, local displays, and rest rooms.

Turn at Wise Point to see:

Eastern Shore of Virginia National Wildlife Refuge, with scenic views across the cape, see page 117 *(Turn right on Seaside Road #600 at Sunset Beach Inn and travel .5 mile)*.

LOWER SEASIDE, tour heading north paralleling Route 13, described in Chapter 11 *(Turn right on Seaside Road #600 at Sunset Beach Inn.)*

THE CAPE. From the Bridge-Tunnel to Capeville, Route 13 parallels the route of an old railroad. The several small villages in this area lie off the highway to the right. **Kiptopeake State Park** *(Turn left on Arlington Road #645, then left on Kiptopeake Drive #704)* occupies the site where the ferries docked from 1950 until 1964, its harbor created by sunken concrete-filled ships resting on the bottom of the bay. Apart from the ships themselves, the view across the Chesapeake here is wide and beautiful. The park offers swimming, fishing, camping, trails, and scenery; fee for parking. The old **Townsend Railroad Station** stands on the left at Townsend Drive #646. ***Pickett's Harbor** *(Turn left on Townsend Drive, then left on Arlington Road #645 and left on Pickett's Harbor Drive #646)* offers an isolated view of the bay.

Arlington and the Custis Tombs *(6 miles above Bridge-Tunnel turn left on Arlington Road #644; at first intersection keep straight on Custis Tomb Drive. Enter Arlington Plantation and turn right; a small sign points to the tombs adjacent to 2157 Arlington Chase Road, 2.3 miles from Route 13)*.

At the edge of a new residential development, in a stately grove of trees overlooking Old Plantation Creek, a brick wall surrounds two ornate old tombstones. This is the burial ground of the Custis family of Arlington, one of the great local dynasties of Eastern Shore gentry. John Custis settled this land and named it Arlington in 1657; John Custis IV inherited the estate in 1714. These are the two men buried here, but the story of Arlington belongs principally to the younger John Custis.

As a wealthy family the Custises maintained a home not only here but also in Williamsburg, and it was there in 1705 that John Custis IV [1679-1750] began wooing the fair Frances Parke [1686-1715]. With elaborate language and courtly letters befitting an 18th-century gentleman he pressed and won his suit, and the two were married, a prominent and handsome couple, in 1706. The marriage proved to be a disaster. Mrs. Custis was a "Tartar, shrewish and curst," while Mr. Custis was easily her equal in eccentric and irascible behavior.

The two grew to dislike each other so much that they would not speak to one another or use each other's name. The faithful butler Pompey was often caught between them. "Pompey, ask your Master if he will have coffee or tea, with cream or sugar," Frances would say. "Tell your mistress, Pompey, that I will take coffee with sugar and cream," John would reply.

One day, quite unexpectedly, John invited Frances to go riding with him in his carriage. She accepted, and they started off in silence towards the bay on what should have been a lovely and leisurely ride. When they reached the shore, however, John Custis did not turn the carriage up the beach but drove straight out into the water. "Where are you going, Mr. Custis?" asked his surprised wife.

"To Hell, Madam," was his reply.

"Drive on, Sir," said she icily. "Anywhere is better than living at Arlington with you."

When the water began to splash around her feet she asked again, and got the same reply, and when the water was almost to the seat of the gig she asked a third time. At this point Custis turned the horse and started back to shore. "If I were to go to Hell and the devil himself were to come out and meet us," said he, never looking at his wife, "I do not believe you would be frightened."

"No, Sir," said she, "I know you well enough not to be afraid of anywhere you may go."

Their marriage reached such an impasse that they finally drew up a long legal document dividing their estate and their daily lives into separate spheres. Mrs. Custis died soon afterwards. John lived in Williamsburg for some years after her death, never remarried, and died in 1750.

The son of this marriage was Daniel Parke Custis, who was the first husband of Martha Washington. The great-grandchildren of John IV and Frances Custis were George Washington Parke Custis and Eleanor "Nelly" Custis, whom George and Martha Washington raised at Mount Vernon. George Washington Parke Custis built a new mansion overlooking the city of Washington on the Potomac, and named it Arlington after this old family land on the Eastern Shore. His daughter married Robert E. Lee, who owned the estate until it was confiscated by the Federal government during the Civil War.

The mansion at Arlington, built about 1670, was in its time one of the finest houses in Virginia, but eventually fell into ruin and disappeared. It was the site of an extensive archaelogical survey (1988-1994), after which the excavation was backfilled in such a manner as to show the size and location of the house; the site is open daily free of charge for self-guided tours. A much later house stands at the end of a long lane as you return to Route 13; this too bears the name Arlington.

There is a tradition that John Custis IV chose to be buried standing up. For certain he carved upon his tomb his insistence that he

> Liv'd but Seven Years
> which was the space of time
> He Kept a Bachelor's house
> at Arlington.

His wife Frances lies buried in Williamsburg, apart in death as in life.

First Baptist Church (*6.5 miles above Bridge-Tunnel*) was founded in 1877 and in this building (1913) Martin Luther King preached once during his years as a seminarian. **Lower Northampton Baptist Church** (*7.5 miles above Bridge-Tunnel*) is the oldest Baptist congregation on the peninsula, founded by Elijah Baker, who preached his first sermon near here on Easter Sunday 1776. This third building on the site dates from 1913. For a view of *Old Plantation Creek turn left on Jacobia Lane #682, 1.1 miles to water. Look to the right for **Kiptopeake Elementary School** (1993), which boasts, curiously, an obelisk that rises just to the left of its front door. This is a gravestone, for the burial ground of the family who donated the land lies adjacent to the entrance. On the left half a mile beyond the school is **Stratton Manor**, sitting well back from the road in the field, a handsome frame house dating from at least as early as 1764.

CHERITON (*9.5 miles above Bridge-Tunnel*) is the first of several railroad towns founded in 1884, larger and more attractive than most of the others, with a tiny but lively downtown business section. It is a town of churches. Just south of town stands *Holmes Presbyterian Church (*Turn right at first traffic signal, then right on Bayview Circle #684, 1 mile below the center of town), erected in 1846; still visible on the eastern side of the building is the "slave door" through which African American worshipers entered and climbed to the balcony. From 1943 to 1953 the pastor of this church was John A. Wood, father of author Catherine Marshall, father-in-law of her renowned husband Rev. Peter Marshall, and husband of Leonora W. Wood, who was the subject of her daughter's novel Christy in 1967. Leonora Wood was an avid fan of Eastern Shore history, and in 1952 published the first guidebook to the peninsula.

In the center of town, Baptist and Methodist churches, both erected in 1920, vie prominently for attention from opposite corners at Sunnyside Road. Older than both is **African Baptist Church** (*4224 Sunnyside Road*), founded in 1869; this building dates from 1892. Still looking churchly, though not always used for that purpose, is the original Baptist building at 21132 North Bayside Road; built in 1898, it has since housed Episcopal and Lutheran congregations.

Tower Hill is not quite visible from Route 13; it is a handsome brick home of c.1750 overlooking King's Creek *(Turn left on Parsons Circle #641, right into gate of Tower Hill Estates, then take two lefts; .9 mi to Tower Hill)*.

Cherrystone Wharf *(At second signal turn left on Townfield Drive #680, then right immediately on Cherrystone Road #663 and travel 2 miles)* has a view worth turning aside to see. Until the railroad bypassed it, this was the principal landing point for the lower Eastern Shore, with regular ferry service to Norfolk and Hampton. In the 1870s a developer laid out a new town around the wharf, and soon Cherrystone could boast a hotel, a church, several stores, and many homes. **Huntington** *(2598 Cherrystone Road)*, the large house behind the fence as you enter the village, dates from about 1800, but stands where the prominent Col. Obedience Robins lived in the early 1600s. Robins, who lies buried beside the house, was visited here frequently by his good friend the "Laughing King" of the Accomac Indians. **Cherrystone Inn** *(2159 Cherrystone Road)* probably dates back to the 1700s; the cannon in the front yard is a 6-pounder of the 1840s, all that remains of the Civil War defenses of the site. The last house on the right is **Cherry Core** *(2127 Cherrystone Road)*, the central section of which dates from the early 1700s, the largest section of which was moved here from Exmore, 17 miles to the north. Across the street is **Kimberley Cottage** *(2132 Cherrystone Road)*, built in 1880 by the man who attempted to develop Cherrystone, and the last remnants of the **Wharf**, whose ancient pilings are still visible at low tide. South of Cherrystone stood *****The Towne** *(Turn on Townfield Drive)*, the Shore's first community, established in the 1630s and abandoned soon afterwards; the site is now occupied by the Cherrystone Campground.

Turn in Cheriton to see:

CAPE CHARLES, the railroad's little resort "city" by the bay, described in Chapter 6 *(Turn left on #184 at the first traffic signal and travel 3 miles)*.

OYSTER, little fishing village, see page 119 *(Take Business Route 13 into center of town; turn right on Sunnyside Road; 1.5 miles)*.

*****CHESAPEAKE** *(3 miles above Cheriton turn right on Cobbs Station Road #636)* is a tiny settlement worthy of note as the *original* place of that name in Virginia. The railroad station established here in 1890 became the nucleus of a little town named Chesapeake, and it still bore that name when, in 1963, a new city on the Western Shore voted to name itself Chesapeake. On June 7, 1963, the village of Chesapeake, population perhaps 50, was required by the U.S. Post Office to relinquish its name to the new City of Chesapeake, and the little village post office was renamed Cobbs. **Tidewater Institute** *(5138 Cobbs Station Road)*, a black private school, operated here from 1907 to 1935, but is no more; an historical marker stands in front of its only remaining building, a dormitory. ***Salem Methodist Church**, described on the historical marker on Route 13, stood on Cobbs Station Road at its intersection with Seaside Road, a mile to the east; only a few graves mark that site.

Eyre Hall *(3 miles above Cheriton turn left on Eyre Hall Lane)* is almost too good to be true. Unquestionably one of the Shore's finest homes, it is so near Route 13 that its entrance gate opens right on the highway. So strong is the tradition of hospitality here that the house is open every year at Garden Week, and its formal gardens are open to the public, free of charge, year round.

Eyre Hall is a Virginia Historic Landmark, "one of the best preserved eighteenth century plantation complexes" in the state. Littleton Eyre built the earliest part of the house in the mid-1700s; his descendants still own the property.

Inside, the house is as impressive as it is outside. The entrance hallway is so large that it constitutes, in effect, a summer parlor, with views of Cherrystone Creek in the distance. Admired architectural details include arched ceilings, carved mantelpieces, and a fine antique wallpaper entitled "The Banks of the Bosphorus," printed in Paris in 1816. Heirlooms abound in every room, including the "Morningstar Bowl," named for a favorite racehorse who so delighted his master that he was given champagne to drink from the family silver. From above the mantels, generations of Eyres look down, painted by the likes of Benjamin West and Thomas Sully.

At the back of the house is the most extensively preserved formal garden on the Eastern Shore of Virginia, a geometrically arranged pattern of magnolia, yew, crepe myrtle, and boxwood. At one side of the garden a brick wall surrounds the family cemetery, where the tombstones are large and horizontal over brick foundations. Adjacent to the cemetery are the ruins of the "orangerie," a substantial brick structure of 1819 which once served as a greenhouse for the estate. During the winters this building housed plants and trees which, during the summers, were moved out into the garden; large windows faced south for sunlight, and two fireplaces, their remains still quite visible, kept the temperature warm enough to protect such tropical trees as oranges and lemons. Vent holes are still visible in the upper walls of the eastern end, facing the garden. The tiny frame structure in the front yard, at the picket fence, is the "dairy," and opposite towards the garden stands the equally ancient smoke house.

It is half a mile from Route 13 up the tree-shaded lane to this plantation, and well worth the trip for those who are serious about seeing the real Eastern Shore.

EASTVILLE *(Turn left on Courthouse Road 5 miles above Cheriton, or left on Willow Oak Road 1.5 miles further north; Business Route 13 parallels Route 13 in and through the village).* The tiny village of Eastville, seat of Northampton County, is a showplace—lovely, historic, quiet, and easily accessible. You can detour off Route 13 here, see the town, and rejoin the highway with no added miles. There is so much to see that the town merits its own Chapter 7.

Holly Brook Plantation *(On the right 1.5 miles above Eastville)* is an old Eastern Shore house of four sections built at different times and in different places. The oldest portion is the section furthest from the road, dating from the early 1700s; the dormered section adjacent to it dates from about 1840. Both of these sections were moved to this site from Keller, some 17 miles away. The "big house" was built about 1750, and the small section next to it was originally a schoolhouse that stood elsewhere on the property.

SHADYSIDE *(3.5 miles above Eastville)* appears to be part of the village of Machipongo, which lies half a mile beyond it. But it had its own post office until 1927, and still retains its separate name among some of the older natives.
Turn in Shadyside to see:
Pear Valley, the Shore's oldest house, erected in 1672; see page 177 *(Turn left on Wilsonia Neck Drive #628, then left on Pear Valley Lane #689; Pear Valley is the one-room house behind the first farmhouse; .5 mile).*
Hungars Episcopal Church, handsome colonial church of 1742; see page 175 *(Turn left on Wilsonia Neck Drive #628 then right immediately on Bayside Road #618 and travel 3.5 miles to church on right. Upon leaving church, turn right on Bayside Road #619, pass through Franktown, and turn right on Rogers Drive #606, rejoining Route 13 at Nassawadox. This detour past Hungars Church is 9 miles long, compared to the 6 miles of Route 13 that it parallels).*

MACHIPONGO *(4 miles above Eastville)* means "Bad Dust" or "Much Dust" in the Indian language. On the left is the new **Barrier Islands Center**, preserving and celebrating the heritage of the islands that line the Shore's seaside. There are interesting exhibits in the stately main building, which is the old Northampton County Almshouse, built in 1803, but two other structures on the site also merit inspection. The smaller single-story frame building was built around 1910 as an annex to the almshouse for the county's African American poor. Even smaller but oldest of all is the old "quarter kitchen," built around 1725 before the farm became the "Poorhouse Farm." *(Open 10:00-4:00 daily except Sundays and holidays; admission charged.)*

BIRDSNEST *(7 miles above Eastville)* was established in 1884 and named for old **Birdsnest Tavern** nearby *(see page 122).*

WEIRWOOD *(8.5 miles above Eastville)* consists of a small cluster of homes, and on the left the old **Machipongo Railroad Station**, now abandoned.

Turn in Weirwood to see:

BAYFORD, attractive waterfront village, see page 174 *(Turn left on Bayford Road #617 and travel 4.2 miles)*.

Red Bank Landing, quiet waterfront scene, see page 122 *(Turn right on Red Bank Road #617 and travel 2 miles)*.

NASSAWADOX *(Traffic signal 9.5 miles above Eastville)*. This relatively new town, founded 1884, bears an old Indian name. **Shore Memorial Hospital**, on your left, is the only hospital on the Eastern Shore of Virginia. The oldest part of town lies to your right. (For more of Nassawadox see page 122.)

Turn in Nassawadox to see:

Brownsville, headquarters of Virginia Coast Reserve, see page 122 *(At traffic light turn right on Rogers Drive, then left on Seaside Road #600 and right on Brownsville Road #608, 2.5 miles)*.

BARRIER ISLANDS, headquarters at Brownsville, see Chapter 4.

FRANKTOWN, tiny country village of 19th-century homes, see page 172 *(Turn left on Franktown Road #609 and travel 1 mile)*.

*HADLOCK is a tiny village, predating the founding of its larger neighbor Exmore; what's left of it clusters just off the highway where the Exmore bypass veers to the left *(Turn left at first traffic signal on Bayside Road #618)*. Nearby, actually on Route 13 in the vacant lot between two businesses just south of the second traffic signal, is an old burial ground where the tombstone of Robert Hadlock [1758-1831] bears a handsome but worn family crest.

EXMORE *(3 miles above Nassawadox)* is the fourth largest community on the Virginia Eastern Shore. Established by the railroad in 1884, its name allegedly comes from the fact that it was the 10th station south of Delaware, thus when trains pulled in here there were "X more" stations still to go. Actually the town's name is simply that of a section of Devon in England.

Downtown Exmore *(Turn right on Business Route 13 at edge of town)* has in recent years lost most of its businesses to the highway; the visitors most likely to find it attractive are antiquers. The **Exmore Diner** *(4264 Main Street)* began life in New Jersey in 1940, and was brought to this site by railroad in 1953. Exmore has two old railroad stations, both of which were moved to town. On the left as you approach downtown is the old Cobbs Railroad Station, awaiting restoration. The **Exmore Railroad Museum** *(On the railroad at end of Bank Street)* is housed in a station (c. 1900) moved from Belle Haven; its exhibits include a caboose.

In downtown Exmore the **John W. Chandler House** *(3342 Main Street)*, built in the Queen Anne style about 1890, still holds its ground though crowded by newer structures. Among the more noteworthy buildings in this section are the old **Telegraph Office** *(12138 Bank Street)*, dating from about 1910, the 1940s **Duer Building** *(3328 Commercial Street)*, and the abandoned **Department Store** at the corner of Main and Willis Wharf. The commercial building at the corner of Main and Westfield began life in 1938 as the **Cameo Theatre**; the last film shown here was "The Red Pony" in 1957.

Turn in Exmore to see:

WILLIS WHARF, fishing village, see page 122 *(From center of town turn right on Willis Wharf Road #603, 1.5 miles)*.

NORTHAMPTON BAYSIDE, tour heading south paralleling Route 13, described in Chapter 15 *(Turn left on Route #183 at traffic signal)*.

PAINTER *(Traffic signal at Route #182, 2.75 miles above Exmore)*, another railroad town, lies largely to your right. **Garrisons United Methodist Church** *(.25 mile off highway to right at traffic light)* is actually two church buildings joined back-to-back; the older front portion was erected in 1855 and moved here in 1927; the newer back portion was erected here in 1905.

Turn in Painter to see:

QUINBY, seaside village with handsome old home Warwick, see page 124 *(Turn right on Route #182 and travel 3 miles)*.

KELLER *(2 miles above Painter)* was established in 1884 and named for a railroad contractor. In its prime it had 3 general stores, 5 grocery stores, 2 clothes shops, 2 barber shops, a barrel factory, a feed store, a blacksmith, and 2 hotels, each of which had a barroom. It is now well past its prime. Two short blocks off the highway on Second Street stands lovely little **Mears Memorial United Methodist Church** (1908). *Hollies Baptist Church *(Turn left on Route #180, then right on Hollies Church Road #620, total distance of 1 mile)*, erected 1792, is the third oldest church building on the Eastern Shore of Virginia, and architecturally unlike any other.

Turn in Keller to see:

WACHAPREAGUE, quiet fishing resort described in Chapter 10 *(Turn right on Route #180 at northern edge of town and travel 4 miles)*.

PUNGOTEAGUE, historic village with Shore's oldest church, site of America's first drama, see page 159 *(Turn left on Route #180 and travel 3 miles)*.

HARBORTON, attractive waterfront village of late 1800s, see page 162 *(Three miles beyond Pungoteague on Route #180)*.

MELFA *(5 miles above Painter)* lies east of the highway and is largely of 20th-century vintage. The **Eastern Shore Chamber of Commerce,** on the left below town, offers information about events and sites on the peninsula, both Accomack and Northampton Counties. **Eastern Shore Community College** offers a two-year Associate Degree in several fields. Once in town look to the right for the old **Railroad Station**, now a private home.

Turn in Melfa to see:

Oak Grove United Methodist Church, pretty country church with nation's oldest Sunday School, see page 126 *(Turn right on Main Street #626, at street's end turn left on Phillips Drive #639, then right immediately on Mapp Road #624; after 1 mile turn right on Seaside Road #600; total distance of 1.7 miles).*

ONLEY *(8 miles above Painter)*, pronounced like the ordinary household word "only," was established in 1884 and named for the nearby home of Gov. Henry A. Wise. Its commercial shopping center area is the largest on the Virginia Shore. **Nandua High School** preserves the name of an Indian village located near here in the 1600s. The handsome **Eastern Shore of Virginia Produce Exchange Building** *(Turn right on Route #179 and follow 1 block past railroad tracks)* is all that is left of Virginia's first, the nation's second farmers' marketing cooperative; chartered in 1900, it handled a quarter of a billion dollars worth of local produce before dissolving in 1955.

Turn in Onley to see:

ONANCOCK, lovely 300-year old town situated on the water, described in Chapter 8 *(Turn left on Route #179 and travel 1 mile).*

TANGIER, the Shore's most isolated community, an island in the middle of Chesapeake Bay reached by passenger ferry (in season); see Chapter 3 *(Follow Route #179 to ferry dock at Onancock Wharf).*

LOWER ACCOMACK BAYSIDE, tour heading south from Onancock, see Chapter 14.

LOCUSTVILLE, tiny early-19th century village on old stage route, see page 127 *(Turn right on Route #179 and follow through Onley 3 miles, then left on Drummondtown Road #605; total distance of 3.5 miles).*

TASLEY *(One mile above Onley)*, arguably the least attractive town on the peninsula, does boast one distinction: Its highway overpass above the old railroad is the highest point on the Eastern Shore of Virginia, a whopping 70 feet or so above sea level.

ACCOMAC *(Turn right on Front Street 2.5 miles above Onley, or right on Courthouse Avenue 1 mile further north; Business Route 13 through the town parallels Route 13).* The seat of Accomack County is one of the jewels of the Eastern Shore, a small village laden with fascinating architecture and history. It is described in detail in Chapter 5.

FISHER'S CORNER *(Traffic signal at Route #176, 7 miles above Onley)*, the intersection for Parksley, was known in the 1780s as

"Poorhouse Corner."

Turn at Fisher's Corner to see:

PARKSLEY, quiet Victorian residential town with a railroad museum, described in Chapter 9 *(Turn left on Route #176 and travel 2.5 miles).*

Zion Baptist Church *(.5 mile above Parksley traffic signal)* juxtaposes two church buildings, a new brick one built in 1917 and, across the road from it, an older frame building of 1852. The black congregation that withdrew from this church in 1877 stands a quarter mile south on the right, known today as **Metompkin Baptist Church**.

Turn at Zion Church to see:

UPPER ACCOMACK SEASIDE, tour heading north paralleling Route 13 (see Chapter 12).

NELSONIA *(Traffic signal at Route #187, 12 miles above Onley)* was once known as Helltown, then renamed for S. R. Nelson, its first postmaster.

Turn in Nelsonia to see:

MODEST TOWN, tiny 19th-century hamlet, see page 133 *(Turn right on Route #187 and travel 1.75 miles).*

Guard Shore, swimming area with wide view of Chesapeake Bay, see page 149 *(Turn left on Route #187; at Bloxom town line turn right on Bethel Church Road #687 and left immediately on Mitchell Road #684 which becomes Guard Shore Road; follow #684 to water; total distance of 5 miles).*

MAPPSVILLE *(2 miles above Nelsonia)* offers nothing pretty to look at, but two things that may be of interest: local produce stands, and one of the several migrant labor camps which house seasonal farm laborers while they are on the Shore. On the left 1.5 miles above the village is old **Conquest Chapel**, still identifiable as a church although since 1930 it has served as store, shop, home, service station, and just about everything else.

TEMPERANCEVILLE *(5.5 miles above Nelsonia)* is so named because the four men who gave the land for the original town center agreed never to sell whiskey on their lands or to permit a barroom. Just off the highway to the right stands the **Lyric Theatre** *(30182 Temperanceville Road)*, the oldest surviving movie theatre on the Shore (1913), silent since the early 1930s.

Turn in Temperanceville to see:

SAXIS, isolated, authentic fishing village, see page 146 *(Turn left on Saxis Road #695 and travel 11 miles).*

OAK HALL *(8.5 miles above Nelsonia).* **Arcadia High School** preserves the name given to this area by Florentine explorer Giovanni da Verrazzano in 1524. The original **Oak Hall** was an old plantation house that stood at the southern edge of the village on the right; it burned in the 1940s, and today the site is occupied by a large southern-style house *(7465 Lankford Highway)*. **Downings United Methodist Church**, on the right, is the oldest of its faith on the Shore, established 1772, erected 1854; this building was used by the Union army as a stable for horses during the Civil War.

T'S CORNER *(Traffic signal at Route #175, 9.5 miles above Nelsonia)* was known as Logg Town in the 1770s; its present name dates from 1936, when T. Edward Mears opened his service station here.

Turn at T's Corner to see:

CHINCOTEAGUE ISLAND, with **ASSATEAGUE ISLAND** the Shore's most famous and visited community, described in detail in Chapter 2 *(Turn right on Route #175 and travel 10.5 miles)*.

WALLOPS ISLAND, NASA installation, see page 135 *(On Route #175 after 4.5 miles)*.

NEW CHURCH *(2.5 miles above T's Corner)* has been settled since the late 1770s, but has little to show for its age. One block off the highway on the left stands **The Garden and the Sea Inn** *(4188 Nelson Road)*, housed in old Bloxom's Tavern. The back part of this building was erected in 1802, the front part, with its lovely Victorian gingerbread porch, about 1900. The **Virginia Information Center**, on the left above town, is a state facility; rest rooms and information are free.

Turn in New Church to see:

FRANKLIN CITY, a "ghost town" on the marshes of Chincoteague Bay, see page 139 *(Turn right on Horntown Road #709 to Horntown, then left on Fleming Road #679 to its end, a total distance of 10 miles)*.

UPPER ACCOMACK BAYSIDE, tour heading south, see Chapter 13 *(At Maryland boundary 1.7 miles above town turn left on Holland Road #705)*.

The tour of Route 13 from south to north ends at the Maryland boundary, 1.7 miles above New Church. Pocomoke City and Salisbury, Maryland, are 6 miles and 35 miles distant, respectively.

THE LIGHTHOUSE, ASSATEAGUE

2 CHINCOTEAGUE AND ASSATEAGUE

Vacation Resort on Ocean and Bay

From Route 13 turn east on Route 175 at T's Corner, 4 miles below Maryland, and travel 10.5 miles.

The island tradition is that its Indian name means "Beautiful Land Across the Water." And from across the water Chincoteague is beautiful. You're still five miles away when you first see it: a wide and peaceful vista of marsh, water, and sky. The island lies flat against the horizon and rises gradually to greet you as you approach over the causeway. It is a pretty sight.

Up close "beautiful" is not necessarily the word for Chincoteague. Chincoteague is many things: sometimes quaint, often prosaic, a little eccentric, increasingly garish, conspicuously neat. But as for "beautiful," we leave that to the eye of the beholder.

Nonetheless Chincoteague is without a doubt the most famous place on the Eastern Shore of Virginia, and the peninsula's number one tourist attraction. Here is the only place on the Virginia Shore where you will encounter real tourism, your pick of lodgings, and more than enough eating places from which to choose. Here as nowhere else on the Eastern Shore of Virginia you'd better plan your trip and your reservations in advance, especially if you want to see the famous Pony Penning. Every year Chincoteague's fame as a vacation spot grows, and you might find yourself sharing the island with 50,000 other people at the height of the tourist season.

Although it is a small town and geographically contained, Chincoteague is in another sense many places and possibilities. Most people come for the ponies, or for the beach on Assateague Island, or for both. Many others come for the fishing and the seafood. And then there is the town itself, noteworthy and charming at any season. In this corner of the Shore there is more than enough to interest the visitor.

This chapter treats Chincoteague Island and adjacent Assateague Island together, because the two are and always have been inseparably tied. Thus it may be in order to begin by straightening out some names:

Chincoteague is (1) the name of the smaller of the two islands, (2) the name of the community on that island, (3) the name of the breed of ponies that live on Assateague Island, (4) the name of the bay that separates both islands from the mainland, and (5) the name of the National Wildlife Refuge that is located on Assateague Island. It is pronounced *Shink'a-tig*, though if you listen closely you may hear some island natives pronounce it without the middle syllable.

Assateague is (1) the name of the larger of the two islands, which is uninhabited, (2) the name of the channel that separates the two islands, and (3) the name of the National Seashore Park which is located on Assateague Island. Assateague is over 30 miles long, and only the southernmost portion lies within Virginia. Another part of the island and its park is accessible only from Maryland, and is not treated here.

History

Chincoteague was a remote piece of property to the early English settlers of the Eastern Shore, inaccessible and, despite the island traditions, unsettled by the Indians. Though Englishmen obtained title to the island as early as 1671, it was not until twenty years later that William Kendall and John Robins laid permanent claim to it. Between them they divided the island into two equal sections, Kendall taking the northern and Robins the southern half. Shortly thereafter Robins sent George and Hannah Blake to his part of the island to take care of his cattle there; the Blakes were probably Chincoteague's first settlers.

Despite the pretty stories about pirates and Spanish galleons, the likelihood is that the famous Chincoteague ponies that still run free on Assateague are descended from stock let loose on the two islands by the early English settlers, for it is known that before the end of the 1600s both islands were in use as a convenient natural livestock range. For more than a hundred years the islands were put to no other use, and the tradition of an annual "penning" undoubtedly dates to the first century of the island's settlement. By 1800 the population had grown to only 60, fully 23 of whom were children. Cattle and farming were still the principal sources of income. In 1821 the worst storm in the history of the peninsula created a tidal wave that swept completely over both islands, bore across Chincoteague Bay, and crashed against the mainland. The simple island homes were destroyed, five people drowned, and some abandoned the island altogether for safer homes on the mainland. Even so, the population began to increase more rapidly at about this time; one story credits the increase to a local fisherman who, cast ashore in far-off New Jersey, bragged so much about the virtues of his homeland that he occasioned an influx of settlers from the North. By 1831 there were 500 people on the island, and 26 substantial homes. In 1833 the Assateague Lighthouse was erected; razed and rebuilt in 1867, it is still one of the oldest structures on the two islands. The rapid growth in people placed a premium on available land for pasture and crops, and caused increasing numbers of people to turn to the sea for their livelihood. Gradually seafood replaced livestock and farming as the main industry, and Chincoteague began early to send the produce of its waters northward to Philadelphia and New York, where there were ready and eager markets.

By the 1850s a central village began to coalesce among the scattered settlements across the island. There were over 100 families, 2 churches, a post office, and after 1858 a physician. Prior to that time islanders had to cross the bay to Horntown for medical aid, and even after the 1850s they still made the trip for most supplies. Mainlanders there laughed at the rustic islanders, and told funny stories at their expense.

In 1861, when the rest of the Eastern Shore of Virginia seceded from the Union, Chincoteague voted 132 to 2 to remain in the fold, and it stayed a part of the Union throughout the Civil War. Southerners on the mainland, considering this an unbearable affront, attempted to storm the island, but the islanders secured aid from the North, where their economic as well as their political allegiances lay. The Union sent the small gunboat "Louisiana" to patrol the bay and protect the island. In October 1861 a battle developed between the gunboat and southern sympathizers from the mainland who were outfitting a schooner as a Confederate privateer; there were no casualties. Throughout the war Chincoteague continued its trade in seafood with the northern cities, and during the war became perhaps the first place in the nation to engage extensively in the private planting of oysters.

The end of the Civil War found Chincoteague no more in touch with the Shore, no less in touch with the North, and not significantly more refined than before. The writer-artist Howard Pyle visited the island in 1876 and described its rusticity to the readers of "Scribner's Magazine": there was neither jail nor law enforcement and little presence of governmental authority, few islanders could read or write, most did not wear shoes, and homes and public services were quite primitive. Pyle was, however, witnessing the end of this simple age, for in that same year a railroad was built from the North to the mainland opposite Chincoteague, where the little town of Franklin City developed. With northern markets even more accessible by railroad, the island entered a period of growth and prosperity. Schools and churches were founded, a newspaper was established, and handsome new homes reflecting the profits that came from the sea arose, many of them still visible today. By the turn of the century Chincoteague had taken its place among the prosperous and progressive towns of the Shore, and the day was past when islanders lived and died in Chincoteague without ever visiting the mainland. The town was incorporated in 1908, and though in 1913 half of the older population still could not read or write, Chincoteague was becoming a proud and modern town, already basking in a certain renown for sports-fishing and ponies.

Two events of the 1920s shaped modern Chincoteague. First in 1922 the automobile causeway to the mainland was opened, resulting in the swift decline of the railroad and Franklin City, and ending the island's long isolation from the rest of the Shore. Then a series of disastrous fires destroyed a major portion of the downtown section, and when the islanders found their fire-fighting equipment antiquated, they organized the Chincoteague Volunteer Fire Company and sought for a way to fund it. It was in 1925 that "pony penning" was expanded to include carnival, pony swim, and a two-week celebration in support of the fire company. Pony Penning was, of course, an immediate success that not only transformed the local fire company into one of the wealthiest among small-town volunteer fire companies in America, but also put that small town on the map. The fame of the island spread, bolstered by news coverage, magazine articles, the publication of Marguerite Henry's children's book "Misty of Chincoteague" in 1947, and Hollywood's filming of the book in 1960. In the years following World War II, Chincoteague also became the Eastern Shore's largest marketer of poultry, and chickens rivaled seafood as the chief industry for a time until the advent of large-scale tourism.

Chincoteague is today the largest community on the Eastern Shore of Virginia, a prosperous place and as always a proud place. The old insular attitudes, like the island dialect, are fast fading, and the whole community seems to be participating in the boom that tourism has brought. What was once one of the most remote and forgotten places on the Eastern Shore is now the very reason many people come to the Shore.

Chincoteague Island

The only access to the island is over the **John B. Whealton Memorial Causeway** [1], named for "Captain Jack" Whealton [1860-1928] who envisioned and built it. The Chincoteague Toll Road and Bridge, as it was first known, opened on November 15, 1922, whereupon immediately after the opening ceremonies 96 automobiles got hopelessly stuck in the mud of its unpaved road and had to be ferried to land. The State Highway Department took over the road and removed the toll in 1930. Though only half of the causeway lies within the bounds of Chincoteague—the town limit lies east of the bridge over Queen Sound—by state law the Town alone controls all the billboards that line the road to the island.

A mile and a half beyond Queen Sound, the road heads left over a new section of the causeway. **Marsh Island** [2], once crossed by the causeway, is no longer connected to the island itself; as late as the mid-1900s, it was still one of those places where the islanders grazed their ponies.

From the new bridge it is a straight shot across the island to Assateague on Maddox Boulevard, but this itinerary will first show you Chincoteague Island itself, visiting each of the island's several neighborhoods. A bicycle tour is a good way to re-visit your favorite sections later.

Chincoteague also offers the "Pony Express," a trolley that covers many, not all, of the routes on this itinerary, available daily June-August and weekends in May, September, and October. Cost is 25 cents per ride. The trolley also offers a one-hour guided history tour for $3. For information, tickets, etc. pick up the trolley at the Community Center, 6155 Community Drive. *(From the bridge keep straight on Maddox to the next light, turn left on Deep Hole Road and travel a quarter mile to the Center on the left.)*

Downtown Chincoteague, survivor of storm, flood, and fire, lies a few blocks south of the new bridge.

Turn right at the traffic signal at the end of the bridge. As you head south down Main Street, most of the structures on the right are built on filled land, for Main Street itself once marked the line between high ground and wetlands. On the left at Poplar Street is **Watson House** [3] *(4240 Main Street)*, built by David Robert Watson in the late 19th century; the mirror-image Inn at Poplar Corner, though similar in appearance, was built fully a century later. Further down the street the mid-1800s homes of the local physician and the local postmaster, who married sisters, are today joined together as a bed-and-breakfast known as **Island Manor House** [4] *(4240 Main)*. As Downtown comes into view, **Miss Molly's Inn** [5] *(4141 Main)*, built in 1886, stands on the right; here Marguerite Henry boarded in an upstairs room and wrote part of *Misty of Chincoteague*.

On the left at Church Street stands the **Marine Bank** [6] *(4116*

Main), completed just in time to fall victim to the 1920 fire, and subsequently rebuilt. The next several buildings on the left were built after the fire and are trapezoidal in shape, to conform to the straightening of the street that occurred during the rebuilding after the fire. Among them are the three-story **Masonic Hall** [7] *(4110 Main)* and the **Bank of Chincoteague** [8] *(4102 Main)*. All of these buildings now house shops, as does **Powell's Opera House** [9] *(4098 Main)*, built in 1923 and renamed the Village Mall.

Misty herself, in bronze by sculptor Brian Maughan, stands on the right as the **Waterfront Park** [10] opens up the view to the water. The park is named for Robert N. Reed, who as mayor fought tirelessly for the bridge to Assateague. Here at water's edge docked most of the boats that connected the island to the mainland prior to the 1922 causeway. Looming over it is the new nautically inspired addition (2009) to the **Library** [11] *(4075 Main)*. The front part of this building was erected in 1890s on a different site; in 1908 it became the barber shop of of Wallace Jester, who then did not stop cutting hair here for 74 years, by which time he had been featured in *National Geographic* and *Ripley's Believe It or Not*. It is one of the few examples of old commercial architecture left unchanged in downtown Chincoteague.

Beyond the Library stand three handsome old buildings: the 1899 two-story **Boatman's Bank** [12] *(4073 Main)*, the old **Telegraph Building** [13] *(4071 Main)*, and the **Watson Brothers Building** [14] *(4065 Main)*, built as an ice cream parlor, now a bookstore.

At the **Island Roxy Theatre** [15] *(4074 Main)*, which opened in 1946, occurred one of the two world premiers of the motion picture "Misty of Chincoteague" in 1961; the other was in Hollywood. Misty's hoofprints are preserved in the sidewalk in front of the theatre. Next door stands the old **Police Station** [16] *(4068 Main)*, built in 1930, now public restroom facilities. Next to it stands the **Earl Watson House** [17] *(4068 Main)*, which was spared in the great fire of 1920, through the rest of the block up to Church Street burned; the original bridge landed on the island just opposite it.

One of the island's most historic homes, the **John A. M. Whealton House** [18] *(4039 Main)*, has been much changed over the years, and now suffers the indignity of housing a laundromat. Behind it is the **Town Dock** [19], opposite Cropper Street. The **Cropper House** [20] *(4034 Main)*, built in 1875 by casketmaker William Cropper, was briefly the home of John B. Whealton, officially a resident of Florida, who lived here while building the causeway. Three doors behind it is the tiny **Old Town Jail** [21] *(6287 Cropper Street)*, built in 1927.

The **Chincoteague Volunteer Fire Company** [22] *(4028 Main)* is the building, and here is the equipment, that the ponies paid for. The wild herds on the Virginia section of Assateague are owned by the fire company, and the "cowboys" who round them up each year are chosen by the local firemen from within their own ranks. Inside the fire

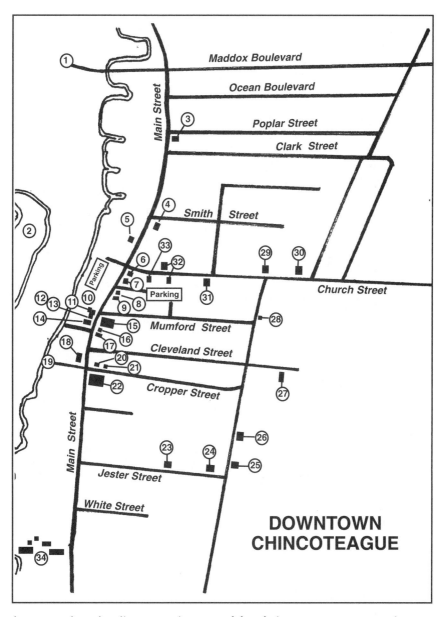

DOWNTOWN CHINCOTEAGUE

house is the island's original piece of fire-fighting equipment, a horse-drawn fire pump dating from 1880.

> *To see more of Downtown, turn left on Jester Street; this itinerary will circle you back to this point. Or, if you prefer to keep straight down Main, skip to "Down the Island" below.*

Jester Street is entirely residential, and was once home to two of the island's more colorful figures. At the **Jester Homestead** [23] *(6369 Jester Street)* lived Wallace Jester, the long-lasting barber who had a bit part in the movie "Misty of Chincoteague." Nearby at the **6419 Jester Street** [24] lived Benjamin F. Scott (1838-1944), a beloved centenarian who fought in the Civil War and lived almost to the end of World War II; in his latter years he operated a small dairy farm from this house.

Jester ends at Willow Street, at the edge of what was once a poor section, quite distinct from Downtown, known as Tick Town. At **3642 Willow Street** [25] lived E. Thomas Mears [1875-1923], undertaker. The **Nancy Fletcher House** [26] *(3676 Willow Street)* is said to date from about 1865. Just off Willow, hidden behind the Seashell Motel, is the old **Freewill Methodist Church** [27] *(6414 Cleveland Street Extended)*, built in 1897 by an African American congregation and now renovated into a private home; its cornerstone is still in place. Except for its happy modern colors the restored house (c. 1865) at **3758 Willow Street** [28] is a typical Chincoteague cottage of the nineteenth century. Facing Willow on Church Street is the old (1901) **Dennard Merritt Store** [29]*(6333 Church Street)*, now a funeral home; Merritt was a sea captain who gave up life on the water for store-keeping after his schooner sank in 1913 and he spent a harrowing 40 hours lashed to its mast before being rescued.

Church Street is aptly named. As you turn left, **Union Baptist Church** [30] *(6365 Church Street)* is visible on the right, built in 1898 and housing the island's largest congregation. **St. Andrew Catholic Church** [31] *(6288 Church Street)* was built in 1887 by the Methodists; directly across the street stands the old Methodist parsonage *(6287 Church Street)*, said to have been built atop an earlier burial ground. **Christ United Methodist Church** [32] *(6253 Church Street)* was built in 1922 to replace the older building (1888) that still stands opposite it. The earlier Methodist site *(6254 Church Street)* is said to be the spot at which the "trading post" of Purnell Watson, perhaps the island's first store, once stood. Just beyond it stands **Channel Bass Inn** [33] *(6228 Church Street)*, built in 1892.

Turn left on Main, retracing your steps through Downtown to:

"Down the Island" is the old local term for the southern part of Chincoteague.

The **Coast Guard Station** [34] *(3823 Main)* is an important facility with a distinguished history. There were once several "life-saving" stations along the coast in this region (an abandoned one still stands on Assateague), but with modern rescue methods only this one is needed today.

The handsome **Daniel Whealton House** [35] *(3760 Main)* was

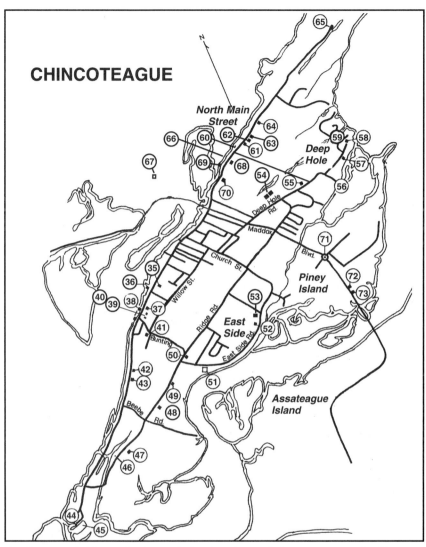

CHINCOTEAGUE

North Main Street

Deep Hole

Church St.

Willow St.

Ridge Rd.

East Side Rd.

East Side

Bunting

Beebe Rd.

Maddox Blvd.

Deep Hole Rd.

Piney Island

Assateague Island

the home of "Squealer Dan," the brother of the causeway builder, so named because his voice was high-pitched. When the Town of Chincoteague was created in 1908, Booth Street marked its southern boundary, and opposite it stands **Charlie Gall's Store** [36] *(3747 Main)*, in which tides rose to four feet in March 1962. Beyond it, the **Carnival Grounds** [37] come alive the last two weeks in July, when the ponies are penned here on their brief annual visit to Chincoteague. Across the street stands the old **Wishart's Point Hotel** [38] *(3639-3641 Main)*, once located on the mainland over 6 miles away; it was floated to this site about 1930.

In the **John Bunting House** [39] *(3608 Main)* lived a man who came to the island as a penniless orphan in 1848 and died its richest citizen. His son's home, the **W. C. Bunting House** [40] *(3594 Main)* stands on the corner of Bunting Road. Just off Main on Bunting Road is the **Greenwood Cemetery** [41] where, just inside on the left, are the graves of Clarence "Grandpa" Beebe [1884-1957], his wife Ida W. Beebe [1888-1960], and grandson Paul Beebe [1936-1957], all residents of the island who were characters in *Misty of Chincoteague*.

Below Bunting Road, street and bay sweep closer together, affording affording pretty views across the water, especially at sunset. **Sunset View** [42] *(3300 Main)* may appear old, but is in fact a modern (1977) rendition of the traditional Chincoteague cottage; for an original to compare it to see **Aquavit** [43] *(3254 Main)*, a few doors to the south. **Inlet View** [44], at the southern tip of the island, will disappoint those who hope for beautiful vistas across the water, but not those who seek fishing, camping, and amusements. **Curtis Merritt Harbor** [45] is named for a local boy who became an accomplished decoy carver despite being blind.

This southern portion of the island, now developed, is where Clarence Beebe, the "Grandpa" of *Misty of Chincoteague*, pastured his ponies. From Inlet View, turn back up Main Street and then right on Seaweed Drive and left on Ridge Road to the site of his home [46], which burned in 1996 *(on the right adjacent to 3008 Ridge Road as the road passes into the woods)*. During the Storm of 1962 (which gave rise to Marguerite Henry's sequel *Stormy, Misty's Foal*), Misty herself took shelter inside the house at **Beebe Ranch** [47] *(3062 Ridge Road)*, not the quaint and beautiful farmhouse depicted in the motion picture (that building was located on Folly Creek below Accomac) but this modest little house behind which stands the even less impressive shed that served as her stable. Visitors may take a self-guided tour of the "ranch" (admission charged) which, thanks to the taxidermist's art, includes the chance to see Misty herself.

The large **Anchor** [48] standing at 3376 Ridge Road was recovered from the sea in 1989 and is thought to be from the Spanish ship *Juno* which sank off Assateague in 1802. The little red building at 3482 Ridge Road is the old **Down-the-Island School** [49], abandoned in 1917. Ridge Road continues up the center of the island, once known as Snotty Ridge, but now a respectable address of new homes. Behind an iron rail fence at the back of the **Thornton Cemetery** [50] at the corner of Ridge and Bunting Road lies William P. Thornton, first resident pastor of Union Baptist Church.

Turn right on East Side Drive to:

East Side faces Assateague Island, with views across the channel to the lighthouse. It is reached from either Church Street in the north or from Bunting and Ridge Road in the south.

Chincoteague Memorial Park [51] is the answer to the question "Where do the ponies swim?" Ordinarily just a community recreational park with a simple monument to war dead, the place comes alive on the day of Pony Penning when thousands crowd the shore here to watch the swim from Horse Marsh, less than a quarter mile away on the opposite shore. Assateague Lighthouse is one mile to the east from here; also visible is Black Point Landing, half a mile to the south on the Chincoteague Shore.

East Side has long been the site of many of the island's seafood companies, one of which shipped 1.3 million clams to market on a single day in 1957. The old **Assateague Chapel** [52] *(7691 East Side Road)* is one of a number of buildings that originally stood on Assateague and which were floated to Chincoteague when that village was abandoned in the 1920s. Another is the home at **7721 East Side Drive** [53].

Just beyond where Ridge Road rejoins your route, turn right on Chicken City Road, its odd name a remnant of the days when Chincoteague had a thriving poultry industry. Just after World War II this neighborhood—which once bore the even more unfortunate name of Buzzard Swamp—was dotted with long, low-roofed chicken houses, and islanders boasted that their town had more chickens per square mile than any other place in the world. Production declined in the 1950s, and virtually ended after the Storm of 1962 flooded the island.

At the intersection of Chicken City Road and Church Street, keep under the traffic signal to:

Deep Hole, a residential section in the northeastern part of the island, is one of the oldest communities of Chincoteague, though there is little visible today to suggest its age. As you turn right on Deep Hole Road, at the end of Chicken City, notice the **Municipal and Civic Center** [54] *(6150 Community Drive)* visible just to the left.

The tiny building adjacent to 5159 Deep Hole Road is the **Old Kingdom Hall** [55], first meeting place of the Jehovah's Witnesses of Chincoteague in the early 1900s and probably the smallest building ever to serve as a house of worship on the Eastern Shore of Virginia. **Fir Landing** [56] offers a somewhat restricted view across Little Oyster Bay to the northern portion of Piney Island. Presumably somewhere out in those waters is the "deep hole" which gave its name to this section.

At 5418 Deep Hole Road stands the **Timothy Hill House** [57], site of one of the island's most sensational tragedies. Here on a fine June day in 1885 Thomas W. Freeman, an employee of the prosperous Mr. Hill, met Mrs. Hill and her daughter Jennie at the front gate as they were leaving to visit the dressmaker. Freeman, a working man of 20, professed his love for 14-year-old Jennie, and when he was rebuffed produced a pistol and at point-blank range shot first Jennie, then her mother, and finally himself. Mrs. Hill survived her wound; Freeman did not, and was buried in disgrace. Jennie lingered in agony for one day, and lies buried in the small cemetery adjacent to the house.

A window dedicated to her memory is still to be seen in the old Methodist church building downtown *(6254 Church Street)*.

The **Tom Reed Wildfowl Farm** [58] *(5446 Tom Reed Lane)* operated for many years just beyond the end of Deep Hole Road. Here Reed raised and trained wild ducks, with which he performed far and wide. Most of his "livestock" flew away during a storm in 1933, but the 100 wild ducks that he sold in 1960 to the producers of "Misty," then filming on the island, were released for a scene in the film and flew straight back home. **Oyster Bay** [59] is the name of the subdivision of homes at the end of Deep Hole Road, as well as of the body of water bordering it. The road here is private and does not (as it seems it should) connect to North Main Street. Instead, retrace your steps and turn right on Hallie Whealton Smith Drive. This road is named for the islander-who gave much of the land on which the island's elementary and high schools stand, acres which had previously been her father's wild goose farm.

North Main Street, extending up the island's west side, was once a separate neighborhood with its own school, churches, and post office, and in some spots it still retains a distinct flavor.

Turn right at the high school, and on the left behind a picket fence stands the **Clarence Tarr House** [60] *(4653 Main)*, a handsome restored Victorian that originally stood on the opposite side of the street. **5010 Main Street** [61] was moved to this location in 1947 from Franklin City, five miles away on the mainland. Its neighbor at **5020 Main Street** [62] was also moved here, from Memorial Park on the East Side. Still standing, though just barely, is yet another house moved to this neighborhood, the abandoned **Hill House** [63], adjacent to 4639 Main, originally from Deep Hole, dating at least to the early 1800s, perhaps to the late 1700s.

Christ's Sanctified Holy Church [64] *(5084 Main)* now has fewer than a dozen members, but it is the mother church of an entire sect of the same name that stretches from Delaware to Oklahoma and numbers thousands nationally. The separation of this congregation from the local Methodists in 1892 and subsequent migration to other parts following their charismatic leader Joseph B. Lynch is one of the most fascinating stories of the Eastern Shore. Worship at this church, where the hymns are still unaccompanied and "lined out" in 19th-century fashion, is now occasional.

The Turntable [65] marks the end of the public road at the northern end of the island. Here once stood Goodwill School; today only the grave of Capt. Joshua A. Chandler [1829-1877] surveys the site. From this point it is a distance of 2 miles to Wildcat Point, the northernmost reach of Chincoteague Island.

From **Donald Leonard Park** [66], opposite the high school, the wide view across Chincoteague Bay includes the superstructure on which the **Killick Shoals Lighthouse** [67] stood from 1886 until 1935. Though long since re-erected, the **Joshua Brasure House** [68]

(4496 Main Street) was toppled to its side by a storm in 1936, its roof thrust into the side of its neighbor to the south. Hiding behind its privacy fence, the **Zadock Carter House** [69] *(4463 Main Street)* is one of the island's oldest, probably dating from just after the great hurricane of 1821. On the corner at Savage Street stands the handsome **Henry Savage House** [70] *(4420 Main Street)*, the late-19th century home of the local postmaster who at one time also operated the store across the street.

> *The circular tour of the island ends at Maddox Boulevard at the bridge. Turn left on Maddox towards Assateague, which after two traffic signals crosses to...*

Piney Island lies between Chincoteague and Assateague, separated from Chincoteague, just barely, by Eel Creek. Except for a small section of residences on Piney Island Road, off East Side Road, most of what is there is new. The island's **Visitor Information Center** [71] is located right in the traffic circle.

The **Refuge Waterfowl Museum** [72] *(7059 Maddox Boulevard)* displays a handsome collection of decoys from all over the country. Carved wooden decoys, used by hunters to attract live waterfowl, have long been a serious business for hunters, and are now an admired folk art. Chincoteague ranks high among those places that have produced decoys of quality. This museum tells all about them, and is well worth the price of admission. Just beyond it stands the **Oyster and Maritime Museum** [73] *(7125 Maddox Boulevard)*, a museum of local life and culture, well worth a leisurely visit (no admission charged).

The bike path that begins at Piney Island offers a pleasant walk or ride over Assateague Channel Bridge to Assateague Island. Beyond the museum there are displays along the route explaining the flora, fauna, and natural history of the region.

Assateague Island: Refuge and Park

The islanders of Chincoteague built the bridge to Assateague in 1962, but the United States government owns Assateague and has shaped the attractions there. Today the bridge across Assateague Channel takes you from the commercial busy-ness of Chincoteague to an unspoiled and largely undeveloped island. Here is the natural coast much as the white man found it centuries ago, a perfect complement to much-peopled Chincoteague. The hopes of the islanders in building the bridge have been fulfilled: Chincoteague has become a popular and successful resort, but in part because Assateague has remained free of commercial development.

The Virginia portion of Assateague Island is composed officially of the Chincoteague National Wildlife Refuge, administered by the Bureau of Sport Fisheries and Wildlife, and the Assateague National Seashore, a part of the National Parks Service. In addition, Assateague Lighthouse is administered by the United States Coast Guard. Such administrative distinctions count for little to the visitor; the whole of the Virginia section of Assateague amounts to one government-owned facility staffed, maintained, and operated with the public in mind. This is clearly one place where government is at work for the people, helping with the not-too-difficult task of enjoying Assateague Island.

There is an entrance fee for Assateague, collected at the toll gate just past the bridge *(Per vehicle admission for 7-day pass)*.

On the left just beyond the curve is the entrance to **Wildlife Loop**, a six mile drive from which can be glimpsed Chincoteague ponies, Sika deer, the large and rare Delmarva gray squirrel, innumerable species of birds, and—yes—an occasional snake. The drive is open from mid-afternoon until sundown, and is especially impressive in the autumn when geese and ducks flock to the area in great numbers.

Assateague Lighthouse stands majestically on the right amid the pines. When first erected here in 1833, it stood near the seashore; the island has grown markedly since then, and now this same site is more than a mile from the beach. In 1866 the old lighthouse was razed, and the present one erected the following year. It is 27 feet across at its base, with walls 22 inches thick, 142 feet high. Lighted at first by whale

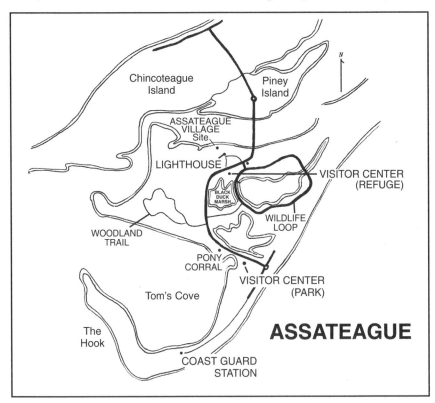

oil, then by kerosene, the light at the top has been powered by electricity since 1932. Wildfowl were so thick on the island in 1869 that the lightkeeper had to install wire screens to keep them from flying into the lanterns atop the tower.

To answer two frequent questions:

(1) The lighthouse, whose light flashes at night with 800,000 candlepower, is painted red and white to make it more visible during the day to ships at sea.

(2) Yes, you can enter the lighthouse and climb its tower. Tours are offered from April thru November; schedules vary from season to season, so check at the Refuge Visitor Center for dates, times, and admission costs. But tickets are not required to wander afoot up Lighthouse Trail to the very base of the structure, where often on weekends local artists display and sell their wares. Camera buffs will delight in the many pretty vistas the structure offers through the pines.

A look towards Chincoteague from the lighthouse will survey the area where once **Assateague Village** stood. Here on the tentative ground bordering the channel lived almost 200 people who tilled the land, kept vegetable gardens, raised livestock, attended a one-room school, worshiped in a small chapel, and bought supplies at a general store. After one citizen acquired most of the surrounding land and made it difficult for villagers to reach the seafood-rich Tom's Cove, the village was abandoned. In the 1920s many of the buildings were jacked up and moved away on barges to various places around Chincoteague.

The **Refuge Visitor Center**, named for the late Congressman Herbert Bateman, is on the left opposite the parking area for Lighthouse Trail. Check in here for information about the wide variety of activities offered by the Refuge, as well as for informative displays and presentations (and restrooms). Tours of the island, and information about them, begin and end here.

Just beyond where the road turns sharply left lies **Black Duck Marsh** on the left, bisected by a bicycle path. **Woodland Trail**, beyond it on the right, is for walking and cycling only; the trail is paved and has observation towers from which, more than likely, you will be able to see some of the wild ponies that forage frequently in this area. Just beyond Pony Trail on the right is **Pony Corral**. No guarantee of ponies here except shortly before Pony Penning in July, for this is where the firemen herd them to wait for the proper tides to swim them over to Chincoteague. The large, usually peaceful, and very shallow body of water that opens to view on the right just beyond the corral is Tom's Cove. This is a new body of water; maps of Assateague as late as 1866 show this as open ocean.

At the seashore you pass out of the Wildlife Refuge into the National Seashore Park; the greatest attraction here—the ocean beach—lies just out of sight beyond the manmade dunes. The **Seashore Visitor Center** has attractive exhibits, publications for free and for sale, a well-informed and friendly staff, but no food. Inquire here about the numerous activities available to the public.

South of the visitor center lies **The Hook**, the tiny southernmost spit of Assateague that has arisen from the sea in the past century and a half. "Oversand vehicles" and permits are required to drive here, and in recent years the area has been closed even to pedestrian traffic in order to protect the mating nests of the piping plover, a threatened local species. From an historical exhibit platform here you can get a beautiful view of Tom's Cove, the remnants of an old fish factory, and the old **Coast Guard Station** (1922), accessible only by foot.

As a final rule of thumb for Assateague, let it be explicitly stated: The Refuge and Park Service personnel, and the publications provided by them, are excellent. It's your facility—ask.

Chincoteague: Events and Festivals

Pony Penning is by far the main, but not by any means the only event that draws people to Chincoteague. A number of other festivals and celebrations, some of them growing rapidly in popularity, are held throughout the year.

Pony Penning *(Last week in July).* The Fireman's Carnival is held the last two weeks in July, Pony Penning itself on the last Wednesday and Thursday. The ponies are rounded up and corralled on Assateague on Monday and Tuesday, and the swim from Assateague to Chincoteague occurs on Wednesday at Memorial Park on the East Side, the time dependent upon the tides but well publicized each year. Ponies are auctioned, branded, and ridden by local bronco-busters on Thursday. The return swim to Assateague, much less crowded, takes place on Friday.

Chincoteague is never more crowded than during Pony Penning week. Make your reservations early! Most rooms on the island, even motels on the mainland, fill up during late July. No parking is permitted at Memorial Park on the day of the swim; plan to use the free shuttle service that the Town of Chincoteague provides from 5 a.m. to 3 p.m. on that day. The shuttle starts at Chincoteague High School and stops at a number of places across the island. For information and inquiries, contact the Chincoteague Chamber of Commerce, P. O. Box 258, Chincoteague, Virginia 23336; 757-336-6161; www.chincoteaguechamber.com.

Seafood Festival *(First Wednesday in May)* was created in 1969 and has just one purpose: Eating. No welcome addresses, no program, and no speeches by attending politicians, who are often prominently present. The festival is held in Tom's Cove Park on the East Side. In one recent year the 4,000 people in attendance consumed 75,000 clams, 97 gallons of fried oysters, 50 bushels of raw oysters, 750 pounds of fish, 6,000 hush puppies, and numerous other trimmings. Tickets to the festival are hard to come by. Those not claimed by members of the Eastern Shore of Virginia Chamber of Commerce, which sponsors the event, must be requested in writing, and as a rule there are so many requests that the recipients are drawn at random. Postmark by October 1, better yet join the Chamber of Commerce. Address all inquires to: Eastern Shore of Virginia Chamber of Commerce, P. O. Box 460, Melfa, Virginia 23410 (Telephone 757-787-2460; www.esvatourism.org).

Oyster Festival *(Saturday of Columbus Day weekend in October)*. Established by the Chincoteague Chamber of Commerce in 1973, this event is held at Maddox Camp Ground on Piney Island. The menu is simply oysters—raw, steamed, fried, stewed, frittered—with a few trimmings, all any ticketholder can eat. For tickets and information write the Chincoteague Chamber of Commerce.

Waterfowl Open House *(Thanksgiving Week)* is held at the Refuge on Assateague Island. For this one week, weather permitting, a 7.5 mile service road is made accessible to automobiles, providing an easy view of the ducks, geese, and swans that normally arrive here at this season. The road is open from 9 a.m. until dark, accessible from Wildlife Loop; stop at the Refuge Visitor Center for information and instructions. Other special activities include guided bird walks and nature walks; advanced sign-up is advised. Local artists demonstrate and display their crafts. Contact Chincoteague National Wildlife Refuge, Box 62, Chincoteague, Virginia 23336 (Telephone 757-336-6122).

Chincoteague Easter Decoy and Art Festival *(Easter Weekend)* gathers waterfowl carvers from far and wide to compete, exhibit, and sell. Wildlife photography is also demonstrated, taught, and sold. Most events are held at Chincoteague High School, some at the Wildlife Refuge, and one—an ecumenical Easter Sunrise Service—at Chincoteague Memorial Park. For information and inquiries contact Chincoteague Chamber of Commerce.

International Migratory Bird Celebration *(Mother's Day weekend in May)* has been held annually on the Refuge since 1995 (and at the National Wildlife Refuge at Cape Charles). Events include bird identification workshops, migratory bird tours, and an opportunity to climb the Assateague Lighthouse. For specific events and information contact the Chincoteague National Wildlife Refuge.

(For a fuller description of Chincoteague's history and sites, see *Once Upon an Island: The History of Chincoteague* by Kirk Mariner, published by Miona Publications.)

3 TANGIER ISLAND

Life in the Center of the Chesapeake

Tangier Island — 2.5 miles long, 1 mile wide, and no more than 7 feet above sea level — sits in the middle of the Chesapeake Bay, a place so remote that neither your cell phone nor your BlackBerry will work there. Fourteen miles from the nearest point on the Eastern Shore, 20 miles from the Western Shore, it is politically a part of Accomack County, but historically and culturally an entity unto itself, dependent upon the waters that surround it, content in its isolation.

Tangier is a celebrated place, visited at one time or another by reporters and photographers from almost every magazine on the newsstand, frequently in the news. No part of the Eastern Shore is more isolated, more colorful, or more demanding of a visit.

How to Get to Tangier

To those with their own boat, Tangier is readily accessible from Onancock, Saxis, or Crisfield, Maryland, on the Eastern Shore, or Reedville on the Western Shore. Most people, however, will need to make specific arrangements for taking one of the several boats that ferry visitors to the island.

The **Joyce Marie II**, a 36-foot converted crabbing boat accommodating 24 passengers, operates between Onancock and Tangier every day except Monday and Wednesday from May 1 through September 30. The boat leaves Onancock Wharf at 10:30 a.m., arrives in Tangier at 11:15, departs from the island at 3:30, and returns to Onancock at 4:45. There is also another daily trip from Onancock at 5:30 p.m., and from the island at 7:30 a.m. Reservations required; round-trip ticket $25 per passenger (2009 rate). For information and reservations, telephone 757-891-2505.

The U.S. mailboat **Courtney Thomas** plies the 14-mile route from Crisfield, Maryland, to Tangier year-round six days a week, except holidays, and takes passengers for a small charge. The boat leaves the County Dock at the foot of Main Street in Crisfield at 12:30 p.m. Monday through Saturday and arrives in Tangier at 1:45. Travelers who take the mailboat must stay overnight on the island, for the captain is an islander and he does not return to the mainland until the following morning. Those who plan to see Tangier by this means should do their sightseeing upon arrival in the afternoon. Telephone 891-2240.

The cruise ship **Steven Thomas**, 100 feet long, accommodates 300 passengers, plies to Tangier from Crisfield daily, including Sundays, May 15 through October 31. The boat leaves City Dock in Crisfield at 12:30 p.m., arrives at Tangier 1:45, leaves Tangier at 4:00, and returns to Crisfield at 5:15. Telephone 410-863-2338.

The cruise ship **Chesapeake Breeze** offers a similar cruise from Reedville, Virginia, on the Western Shore from May through October 15. The boat leaves Buzzard's Point Marina in Fairport at 10:00 a.m. and returns at 3:45 p.m. Reservations required. Contact Tangier & Chesapeake Cruises Inc., Route 1, Box 1332, Reedville, Virginia 22539, or call 804-453-2628.

When the day is bright and sunny the cruise boats offer a splendid view of the Chesapeake, and with a little cooperation from the weather getting to Tangier can be half the fun. Most people taking the tour boats to Tangier indulge in the giant seafood feast at the Chesapeake House, which is not included in the cost of the passage. For those more interested in sightseeing than eating, there are also smaller restaurants and snack bars on the island.

History

When first sighted by Captain John Smith in 1608, the islands in the center of Chesapeake Bay were considerably larger than they are today, wooded with high, fertile ground, useful to the Indians but not inhabited by them. Though tradition has long held that Smith "discovered" Tangier, there is no certainty that he stopped at this particular island. And though tradition insists that he himself named it Tangier because it reminded him of the city of that name in Morocco, that name does not appear in any written record of the Chesapeake region until more than a century after his visit.

Only towards the end of the 1600s did Eastern Shoremen lay claim to the island that had come to be known as Tangier, not as a place to settle but as a range for livestock, and for the greater part of a century the only human inhabitants were tenants who tended the cattle of rich mainland "planters." When the American Revolution began, Tangier and the adjacent islands were still isolated and sparsely populated, and became a notorious hide-out for Tories, pirates, and British sympathizers who used them as a base to prey upon American shipping. It was during the late 1700s — not, as local tradition maintains, a century earlier — that Joseph Crockett bought land on Tangier, moved his family from Smith Island, settled in Canton, the easternmost "ridge" of high land on the island, and became the first permanent resident.

The census of 1800 found 89 people living on Tangier and the adjacent islands, most of them bearing one of the family names still so prominent on the island: Crockett, Parks, Evans. Another resident in that year was Joshua Thomas, a simple waterman who, after his conversion during a Methodist camp meeting in 1805, rose to fame throughout the region as "the Parson of the Islands." Though almost illiterate, Parson Thomas brought Methodism home with him, and the first of many revivals swept through the community, transforming it into a place of almost fearsome uprightness. After 1808 it became, as well, the site of a great camp meeting held annually in the summer on the beach at the southern end of the island.

British troops occupied Tangier during the War of 1812. A fort was erected near the camp meeting grounds, and several thousand troops used the island as a base for raids against the Eastern and Western Shores. It was from Tangier that British forces moved against Washington and burned the city, forcing President James Madison to flee. When it became obvious that a similar campaign was being prepared against Baltimore, Parson Thomas was summoned to preach to the British troops. His sermon, on September 11, 1814, predicted to his British audience that they would not succeed in capturing Baltimore. Two days later the American defenses in that city held strong against the British attack, as Francis Scott Key, who witnessed the battle, penned the words that became the national anthem. The Parson's sermonic prediction elevated him to near legendary stature throughout the Chesapeake region. He later moved to Deal Island, Maryland, to promote Methodist revival there.

In 1815, at the close of the war, Congress considered Tangier as the site for a great new naval base, but after Norfolk was chosen Tangier slipped back into obscurity. In 1821, when the island's population totaled only 74, the camp meeting attracted 6,000 people, and soon after it closed a terrific hurricane raised tides that completely inundated the island beneath five feet of water. Though the islanders continued to raise most of their own food, a new industry — oystering — was in full swing by the 1830s, and with the profits from seafood came a growing population, a church (1835), and the first general store (1840).

Tangier remained loyal to the Union during the Civil War, and prospered on seafood during the conflict only to be struck by an epidemic of cholera in 1866. In that same year a new railroad was built down the Eastern Shore to a new town called Crisfield, Maryland, and the seafood trade, spurred by the possibility of swift shipment to northern urban markets, boomed. Tangier's mainland contacts shifted from the Virginia Eastern Shore to Crisfield, and the island entered a prosperous period that saw the erection of a number of the homes still standing today.

By 1900 Tangier had a population of 1,500 located in several communities, or "ridges." A lighthouse erected in 1890 beamed from the island's southern tip; there were two public schools and, in time, two local movie houses. Telephone service became available in 1907, electricity in 1910, though not for decades would either be up-to-date by mainland standards of that day. Many islanders were intensely religious, all Methodists, and the present church, the fourth one on the island, was completed in 1899.

In 1917 and 1922 the government dredged a deeper harbor, in the process building up land at the northern edge of Main Ridge, and that part of the island quickly became the central "downtown" even as other more out-lying ridges faded. Canaan Ridge, on the northernmost shore, was abandoned in 1928, victim of steady erosion, and Oyster Creek Ridge, the westernmost, in the 1930s. The island's once-scattered population coalesced on three "ridges" — Main, West, and Canton — which are now connected by bridges and paved roads, and constitute the only inhabited portion of the steadily shrinking island.

Despite its isolation, it seems to be the island's lot to become the subject of a flare-up of publicity from time to time. The publicity surrounding the need for a doctor, after the resident physician of many years retired in 1954, was nothing short of worldwide. Storms and tides and winter freezes have kept the island in the news, as has the steady erosion that has gobbled up the western side of the island as much as 35 feet a year; a stone "seawall" completed in 1990, designed to stop the erosion, now hugs the island's western shore. The ecological problems of the Chesapeake have not only affected the island, which has long since depended upon the crab instead of the oyster, but also kept it in the public eye. And Tangier was once again thrust into the limelight in 1998, when the Town Council con-

sidered the possibility of using the island as the location for the motion picture "Message in a Bottle," but spurned the offer upon learning that the script included drinking and foul language.

In the early 1900s Tangier Islanders had a reputation for stand-offishness, even unfriendliness to visitors — perhaps because the islanders initially mistook the entourage of President Woodrow Wilson for German spies when he visited the island in 1916. Visitors sometimes found townsfolk sensitive about being photographed, unhappy that their "accent" was remarked upon, and resentful when their practice of burying family dead in the front or back yard was labeled "quaint" (in fact, that custom is not limited to Tangier and is frequently seen on the Eastern Shore mainland). No such attitudes greet today's visitors, who are gently tolerated and even welcomed. As many as 20,000 people a year visit Tangier, but the tour boats come and go in the same day, leaving few behind, and Tangier remains visibly, even defiantly "un-touristy."

Tangier Island meets the expectation of almost no one. Those who expect the picturesque find it prosaic, those who expect it to be awful find it quite pleasant, those who anticipate the antiquated find it up-to-date. It is, nonetheless, a remarkable place.

A Walking Tour of Tangier

It *is* possible to take a riding tour of Tangier, in the golf-cart "buses" of enterprising islanders who will show you around for a fee. On the other hand, Tangier's roads are meant for walking and are not extensive, and interpretive historical markers (in distinctive yellow and blue) in front of many of the island's homes and sites deserve close scrutiny.

Though the town's homes and businesses largely turn their backs to the water, **the Harbor** [1], where your boat will dock [the Onancock boat docks at the County Dock, see #36 below], is still the busiest place in town, usually buzzing with activity. To the north, across North Channel, lies fully half the land area of Tangier Island, once inhabited, now abandoned marshland. To the east lies Port Isobel Island, owned by the Chesapeake Bay Foundation, and on the horizon uninhabited Watts Island. Most of the buildings in and around the harbor are crab houses, where island watermen watch for "peelers" — crabs about to shed their hard outer shell — until just the right moment for shipping.

From the harbor all lanes lead to Main Ridge Road, the island's principal thoroughfare. Turn left, and as you head south the homes and buildings on your left are for the most part recent because they stand on "new land," built up with shells and fill from the dredging of the harbor. Buildings on the right are older, including an old **Oyster Creek House** [2] *(16140 Main Ridge Road)* moved to this spot from a part of Tangier now under water, and the **Double Six Sandwich Shop** [3] *(16146 Main Ridge Road)*, a favorite hang-out of local watermen that was depicted in the 1973 *National Geographic* article on Tangier.

Swain Memorial United Methodist Church [4] *(16164 Main*

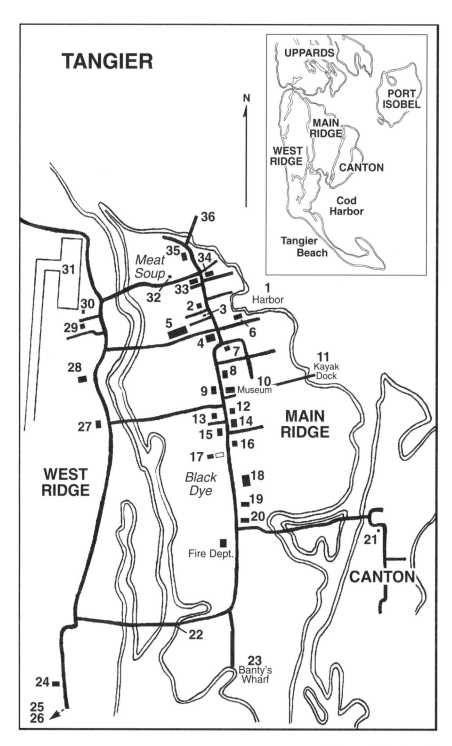

TANGIER

N

UPPARDS

PORT
ISOBEL

MAIN
RIDGE

WEST
RIDGE

CANTON

Cod
Harbor

Tangier
Beach

36

35   34

*Meat
Soup*

33

32

31

30

29

2   3

5

6

4

28

27

7

8

9   Museum

11
Kayak
Dock

10

12

13   14

15

16

17

*Black
Dye*

18

19

20

21

WEST
RIDGE

MAIN
RIDGE

CANTON

Fire Dept.

22

23
Banty's
Wharf

24

25
26

1
Harbor

Ridge Road) dominates almost any view of Tangier. The church is named for Charles Swain, the young pastor who died suddenly after overseeing its construction in 1899. There are more than 400 members, and many of them attend "class meeting" (look for it on the signboard out front), a weekly gathering that has disappeared virtually everywhere else in American Methodism. The oldest part of the church cemetery is behind the building on School Road; it is easy, by noting the dates of the tombstones, to see how the cemetery has expanded over the years. **The Tangier Combined School** [5] — "combined" because it is attended by all the island students, kindergarten through grade 12 — is the most recent (1998) of the several school buildings which have stood near the church.

Janders Road is named in honor of Henry Jander, a Connecticut contractor who moved his family to the island in the 1940s and became instrumental in obtaining up-to-date electrical power for the community; the **Electric Plant** [6] *(4443 Janders Road)*, built in 1947, displays a number of photographs of the island from that period. The road beside the **Post Office** [7] turns a sharp right and becomes Ponderosa Lane, named for the location of a TV western that was popular when this part of the island was developed; the "new land" on which its homes stand, built up with fill from dredging, was said by the islanders to be "as big as the Ponderosa."

Some of the island's oldest and largest homes line the street south of the church, among them the **Edward Crockett House** [8] *(16199 Main Ridge)* and the **Joshua Pruitt House** [9] *(16216 Main Ridge)*, both of which served at times as "hotels" or boarding houses.

An essential stop for all visitors to the island is the **Tangier History Museum** [10] *(16215 Main Ridge)*. In what was once an old store, the museum now offers an impressive and engaging presentation of the island's history and culture, past and present (no admission charged; donations welcome). Behind the museum is the **Public Kayak Dock** [11], reached by a boardwalk stretching across the marsh. The view here is a good one, and the kayaks and canoes may be used free of charge; a brochure charting several water trails around the island is available in the museum.

Below the museum, the **Milton Marshall House** [12] *(16233 Main Ridge)*, now housing a gift shop, and the **Peter Dise House** [13] *(16230 Main Ridge)*, which was moved to this location from the northern end of the island, both once boasted wells in their yards; another well adjacent at 16235 Main Ridge was widely used by the community before the advent of the town's water supply.

The **Chesapeake House** [14] *(16243 Main Ridge)* began in 1944 in the old **Peter S. Crockett House** [15] *(16246 Main Ridge]*; today one house serves as restaurant, the other as "inn." Two doors below at 16251 Main Ridge stands the **Doctors' House** [16], home to several consecutive island doctors; their little office still faces the back yard behind the next house to the south. On the right two doors beyond Dise Lane, behind the new house at 16276 Main Ridge, stands the **Old**

Jail [17], a tin building where the town kept its lock-up cell. One of the last prisoners here, convinced that the jailer had forgotten to bring him lunch, simply climbed out through the roof, went home to eat, and climbed back in to resume his sentence.

Below the Old Jail, the road passes into a part of town known (for reasons long forgotten) as "Black Dye." The **New Testament Congregation** [18] *(16289 Main Ridge)* was founded in 1946 from the Methodist church in a schism so heated that it was featured in *Newsweek*. A few doors further south stands the **Patrick Benson House** [19] *(16307 Main Ridge)*, a handsome home of the late 19th century. **Parks Store** [20] *(16315 Main Ridge)* operated until 2006; its closing left only one grocery store on the island.

Just beyond Parks Store, Canton Road leads eastward to Canton, the smallest of Tangier's three "ridges," and the first to be settled. Most homes in Canton today are recent ones, but in the corner of the cemetery is a marker indicating the probable **Site of the Island's First Church** [21], erected 1835.

At the southern end of Main Ridge, the road turns westward and crosses the **Hoistin' Bridge** [22], which is now fixed but once had an opening in the center that allowed the masts of sailing vessels to slip through; a loose plank across the opening, removed for boats, was put back for pedestrians (and sometimes removed at night by youthful pranksters). From the bridge can be glimpsed, toward the south, the waters of Cod Harbor, where once the steamboats docked; **Banty's Wharf** [23] was then the chief landing spot for the island. The view towards the north is of the "Big Gut" as it meanders through the marshes separating Main Ridge from West Ridge.

A short distance down Hog Ridge Road, to the left once at West Ridge, is the **Muddy Toes Library** [24] *(16680 Hog Ridge),* a privately owned free lending library for the island; the home opposite it at 16685 Hog Ridge, also known as Muddy Toes, boasts the island's first and only heli-pad. An unpaved road and bridge beyond the pavement leads to the place where the southern end of **the Seawall** [25] meets the northern end of **Tangier Beach** [26]. From this point there is more than a mile of beach to the island's southernmost tip; at points there may be little more than 15 feet of dry land between water on both sides, as wind, storm, and waves constantly shift the terrain. The beach, which is usually deserted, is much diminished from the days when thousands of British troops camped here in 1814, and the Methodist camp meeting attracted thousands annually until 1857.

Prominent among the houses of West Ridge are the large 19th-century **John Thomas House** [27] *(16448 West Ridge)*, facing Wallace Road, and the much-admired **Sidney Wallace House** [28] *(16408 West Ridge)*, built in 1904. The Parson of the Islands lived from 1799 to 1825 at **4300 Joshua Thomas Lane** [29], where today a modern chalet stands next to a former naval "spotting station" that now houses the **Town Office** [30] *(4301 Joshua Thomas Lane)*. The Parson's home was not unlike the old abandoned house still standing at the end of Long Bridge Road, which was moved here from Oyster Creek Ridge when that community was abandoned. The **Tangier Airstrip** [31] was dedicated in 1969; beyond it the Chesapeake, now 1,000 *feet* from the tarmac, was then more than 1,000 *yards* distant.

Northernmost of the four bridges over the Big Gut is the New Bridge, or Long Bridge, which leads back to a section of Main Ridge known as "Meat Soup." On the left is the **Old Cemetery** [32], dating from 1858 and containing many of the island's most interesting old gravestones. At the busy corner on Main Ridge stands the **Peter Williams House** [33] *(16116 Main Ridge),* now bereft of the "gingerbread" that once adorned its eaves and porch, and **Daley's Grocery** [34] *(16115 Main Ridge),* built in the 1920s. The **Methodist Parsonage** [35] *(16094 Main Ridge)* was erected in 1887, and just beyond it the **County Dock** [36] juts into the harbor at the point where it was once crossed by a bridge to the northern part of the island, known as "Uppards." Canaan Ridge, once a thriving community with its own stores, school, and church, lay a mile north of this point; it was abandoned in the 1920s.

(For a fuller description of Tangier's history and sites, see *God's Island: The History of Tangier* by Kirk Mariner, published by Miona Publications.)

PARRAMORE ISLAND DUNES

4 THE BARRIER ISLANDS

Nature Untamed

It is not easy to visit the Barrier Islands, but those who do will see one of the most celebrated yet unfrequented portions of the Eastern Shore of Virginia.

They are celebrated for their natural beauty and tremendous ecological value. Designated a National Natural Landmark by the Federal government and a Biosphere Reserve by the United Nations, the islands have been pictured in full color in such national magazines as *Life* and *Smithsonian*, and are today more than ever in the news.

They are unfrequented because they remain untouched by development, inaccessible to automobiles, and beyond the reach of all who do not travel by boat. In fact, if you plan to do all of your sightseeing from the car, you might as well skip this chapter.

The Barrier Islands—the term is a modern one, and refers to all the islands that line the Atlantic side of the Eastern Shore, from Fisherman Island in the south up to and including Assateague Island in the north—are the one part of the Eastern Shore of Virginia that man has never tamed. A wild maze of marshland, beach, shallow water, and shifting channel, they comprise a giant protective buffer between the Shore and the relentless Atlantic. Since before the time of man, storm-driven waves have expended their energy on these lonely islands, unable to vent their full wrath on the mainland behind them. The happy result for the Eastern Shore is that it has remained impervious to the ocean's onslaught, but the islands themselves are a mosaic of almost constantly changing shapes. As man has discovered when he has dared to build here, the shoreline never stays still, but is constantly being eroded away in one spot only to be built up in another.

Since they act as giant sponges that absorb most of the ocean's tides, the Barrier Islands are immensely rich in plant and animal life. Biologists have estimated that the marshes that link the islands to the mainland are among the richest and most productive in the world, and that as much as 90% of the fish and shellfish harvested in this region are dependent, at some time in their lives, upon the wetlands of the Barrier Islands. Large concentrations of birds, including migrating and wintering waterfowl, are to be seen here; ten species of hawks inhabit the islands, including the endangered Peregrine falcon.

In 1970 a development company announced its intention to turn three of the islands—Smith, Myrtle, and Ship Shoal—into "King's Beach," a residential and recreational community complete with convention center, shopping malls, airports, bridges, and subdivisions. Alarmed by this prospect, the Nature Conservancy, an Arlington-based conservation organization, purchased nearby Godwin Island and launched negotiations to purchase the three islands slated for development. Today the Virginia Coast Reserve, a preserve of the Nature Conservancy, owns most of the islands, nearly 40,000 acres in all. With the exception of a portion of Cedar, which is privately owned, and Assateague, Wallops, Assawoman, Wreck, and Fisherman Island, which are owned by various agencies of the government, most of the rest of the Barrier Islands are now Nature Conservancy property, and the owners are bent on letting nature have her way with them.

Three of the islands are off-limits to the general public: Parramore, Revel's, and Ship Shoal, the last of which was once a bombing range and may be unsafe. Public use of the rest of the islands is permitted during the day for hiking, beachcombing, swimming, surf fishing, photography, and nature study. Hunting is restricted to the low saltmarsh areas and to the use of steel shot, and hunters must contact the Coast Reserve headquarters prior to using the islands. Shellfishing is possible in some areas. "Take only pictures, leave only footprints," and the islands' owners are happy for you to use them.

Not permitted on the islands are airplanes, motor vehicles, overnight camping, campfires, domestic animals, and destruction of plant and animal life. Visitors are asked to stay close to the water's edge so as not to disturb the nesting birds.

The headquarters of the Virginia Coast Reserve are at **Brownsville** *(From Route 13 turn east in Nassawadox at light, then left on Seaside Road #600 and right on Brownsville Road #608, a total distance of 1.6 miles)* The staff here welcomes inquiries about the Conservancy and its programs. Check in (9:00-4:30 Monday-Friday) for a self-guided walk out to the hammocks overlooking Hog Island Bay.

Membership in the Virginia Coast Reserve is not required, but all members receive regular mailings about upcoming events and tours. Write: Virginia Coast Reserve, P. O. Box 158, Nassawadox, Virginia 23413, phone 757-442-3049.

A separate entity is the **Barrier Islands Center**, located not on the islands but on Route 13 at Machipongo, which houses the efforts of a local foundation to "preserve and perpetuate the culture and history of the Virginia barrier islands through education, protection and collection or artifacts, and interpretation of that way of life." *(See page 21)*.

FISHERMAN ISLAND, the southernmost of the Barrier Islands, is one of the few accessible to the automobile, since it is crossed by the approaches to the Chesapeake Bay Bridge-Tunnel. Because it is, however, a wildlife refuge owned by the Federal government, access to the island is generally restricted to special tours on Saturdays, October through March; for schedules and information check at the Eastern Shore of Virginia National Wildlife Refuge Visitor Center *(Entrance on Seaside Road just east of Route 13 at the Bridge-Tunnel; 331-2760)*.

The earliest maps of the Eastern Shore show no island at this point, because Fisherman Island was simply not there. The island has taken shape within historic times. According to local tradition, a ship with a cargo of linen sank east of the island centuries ago, and the sand that collected around it became a sandbar, "Linen Bar," that ultimately built up into Fisherman Island. In fact, the constant eroding away and building up of land throughout the Barrier chain tends to build up the southern end at the expense of the northern end, a tendency visibly illustrated by Assateague Island's "Hook." The same process seems to be at work at this end of the island chain, where Fisherman Island is taking shape at the expense of adjacent Smith Island, which during historic times has been broken into separate portions.

SMITH ISLAND. With characteristic modesty, or lack thereof, Captain John Smith named this island for himself when he explored the Eastern Shore in 1608. Smith Island proved valuable to the early colonists because salt could be so easily obtained there; in fact, salt-making operations on the island brought the first, though impermanent, English settlers to the Eastern Shore in 1614. The island was also strategic because of its location at the entrance to Chesapeake Bay, and to it the colonial government dispatched look-outs to "Range & Scout at least once a week" for enemy vessels. Pirate captain Edward Teach, known as Blackbeard, selected Smith Island as the place to clean the fouled hull of his ship in 1717; the cove at the southern end of the island is still known as **Blackbeard's Cove**.

Cape Charles Lighthouse, erected in 1895, is the third lighthouse to stand on the island. The first, built of brick in 1828, early proved inadequate and a source of complaint. A new one was begun in 1856, was plundered by Confederate raiders before it was finished, and was finally lighted in 1864. It stood a mile east of the present one, and ultimately succumbed to the ever-encroaching sea. The present lighthouse, automated in 1963, is the brightest in the Chesapeake region, with 1.2 million candlepower; its original lens is now on display at the Mariner's Museum in Newport News.

Landlubbers may glimpse the lighthouse while crossing Fisherman Island on the Bridge-Tunnel, or from Cushman's Landing on the Lower Seaside *(see page 119)*.

COBB ISLAND *(Accessible by boat via Sand Shoal Channel from Oyster)* was for many years known as Great Sand Shoal Island, a distant and inaccessible place that seemed to prey upon passing ships. Among the many people who were cast ashore in these treacherous waters were Nathan and Nancy Cobb and their family, as they sailed southward from Massachusetts in the 1830s looking for a more healthful climate for the ailing Mrs. Cobb. In 1839 the Cobbs bought this island, allegedly using as part payment a wagonload of salt gathered from the beach here, and thereafter the island bore their name.

Nathan Cobb moved his family to Cobb Island for the express purpose of going into the salvage business. In those days before the Coast Guard, someone had to rescue crews and cargoes of the ships that frequently went down offshore. Though they never charged a fee, Nathan and his sons often collected as much as 60% of what they managed to save, and the Cobbs prospered. Game was plentiful on their island; the Cobbs killed more than they could eat, and shipped the rest out at a profit. When this caused the island's fame as a hunting ground to spread, Nathan erected a large hotel to accommodate the sportsmen who came to sample it. By the 1880s the Cobb Island hotel had entertained guests from as far away as Canada, France, and England, was connected by a stage to the Cobb's Station on the railroad nearby, and was supplied by family-owned farms and mills on the mainland. The descendants of Nathan Cobb multiplied sufficiently to necessitate the erection of their own village church in 1882.

Nathan Cobb died in 1890, and the following year his island began to wash away. The Cobb brothers moved their families to the mainland as erosion rapidly reduced the size of the island; the last to go were Nathan Jr. and his wife Sally, who were removed by the Coast Guard in 1896. Not long afterward the ocean cut a channel through the island at exactly the point where the hotel had once stood. Today Cobb Island is only a fraction of what it once was, and offers no evidence of its once prosperous settlement. Among the most sought-after remnants of life on this island are the decoys carved by the hunting brothers Nathan Jr. and Albert. Widely admired by the collectors of this form of folk art, they are among the earliest Eastern Shore decoys. In 1983 a single Nathan Cobb decoy sold at auction for $28,000; other examples of his work are on display at the Refuge Waterfowl Museum in Chincoteague. The last Coast Guard Station of Cobb Island now stands on the mainland near Oyster *(see page 120)*.

HOG ISLAND (*Accessible by boat via Great Machipongo Channel from Willis Wharf, or via main channel from Quinby*) has been so named since before it was settled, probably because early mainland settlers turned their hogs loose on this island to forage for themselves. The first resident here was Thomas Coffin in the 1680s. Peter Doughty, whose progeny became in time the largest family on the island, moved here in 1752.

During the American Revolution, the British under Captain John Kidd established a base on Hog Island, and from it made frequent nightly raids on the plantations of the mainland for livestock and food to supply their warships.

It was only after the Revolution that Hog Island's population began to grow. A Methodist congregation was established among the islanders in 1795, only to fade out by the 1830s. A lighthouse was erected here in 1852, a life-saving station in 1874. After 1880 the island entered its prime. A new church was built in 1883, and in 1886 a hunting club whose guests included President Grover Cleveland. In 1892, the year when the crew of the life-saving station saved 25 lives from a sinking Spanish ship, a new lighthouse was erected. By 1900 the population had reached 160, and islanders were shipping 150,000 bushels of oysters a year at considerable profit.

Life on Hog Island, or Broadwater as the village was called, was a constant battle with the sea. In 1903 a storm, the same storm in which Orville and Wilbur Wright first flew their aircraft at Kitty Hawk in North Carolina, raised tides that completely covered the island. By then it was the local custom to open front and back door of the house during a storm, so that the waves could wash completely through, sparing the house itself. Many an island home was erected with lumber washed up from the sea, and some were furnished with furniture, silverware, lanterns, and chronometers also cast up on the beach.

The sea began to win its battle in the early 1900s. As erosion set in, islanders one by one floated their homes over to the mainland, to Oyster and Willis Wharf in particular. By 1919 the population had dwindled to 70, and years later, after the great Storm of 1933 took 60 feet of the beach at one bite, only 40 people remained. By 1940 the island was virtually abandoned, except for Southey "Sud" Bell, who lived there alone for many years, departing only to create a name for himself in New York and Richmond playing banjo and clowning for crowds who considered him a colorful eccentric.

In 1948 the ocean finally reached the base of the lighthouse, which had once stood a mile from the sea; the government had it demolished in that year. In 1956 a Coast Guardsman walking in the region of the abandoned town cemetery found the petrified torso of an islander buried in 1931, so perfectly preserved by minerals from the sea that he was identified by his friends and reburied on the mainland. A few years later even the Coast Guard abandoned Hog Island.

Hog Island today betrays almost nothing of its former life. Erosion has diminished the island and constantly changed its shape, and waves lap upon what once were front lawns and well-tended gardens. In Willis Wharf, however, stand 18 homes which were once located on the island, one of which also served as the Broadwater Post Office. And in the village of Oyster the little church that once served Broadwater still stands at the back of the Methodist chapel there.

PARRAMORE ISLAND *(Accessible by boat via the main channels from Quinby or Wachapreague)* takes its name from Thomas Parramore, who purchased it in 1750. Legends persist that Blackbeard, Edward Teach, frequented this island, and even buried a treasure here. But early maps call it Feaches' Island, and the legends are likely rooted in nothing more than a confusion of names.

There has never been much settlement on Parramore, largest and most heavily wooded of the Barrier chain below Assateague. A club house for sportsmen functioned here from the 1880s until 1933, and there is still a private hunting lodge. The island looms quite visibly on the horizon from the waterfront in Wachapreague; the Coast Guard once stationed on Parramore Island now operates out of a boat berthed in that town. Because of certain "legal constraints," the Nature Conservancy does not open Parramore Island to the general public.

CEDAR ISLAND lies closer to the mainland than most of the other Barrier Islands, across the marshes from Daugherty, south of Accomac. As a result, people have always tried to develop it. In 1683 the island's first owners petitioned for "a convenient road to a point where we can embark for the Island recently patented by us." A. H. Gordon Mears, builder of the hotel in Wachapreague, erected a hotel on the southern spit of the island early in the 20th century, but it was destroyed during a storm. More lasting was the Snead's Beach Clubhouse which operated on a high point in the center of the island until the middle of the twentieth century.

In the early 1960s, when local developers envisioned a resort named Ocean City, Virginia, over 2,200 building lots were sold on Cedar Island, and a hotel opened in an abandoned Coast Guard station. Small boats regularly plied the route between Cedar Island and Folly Creek Landing, but a projected bridge was never built, and only a few cabins ever erected. In the late 1980s the island again became the center of controversy between those who hoped to develop it and those who hoped to see it left as it is.

There have been two Coast Guard stations on this island. The earlier was located at the southern end, swept away in 1933, and replaced by one on Parramore Island. The second still stands at the northern edge of the island on Metompkin Inlet, a privately owned hunting lodge that also served as the Cedar Island Sports Club Hotel in the short-lived Ocean City.

Cedar Island, which is privately owned, can be glimpsed from the Wachapreague waterfront, but is better seen from Burton's Shore *(see page 129)*, where the second **Coast Guard Station**, now abandoned, and a number of beach cottages can be seen, clinging to man's tenuous hold on the sands of this restless island.

METOMPKIN ISLAND *(Accessible by boat from the public landing at Gargathy Creek),* northernmost of the islands owned by the Nature Conservancy, has in the past 300 years had several other names: Ship Rack Island, Rack Island, Justis Beach, or just The Beaches. There has been little building here. A Coast Guard station was established on the south beach, but washed away during the great Storm of 1933; after being relocated on Cedar Island, it was still known as the Metompkin Inlet Station.

Metompkin Island can be glimpsed from Gargatha Neck *(see page 131),* where most of the cottages that punctuate the horizon in the distance stand on the Metompkin shore. Also visible from the same spot is **Wallops Island**, identifiable by its tall NASA installations. Between Metompkin and Wallops lies **Assawoman Island**, never inhabited; this only view of it from the mainland finds it blended into the horizon, utterly indistinguishable from its neighbors because nothing is built on it. It is Federally protected as part of the Chincoteague National Wildlife Refuge. Wallops Island and **Assateague Island**, the northernmost of the Barrier chain, are described in detail in Chapters 12 and 2, respectively.

ACCOMAC COURTYARD

5 ACCOMAC

Historical Jewel of the Eastern Shore

*From Route 13 turn east in the center of Accomack
County, 20 miles below Maryland or 15 miles above
Exmore.*

It is said that among Virginia's old towns only Williamsburg has
more historic architecture than Accomac. Certainly few places in
Virginia, and none on the Eastern Shore, surpass the county seat of
Accomack County in preserving handsome buildings from the past. A
Virginia Historic District was created here a few years ago, and
Accomac is so historic that almost the whole town was included in it.

To surround its collection of remarkably fine historic homes,
churches, and public buildings, Accomac uses tree-shaded streets, pretty gardens, well-tended lawns—just about everything needed to make
the place picture-perfect. Only those totally oblivious to the past can
afford to pass up this little town; for most others, it will be one of the
premier attractions of the Eastern Shore.

History
*Because of its central location, the site of Accomac was chosen
for the county seat in the 1600s. This neighborhood was then*

known as Metompkin, and John Dye, the first white man to settle here, complained to the authorities in 1664 that "the King of the Matompkin [Indians] and his great men have beaten and abused him." Even so, white residents gradually filled the area, pushing the Indians out, and by the 1690s the Accomack County Court had settled here for good.

In 1786, when the site was owned principally by a man named Richard Drummond, Virginia established here "a town by the name of Drummond." The present configuration of streets dates largely from that time, and it was then that the homes and buildings so admired today began to be constructed. In a tavern that stood across the street from the courthouse was born Henry A. Wise [1806-1876], three-term Congressman, U.S. Minister to Brazil, and the only Eastern Shoreman ever elected Governor of Virginia. By 1835 Drummondtown was a thriving village of 240 inhabitants, 39 homes, one church, and a host of small businesses. In 1860 the Shore's first newspaper, the "National Recorder," came off the press here.

In 1861 when the Eastern Shore of Virginia was occupied by the Union army, Drummondtown was chosen as the headquarters of its commanding officer, General Henry H. Lockwood. Though the town survived the Civil War with little physical damage—except to the Methodist and Presbyterian churches, which Union soldiers used as barracks and stables—southern sentiment in Drummondtown was strong, and the occupation was an uneasy one. One anonymous Yankee writing in the army's own local newspaper, the "Regimental Flag," labeled the place a "one-horse town." Not until the early 1870s did the townsfolk see the last of the army of occupation.

In 1884 the railroad came to the Eastern Shore of Virginia and by-passed Drummondtown, creating Accomac Station, now Tasley, just to the west. Throughout the last two decades of the 1800s there was considerable agitation to move the courthouse from Drummondtown to the new town of Parksley on the railroad; a county-wide referendum on the issue in 1895 decided in favor of the older town. By then Drummondtown had been officially renamed Accomac, in 1893, to the continuing confusion of untold numbers of people from off the Shore ever since. By official legislative act, the proper spelling of the town is Accomac, without the final "k," while the county is spelled Accomack.

Today Accomac is, at it has always been, a small place, population 466. But it has always had a local significance disproportionate to its size, and the visitor will likely find it, small or not, charming and memorable.

A Walking Tour of Accomac

Accomac is best seen afoot. There is free parking in the center of town near the Courthouse.

This walking tour covers about 1.5 miles. Homes on the route are private residences not generally open to visitors. Public restrooms are located in the County Office Building behind the Courthouse.

Start at the town's most famous building the **Debtor's Prison** [1]. Erected in 1783 as a residence for the county jailer, it stands in what was once the corner of the large walled "prison bounds," and in 1824 was made over into a jail for segregating imprisoned debtors from other inmates. Heavy wooden doors and iron bars over the windows are still to be seen. The building is a Virginia Historic Landmark, listed in the National Register of Historic Places.

The **Courthouse** [2] was erected in 1899, replacing an earlier and prettier one on the same site built in 1756. You may enter and inspect this public building, but perhaps more interesting is the Victorian brick Clerk's Office, largest of the small buildings that line the west side of the Courthouse Green. Here you can see books dating back to 1663, the second oldest continuous court records in the nation (only those in Eastville are older). In a giant volume labeled Accomack County Orders 1714-1717 are two ancient graffiti on the original flyleaf: *"God Save the King"* is written in one hand, and beneath it in another, *"God Damn the King."*

The old cannon on the Green is one of several in town from the American Revolution. Across the street from it, at the edge of the service station lot, is another one standing perpendicular next to a telephone pole. To this cannon visitors used to be sent if they wished to return some day to Accomac, there to intone:

Whoever doth this ancient gun embrace
Will surely to the town his steps retrace.

Across Front Street from the Green, on the site of an older tavern that burned in 1921, stands the **Accomac Hotel** [3], now a private home. Here was born Henry A. Wise (1807-1876), the Shore's most prominent son, a political leader of national stature in the mid-1800s.

Seymour House [4] *(23292 Front Street)* stands a few doors west of the Green on the south side of the street, a perfect example of the Shore's characteristic "big house, little house, colonnade, kitchen" architecture *(see illustration, page 9)*. Its construction was begun in 1791, and it is said to contain an undiscovered buried cache of money and no fewer than three ghosts. Just east of the house is a well preserved icehouse, built low into the ground for the storage of great blocks of ice for family and town use. On the corner beyond Seymour House stands **Rural Hill** [5] *(23254 Front Street)*, dating from 1816; this is "Meetinghouse Lot," site of an early Presbyterian church from 1765 to about 1790.

Turn down Drummondtown Road #605 to **St. James Episcopal Church** [6], one of the architectural gems of the Shore. The first build-

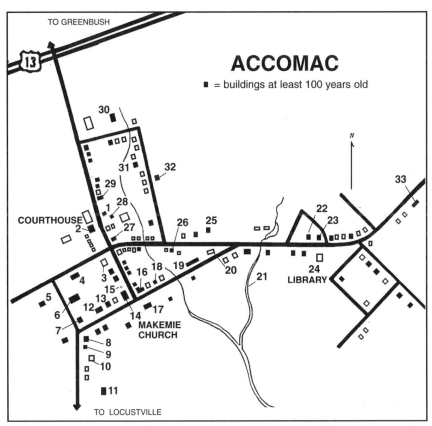

TO GREENBUSH

ACCOMAC

■ = buildings at least 100 years old

N

33

COURTHOUSE

22
23

26   25

20   21

24
LIBRARY

16 18 19

4   3
15
13
12
6
7
14
MAKEMIE
CHURCH

8
9
10

■11

TO LOCUSTVILLE

ing of this congregation was erected a mile south of town in 1767, before Drummondtown was founded. In 1838 the Episcopalians decided to move to the village to compete with the Methodists and the Presbyterians, so they dismantled their old building, carted the bricks to this site, and built this handsome Greek Revival church, the walls of which are in some places 20 inches thick. About 1855 a traveling artist named Jean G. Potts was commissioned to decorate the interior, and he did so with an exceptionally fine display of illusionistic, or trompe d'oeil, painting: columns, pilasters, panels, even hallways and doors that are actually fakes painted on a flat surface. Potts' painting has been restored, but on the south wall under the balcony one section was left untouched to show his original work. St. James is another Virginia Historic Landmark.

Bloodworth Cottage [7] *(23283 Back Street)* stands on the corner of Locustville Road and Back Street, a charming home of the early 19th century, now restored and pleasing from every angle inside and out. Most of the houses beyond it on the Locustville Road are "new," that is, late-19th century. **23433 Drummondtown Road** [8], with its big front porch, was built in 1890. Next door to it is **Woodbridge** [9] *(23443 Drummondtown Road)*, a tiny two-room home with no front door; originally erected miles away in Northampton County in the 1700s, this house was moved to this site in the 1960s. **Drummondtown United Methodist Church** [10] is the third building on this site; the first was built in 1793, soon after Bishop Francis Asbury preached here. The present building, with stained glass windows by Tiffany protege George Hardy Payne, dates from 1918. **Roseland** [11] *(23340 Drummondtown Road)* sits back from the road two doors south of the church, almost hidden by its trees and shrubs. It is composed of five sections, the largest of which was built in 1826, the oldest of which dates from the 1750s, making it possibly the oldest house in Accomac.

Back Street is considered by many to be the loveliest street on the Eastern Shore. Two doors past Bloodworth Cottage stands **The Rectory** [12] *(23309 Back Street)* of St. James Episcopal Church, built about 1811. This is the house selected by Union General Lockwood as his headquarters in 1861. The small frame building in the front yard was his telegraph office; it was erected in the 1850s by Peter Browne, a physician who used it for his practice. A careful glance at the east end of the "big house" of The Rectory will reveal an upstairs outside door, suggesting that the "colonnade" was once flat-roofed. Next door is **Parramore House** [13] *(23319 Back Street)*, built in 1881.

Makemie Presbyterian Church [14] is the oldest of this denomination on the Eastern Shore of Virginia, organized and erected in 1837 and named for the Reverend Francis Makemie. There were all of two charter members when this church was founded, but one of them was from New York City, and he obtained for the new building the pulpit furnishings of Brick Presbyterian Church in that city. Though severely damaged during the Union occupation, the church has been carefully restored to its mid-19th century appearance. Behind the church is a Statue of **Francis Makemie** [15], the "Father of American Presbyterianism." Erected in 1908, the statue originally stood at the Makemie Monument Grounds near Sanford *(see page 145)* and was moved to this site in 1984 to protect it from vandalism.

Seven Gables [16] *(23381 Back Street)*, on the corner by the church, was begun by Matthias Outten soon after 1788; succeeding owners kept adding to it, and the result is the U-shaped house of today, much admired for exterior and interior details. Behind the house is the one-room building that served as the office of Dr. Edward Young, who lived here in the 1840s.

Fletcher House [17] *(23368 Back Street)*, across from Seven Gables, was erected soon after 1817, and closely resembles The Rectory. The white lintels above its windows and doors are actually of wood, painted to resemble stone; the eastern end of the "little house" has been enlarged, as the brickwork at the side reveals. Diagonally opposite it stands **Tanyard House** [18] *(23385 Back Street)*, erected about 1800 for the owners of the tannery that once operated next door on the branch. One of its old sycamores is officially labeled a "Bicentennial Tree," complete with bronze plaque.

Across School Branch stands **The Haven** [19] *(23454 Back Street)*, composed of six sections that total half a football field in length. The original section, begun by Benjamin Potter about 1794, is the entrance hall facing Back Street. The detailed woodwork of this house is quite fine inside and out. **Drummondtown Baptist Church** [20], unusually formal for the Eastern Shore, dates from 1913, replacing an older building on the same site dating from 1870. In the yard of the church is a monument to Elijah Baker, founder of the Baptist faith on the peninsula.

At its mouth a wide and significant stream, **Folly Creek** [21] is here hardly more than a ditch, but the pond on it makes a handsome setting for a modern house that is a copy of the old estate Shirley in Hacks Neck. **Little House** [22] *(23601 Front Street)* is a charming representative of the "double house" that was so popular on the Shore up until 1850 *(see illustration, page 9)*. Next door to it is **The Glade** [23] *(23613 Front Street)*, part of which dates from the 1700s, part from about 1845; despite its charm, one room of this building may originally have been built as a barn. **The Eastern Shore Public Library** [24] is hardly old, but it is the best place on the peninsula for the study of regional and local history; there is an extensive collection of local materials, and a friendly and helpful staff.

Returning to downtown via Front Street, one encounters the **Bayly House** [25] *(23463 Front Street)*, built about 1810 for Congressman Thomas M. Bayly; his son Thomas H. Bayly, raised here, was also a Congressman. The cannon in the front yard marks one of the four corners of the area within which trusted prisoners from the jail were allowed to wander. **Milliner House** [26] *(23428 Front Street)*, now an office building, is another "double house" from the mid-1800s. On the corner is the **Old Mercantile Building** [27], built in 1816; over the years it has served as store, post office, bank, and office of the justice of the peace. Its cornices are exceptionally fine, deserving notice. Two old buildings adjoining the public parking lots were moved here from other places: the **Old Law Office** [28] (c. 1835) behind the Debtor's Prison once stood south of Tasley; the front part of the real estate office is an Old Schoolhouse [29], erected about 1870 in the village of Daugherty and moved to this location in the 1960s.

Around Accomac by Car

On School Street, behind the Accomac School, stands **Bayly Memorial Hall** [30], named for Congressman Thomas H. Bayly [1810-1856]. This is the original building of Drummondtown Baptist Church, erected in 1870 and moved to this site in 1913. Beyond it lies Lilliston Avenue, a late 19th-century street lined with large homes that are, by Accomac standards, "new." Among its more admirable homes are **23208 Lilliston Avenue** [31], a handsome Queen Anne style house of 1892, and **23227 Lilliston Avenue** [32], erected c. 1900 as Drummondtown Academy, a private school.

At the eastern end of town stands **Woodbourne** [33] *(24118*

Front Street), the largest section of which was built by George Wise soon after 1859. Wise joined the Confederate army and was killed at Petersburg, and the Union army, when it occupied Drummondtown, used his home as a hospital. There was a cemetery for Union soldiers at the back edge of the property, and for many years thereafter "Miss Etta," Wise's daughter, always ordered that the dead animals from the family barnyard be buried in that graveyard atop the soldiers—her way of having the last word with the Yankees.

Courthouse Avenue leads out of Accomac across Route 13 towards Greenbush, where the most prominent house is the **Bull Place** *(22401 Accomac Road)*, on the right a quarter mile beyond the highway. When Carter John Bull built the taller portion of this house around 1800, the lower brick section was already standing. Carter John was a slave trader who kept slaves chained in cells in the high basement beneath the newer part of the house. In his day it was customary for slaveowners to take their slaves to Drummondtown on court days to rent them out to other farmers, and Bull is said to have asked to be buried close to the road so that he could hear the tramping of the slaves on their way to the August court. After passing two nineteenth-century "double houses," this road ends in the village of Greenbush, where just across the railroad track is the tiny **Greenbush Post Office**, a charming little one-room building.

From this point it is three miles to the town of Parksley *(see Chapter 9)* on Route 316.

THE PAVILION, CAPE CHARLES

6 CAPE CHARLES

The Railroad's Once-and-Future "City"

From Route 13, turn west at the Cheriton traffic light, 9.5 miles above the Bridge-Tunnel, 56 miles below Maryland.

In Cape Charles, streets cross each other at perfect right angles to form regular city blocks, and houses stand close together as if transplanted from some more urban setting. Cape Charles City, as it was once called, was in its time the largest and busiest place on the Eastern Shore of Virginia, the other end of a railroad line that began in Manhattan, a Yankee outpost at the southern end of the peninsula.

Over the years the south domesticated this northern intrusion, as evidenced by the grand row of crepe myrtles lining today's main road into town. But then the railroad declined, and the highway moved elsewhere, and by the time it celebrated its 100th birthday Cape Charles had fallen into serious decline. Yet in this town civic pride is strong, and even as its downtown emptied and its grand old houses slipped towards decay, there was always a strong insistence that the town would bounce back.

Today that long-awaited renaissance is in full bloom, as once-sleepy Cape Charles has been rediscovered. Once again the town is at the center of new development, and once again what is happening there is unlike what the rest of the Eastern Shore of Virginia has ever witnessed. What was originally true of Cape Charles at its founding still seems true today: Cape Charles may be *on* the Eastern Shore, but it is not quite *of* it.

History

Cape Charles owes its birth to the railroad. In 1883, when it was known that this was to be the site for the southern terminus of the new railroad, Pennsylvania Congressman and multi-millionaire William L. Scott bought the land for the staggering sum of $55,000 and created a town from scratch. He laid out roads that formed a perfect square, with avenues named for famous Virginians crossing streets named for fruits and trees. The neat city blocks contained space for a central park, a school, and 644 new homes. In 1883, even before the railroad reached Cape Charles, the town began to take shape (the first building was a tavern on the eastern corner of Strawberry and Mason). Three short years later the town incorporated, by which time it contained 2 hotels, a tavern, a post office, a livery stable, several barrooms, several stores, a growing number of homes, and a newspaper named "The Pioneer."

The central attraction was the harbor, largest on the Shore between Norfolk and Maryland, where the rails ended right at the water. The railroad chartered the boat "Jane Mosely" to make the run to Norfolk, and by 1885 had added the steamer "Cape Charles" to ferry passengers and the tug "Norfolk" to pull freight. In 1886 another steamer line was opened connecting the town to Hampton. Whenever the train pulled in from the North, there was a steamer in the harbor waiting to shuttle passengers across the Chesapeake. By 1907 there were two round trips daily, and in Cape Charles the railroad employed almost 2,000 people in its machine shop, roundhouse, and network of trains and ships.

The Eastern Shore of Virginia had never experienced a town so prosperous, or one so oriented to the urban North, as "Cape Charles City." Here Eastern Shore natives and "come-heres" from the North mingled amicably. The town saw the first Roman Catholic and the only Jewish congregations ever assembled on the Virginia Shore. The most famous resident of the 1890s was a Baptist preacher who lived here and commuted weekly by train to his congregation in New York City.

For more than half a century the town prospered simply because anyone who traveled up or down the Shore had to pass through Cape Charles. The automobile ferry "Virginia Lee" went into service between Cape Charles and Little Creek in 1928; by 1930 there were three round-trip ferries daily, and a second ferry line to Ocean View. By the middle of the 1940s as many as two million people were passing through the town each year, and during holiday seasons traffic would back up in two lanes to the town limits waiting for the ferries. In 1947 the town was the location for a motion picture, "The Story of Mr. Hobbs," which starred noted film actress and producer Nell Shipman.

The decline began at mid-century. In 1950 the ferry moved its terminal out of Cape Charles to Kiptopeake Beach, six miles to the south. Four years later the railroad ceased to carry mail and passengers. Cape Charles, once the jumping-off-place for virtually all the Shore's travelers, found itself three miles off the beaten path. Commerce, and the population with it, began to dwindle.

A few years ago, when most of old Cape Charles was designated an Historic District, fewer than 40 of the more than 500 buildings in town were less than 50 years old. In the past decade the town has extended its boundaries to include Bay Creek, an extensive new residential development that almost surrounds the old town with upscale housing, shops, and golf courses. Today Cape Charles is a town in transformation, as the old section puts on a new face, the new sections continue to arise, and once more, as in the beginning, the place threatens to take on the air of a city.

Cape Charles by Car

Cape Charles is great for walking, but your first view of it should probably be by car. (Or rent a golf cart—Cape Charles is one of the few places in Virginia where such transportation is legal on public streets.) This itinerary will show you most of what the town has to offer with a minimum of doubling back in your tracks.

First stop, just beyond the town water tower that masquerades as a lighthouse, is the **Cape Charles Museum** [1], housed in an electric generating plant of 1947. The exhibits here change with some frequency, but always on display is the original giant Busch-Sulzer diesel fuel injection engine (16.5 inch bore), which can be cranked up and viewed close at hand. The museum includes a restored railroad station (originally from Bloxom), and a growing collection of railroad cars.

From Route 13 you enter Cape Charles on Randolph Avenue, and the downtown section, a row of stores facing the harbor, is on Mason Avenue, a block to the left. Downtown will be the ultimate test of how attractive the new Cape Charles can become. Though individual buildings are being refurbished, collectively they still face the railroad yard which was once, but is no longer, almost park-like, its lawns manicured and landscaped. Where once trains pulled into a giant railroad depot alongside steamboats, today one tiny office building occupies a near-empty railroad yard. Yet a taste of the railroad's glory days is available in the 1913-vintage **Bay Creek Railway Dining Car** [2], which offers dinner excursions. *(Parking and information on left between Peach and Strawberry streets)*.

The **Oldest House in Cape Charles** [3] *(515 Mason Avenue)* dates from 1883 and originally served as a hotel. It stands next to the **Municipal Building** [4], the oldest part of which is in the Art Deco style. The local fire department located here, organized 1888, still owns its first piece of motorized equipment, a 1924 American LaFrance engine, which is housed on the first floor of the Municipal Building, and is still used in parades. The **Palace Theatre** [5] *(305 Mason Avenue)* was built in 1941, once hosted the state-wide "Miss Virginia" pageant, and is now used for drama, ballet, and live performances. Inside are rare and unique murals of the Art Deco period. The town's oldest surviving commercial building is the corner store at **301 Mason Avenue** [6]; built in 1891, it is much changed on the ground floor but not on the second, as its Italianate windows attest.

The old **Wilson's Department Store** [7] *(245 Mason Avenue)*, now converted to condos, was in its time the largest department store on the Eastern Shore of Virginia. Among the most beautifully restored buildings of old downtown are the **Cape Charles Coffee Company** [8] *(241 Mason Avenue)* and the **Cape Charles Hotel** [9] *(235 Mason Avenue)*, both of which now reveal an elegance long obscured. On the corner of Mason and Pine a restaurant occupies the **Old Bank** [10] *(133 Mason Avenue)* built in Romanesque style in 1907, abandoned in 1921 for the newer one, in the Beaux-Arts style, across the street *(201 Mason Avenue)*.

The original Cape Charles ended at Pine Street, and when the town was founded the land between here and the bay was low and swampy. This area was drained, filled, and annexed to the town in 1911, when it became known as the Sea Cottage Addition. The first building in it was the **Cape Charles Ice & Lumber Company** [11] *(117 Mason Avenue)*, built about 1901 and now restored to its former appearance; it was the first downtown building to recover its second-story porch.

The **Northampton Hotel** [12] *(1 Mason Avenue)* was originally a home built c. 1900; it was enlarged into a hotel in 1940, but no longer functions as such. Just beyond it the town meets Chesapeake Bay; here the **Pier** [13], erected in 1995, juts out into the bay atop the jetty built by the government when the harbor was created in the 1880s, and the

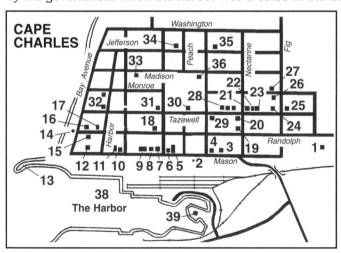

Boardwalk leads to **The Pavilion** [14] at Randolph. The beach is free and public. Turn down Randolph Avenue to see **Sunset View** [15] *(2 Randolph Avenue)*, built in 1920 by a retired

sea captain who outfitted it with no fewer than 53 windows. Across the street stand two **Sears Houses** [16] *(1 & 3 Randolph Avenue)*, built in the 1920s from ready-to-assemble materials marketed by Sears and Roebuck. In the same block is **Sterling House** [17] *(9 Randolph Avenue)*, the 1913 home of a former mayor. Two blocks beyond stands **237 Randolph Avenue** [18], a Victorian-era house in the Gothic Revival style with a handsome and, for these parts, rare cast-iron fence.

St. Charles Roman Catholic Church [19] *(545 Randolph Avenue)* was the first, and for 60 years the only Catholic church on the Eastern Shore of Virginia. Monsignor Edward Mickle, who built it in 1889, single-handedly planting Catholicism on the overwhelmingly Protestant peninsula, lies buried in the churchyard next to the rectory, which he also built in 1894. His is the only grave within the old town limits of Cape Charles. Behind the church on Tazewell Avenue at Nectarine is the **Convent of the Holy Family** [20], the only Catholic parochial school ever to function on the Eastern Shore of Virginia. It was built by Mickle in 1898 and opened with only four scholars; when enrollment reached 100, fully 85 of the students were Protestants. The school closed in 1935.

Diagonally opposite the convent stands **Emmanuel Episcopal Church** [21], erected 1893, and next to it **Henrietta's Cottage** [22] *(611 Tazewell Avenue)*, erected in 1895 by the superintendent of the railroad. **Honeysuckle Lodge** [23] *(629 Tazewell Avenue)* dates from the 1890s, and from 1894 to 1896 was the home of Thomas Dixon Jr. [1864-1946], Baptist minister, lawyer, writer, actor, who lived here while he was the popular pastor of a congregation in New York City. Dixon is best remembered as the author of the novel *The Clansman* (1905), from which D. W. Griffith, with Dixon's aid, made the epochal motion picture *The Birth of a Nation* (1915). While in Cape Charles, Dixon engaged in many local businesses and civic activities, and served on the Town Council. **Cape Charles House** [24] *(645 Tazewell Avenue)* was built in 1912 by attorney Tucker Wilkins, and occupies the site of the town's first one-room school house (1886). **711 Tazewell Avenue** [25], at the corner of Tazewell and Fig, was built in 1899.

Circle back by turning left to Fig, then left to Monroe, passing large **Kellogg House** [26] *(644 Monroe Avenue)* on the left (1924) and on the right the town's oldest surviving **School Building** [27] *(635-637 Monroe Avenue)*, which was built in the 1890s and enlarged shortly thereafter. On the north side of Tazewell between Nectarine and Plum are eight houses known as **Cassatt Row** [28], for Alexander J. Cassatt, engineer and railroadman (and brother of Impressionist painter Mary Cassatt) who brought the railroad to the Eastern Shore and chose the site of Cape Charles as its terminus. There were originally ten identical houses, built for railroad employees; eight remain, at opposite ends of the block, still sufficiently similar to be distinguished from their neighbors. **Northampton Memorial Library** [29], at Tazewell and Plum, was dedicated in 1927 to the memory of local men who died in World

War I, the first memorial library in Virginia; it occupies the building erected as First Presbyterian Church in 1901. The **Wilson-Lee House** [30] *(403 Tazewell Avenue)* was built in 1906 by noted Norfolk architect James W. Lee for local merchant W. B. Wilson. **First Presbyterian Church** [31] *(Corner of Tazewell and Strawberry)*, erected in 1926, was in its time the most expensive church building ever erected on the Eastern Shore of Virginia ($70,000); its congregation is no longer functioning. Closer to the bay stands **Seagate** [32] *(9 Tazewell Avenue)*, erected 1910, the first of the town's bed-and-breakfast inns. Further north stands **Chesapeake Charm** [33] *(202 Madison Avenue)*, built in 1921, and **225 Jefferson Avenue** [34], another documented Sears house.

Bounded by Washington, Fig, Madison, and Strawberry is a venerable predominantly African American part of town known traditionally

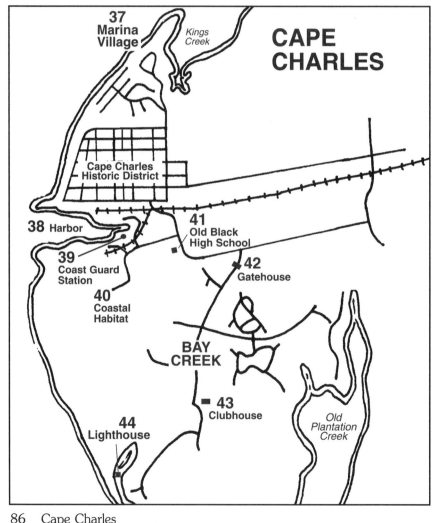

as "Jersey," and in it **St. Stephens A.M.E. Church** [35] is the oldest church building in Cape Charles, erected 1887 and moved to this site in 1912. Though it bordered this section of town, the old **High School** [36] *(Corner of Madison and Plum)*, built in 1921, was for whites only. Cape Charles was one of the few towns in Virginia to have its own school system, separate from the county; it merged with the Northampton County system in 1987 and closed in 1993. The building now functions as a civic center, while the grounds have been reclaimed as Central Park.

Washington Avenue marked the northern border of the original town, and at the northern end of Fig Street was a small marina on King's Creek. This has now become **Marina Village** [37], the northernmost part of the new Bay Creek that almost surrounds the town. The residences here are to become a "gated" community, but the road to the new marina, the shops, and the lovely view are all public.

To get to the **Harbor** [38], head back down Fig to Mason, and turn left up the overpass known locally as "the Hump" *(Old Cape Charles Road #642)*. The harbor is not natural but man-made, dredged by the railroad in 1884 from what was originally a tiny creek. Sizable ships, including tankers, can and do dock here, and during the winter the boats of Tangier Island crabbers are often to be seen. At the eastern end of the harbor is a public boat dock and the **Coast Guard Station** [39]. At the end of the road is the **Coastal Habitat Natural Area Preserve** [40], where a boardwalk wanders out over the wetlands and into the woods. Further south on Old Cape Charles Road is the **Old Black High School** [41], built in 1929, awaiting restoration.

Old Cape Charles Road was originally the main entrance into Cape Charles, and just beyond the school it turns to pass the entrance to **Bay Creek**, the largest part of the new golf and marina resort; this part of it occupies the estate which was the home of William L. Scott, the founder of Cape Charles. Bay Creek is a gated community with restricted access, but visible to all just outside the gatehouse is an admirable life-size bronze **Sculpture** [42] by Ken Herlihy (2006) of two watermen crabbing from a "Hancock scow." Visitors who are planning to eat at the restaurant in the central **Clubhouse** [43] *(1 Clubhouse Way)* may obtain a pass to enter simply by asking at the gate. The Clubhouse sits at the intersection of the resort's two signature golf courses, designed by Arnold Palmer and Jack Nicklaus. Visible in the distance to the right as you turn into the Clubhouse, or straight ahead as you leave, is the reconstructed **Old Plantation Flats Lighthouse** [44]. The original of this "screwpile" structure stood a mile out into the Chesapeake, where it operated from 1886 until 1962; this is an exact replica. Future development plans for Bay Creek include an area near the lighthouse that will contain shops, restaurant, and boardwalk and which, like Marina Village, will be open to the public, with public access to the lighthouse itself.

EASTVILLE COURTYARD

7 EASTVILLE

History Lives Just Off the Highway

From Route 13 turn west in the center of Northampton County, 15 miles above the Bridge-Tunnel, 49 miles below Maryland.

Most people who travel up and down the Eastern Shore of Virginia spend about 14 seconds in Eastville. That's approximately how long it takes to zip through that part of town that is crossed by Route 13.

Little do they know, apparently, that just off the highway lies a charming and lovely and very historic little county seat. It is half a mile, and maybe a hundred years, from Route 13 to the Courthouse in Eastville. And Eastville is well worth turning aside to see.

History
Eastville was nothing more than a single home, the "place called the Hornes where Henry Matthews now liveth," when it entered the pages of history. In 1677 the residents of the upper end of Northampton County, distressed that the court convened so far down the peninsula, requested a more convenient central location for the court, and suggested Matthews' home. Later that year the court convened at "the Hornes," and the place gradually evolved

into the permanent county seat.

What is now the Courthouse Green began to take shape around 1715, and from the very first it was the center of the little village that grew up around it. But growth was slow, because county government was the only industry at the Hornes. In 1773 John Tazewell, who owned land adjacent to the courthouse, divided it into building lots and began selling them; much of the present shape of the town dates from Tazewell's plan. On August 3, 1776, the Declaration of Independence was read publicly from the steps of the courthouse, having taken five weeks to travel from Philadelphia to the village. By then the village was known as Peachburg; not until about 1800 did the name Eastville become current.

In the early 1800s Eastville began to grow more steadily, and by 1835 it had a population of 217 inhabitants who were "not to be surpassed for their morality and hospitality to strangers." The village was the southern terminus of the main stage line down the shore. Overland passengers traveling to all points north had only one stage a day, and it left from the Green promptly at 6:30 every morning, scheduled to arrive in Horntown in Accomack County, 55 miles away, 12 hours later. Among the trades practiced in Eastville in the 1830s were coachmaker, harnessmaker, shoemaker, tailor, house and sign painter, hatter, cabinetmaker, blacksmith, plus attorneys and physicians. In addition to church, school, and county buildings the town could boast 4 stores, 2 taverns, 21 homes, and 3 "castor oil manufactures."

In 1884 the railroad passed about a mile east of the courthouse, and the little village experienced a final spurt of growth. Eastville Station, at the railroad tracks, became a busy shipping point, and by the turn of the century what had been the country road linking courthouse and station was lined on both sides by handsome new houses that stretched out the entire mile. Eastville was, however, quickly eclipsed in size and commercial importance by other new towns that sprang up along the railroad, principally Cape Charles and Exmore, and settled into its routine as the sleepy little county seat.

Today Route 13 bisects the Town of Eastville, and most cars rush through with hardly a notice. But sleepy, historic Eastville should not be missed by those who appreciate times past.

A Walking Tour of Eastville

Begin and end your visit at the Courthouse Green, .5 mile west of Route 13. Parking here, on the street or in the lots that begin next to Eastville Inn, is ample and free.

This walking tour covers approximately 1.25 miles. Homes on this route are private residences not generally open to visitors. Public restrooms are located in the Courthouse.

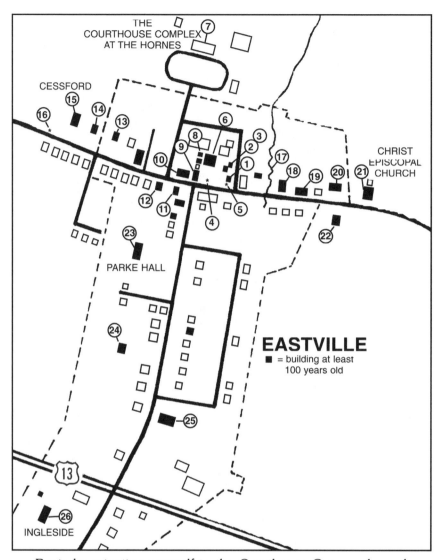

THE
COURTHOUSE COMPLEX
AT THE HORNES

CESSFORD

CHRIST
EPISCOPAL
CHURCH

PARKE HALL

EASTVILLE

■ = building at least
100 years old

INGLESIDE

Begin by orienting yourself to the Courthouse Green, whose three oldest structures can be examined from the inside. If not already open, access to them can be obtained by request at the Clerk's Office in the new Courthouse Complex (#7 below).

The first building on your right is the **Old Courthouse** [1], erected in 1732, abandoned in 1795, and after that used for a variety of purposes, including a saloon. In 1913 it was moved to this site to make way for the Confederate Monument. It is maintained by the Association for the Preservation of Virginia Antiquities, and is furnished much as it would have been when in use. Next to it stands the **Old Clerk's Office** [2], erected in the 1830s to hold the court records. The A.P.V.A. maintains a small museum inside which includes, among other things, a rod for measuring slaves.

Behind the Old Clerk's Office stands the **Debtor's Prison** [3], and the wall connecting the two is all that is left of the old prison yard wall. This building was erected about 1814, and was used to segregate from the general criminal populace those who were, according to current custom, imprisoned only for failure to pay their debts. This building is also maintained—unfurnished and prisonlike—by the A.P.V.A.

The newest structure on the Green is the **Confederate Monument** [4], dedicated in 1914. Notice also the low stone marker to the right of it, a **Monument to the "Laughing King"** [5], here misnamed Debedeavon. Unlike most of his contemporaries, the "Laughing King" of the Eastern Shore Indians befriended the English, welcomed them as settlers, and never went to war against them. The land on which Eastville is situated was given by him to Thomas Savage, the first permanent white settler on the Shore, about 1620.

Dominating the Green is the **Courthouse** [6], the sixth for Northampton County and the fourth in Eastville—but no longer the current one. Built in 1899, it was replaced by the new **Courthouse Complex at The Hornes** [7] in early 2006. Relocated into the new courthouse is the County Clerk's Office, from which can be obtained access to the older buildings on the Green, and which is the location of one of the greatest treasures of the Eastern Shore: the oldest continuous court records in the United States.

Having escaped fire, vermin, and neglect, Northampton County's records date from 1632 without a break. They are all still accessible to the public and can be handled and examined simply by inquiring at the Clerk's Office. The oldest record book, dating from 1632, was restored in the early 1900s; its first page is now so badly mutilated that the date on it is no longer legible, but students of the records attested to its date—back in 1855, when the records were already over two centuries old! In the fourth book you can see and touch the "signature" with which the local Indian leader Ochiawampe signed a deed of land in 1650—a rare pictographic version of himself.

The left side of the Green is lined with the small frame buildings of **Lawyers' Row** [8], built over the years between 1822 and 1910, and the side of the old **Brick Store** [9], which stands on one of the lots laid out by John Tazewell in 1773. Built about 1820, the store originally had two front doors, one directly above the other. The second-story door is still in place, and to it by pulley merchants would hoist their wares for storage; the spot where the pulley was located is still visible above the door.

Elias Roberts lived just south of the store and operated a tavern in his home as early as 1720, but **Eastville Inn** [10] was probably not erected until about 1760. It was built by James Taylor, and for more than a hundred years was known as Taylor House. It has been much changed over the centuries, both inside and out, the latest change a thorough restoration. On display inside are artifacts from Eastville's long history.

Opposite the inn is the mid-1800s **Old Drug Store** [11] which like the Brick Store had a door on the second floor for receiving goods. Just down the street from it is another **Old Store** [12] of the nineteenth century, from 1890 until 1936 the home of the local African American chapter of the Odd Fellows; when in 1936 the town was installing sidewalks, its new owner removed the front part of the first floor so that the building would not have to be moved.

From "downtown" Eastville it is a short walk to the southern edge of town, past **Littlecote House** [13] *(16476 Courthouse Road)*, dating from the early 1900s, and the **Rectory** [14] *(16494 Courthouse Road)* of Hungars Parish to **Cessford** [15] *(16546 Courthouse Road)*. Erected by John Kerr in 1832 and named for his ancestral home in Scotland, Cessford was relatively new when General Henry Lockwood chose it for his Northampton headquarters in the Civil War; hanging in the house is his order requisitioning the place, written in his own hand. At the edge of the property is the **Historical Marker** [16] concerning Thomas Savage [1595?-1633?], the first white settler of the Eastern Shore. Savage lived west of here, and Eastville stands on his original land grant.

North of the Green, almost obliterated by the road but visible from the west side of the street, is a tiny little stream known as **Sugar Run** [17], which may have formed one of the "horns" from which Eastville took its early name. The little house adjacent to it is undoubtedly one of the 21 homes that stood in the village in 1835. The **Westcoat House** [18] *(16374 Courthouse Road)*, turned perpendicular to the street, was built about 1845; it was originally a store, and still has a second-story front door similar to that of the Brick Store down the street. **The Maria Robins House** [19] *(16358 Courthouse Road)*, sitting almost in the road, was erected about 1825, and bears the name of an early occupant.

Two doors north of the Robins House stands stately **Coventon** [20] *(16338 Courthouse Road)*, with its formal boxwood garden. Erected by Coventon Simkins about 1795, it was, like Cessford, commandeered by Federal troops during the Civil War, and beneath the paint on the doors upstairs can still be seen the words "Artillery Harness" and "Chaplains."

Christ Episcopal Church [21] is the fourth oldest church building on the Eastern Shore of Virginia, and one of the loveliest. It was erected in 1828 at a cost of $2,960. Changes to the building since then have been few: the steeple is a later addition, and the altar wall has been extended. The stained glass windows were made in Germany and are among the most valued on the Shore. The church's interior was restored to its original appearance in 1906. The adjacent burial ground is an interesting one, containing some of the above-ground vaults often found on the Shore. Across from the church stands the **Old Rectory** [22] *(16310 Courthouse Road)*, built in 1908 and now housing a gallery. From here can be seen, outside the town limits and beyond the range of this walking tour, *Selma, erected in the 1790s, now the center of new residential development.

The "new" road to Eastville Station is now named Willow Oak Road, intersecting Courthouse Road in front of the inn. Here **Parke Hall** [23] *(5264 Willow Oak Road)* sits back in a large yard with a circular drive. The large section of this house was built by Griffin Stith about 1784, the smaller portions may be even older. This is the oldest house in Eastville, and like Coventon once boasted a formal garden. **Windrush Farm** [24] *(5350 Willow Oak Road)* was indeed a farmhouse, and outside of town, when built in the mid-19th century.

Eastville Baptist Church [25] is .4 mile from the Courthouse Green in the "newer" part of town, where houses are more Victorian than colonial in style. The church was erected in 1878 and renovated extensively in 1904.

> *The next several sites in Eastville lie beyond the busy 4-lane Route 13, as much as .5 mile beyond Eastville Baptist Church. They are best seen from your car.*

The handsome home that lies just beyond Route 13 on the right, behind the bank, is **Ingleside** [26] *(5516 Willow Oak Road)*, the oldest portions of which date from about 1800, the largest from the 1830s. Inside are wallpapers printed in Paris in 1814 depicting French troops in Egypt during the Napoleonic Wars. A large portion of Ingleside's formal garden is still intact behind the house, and can be glimpsed from Route 13. Two doors beyond is **Eastville Manor** *(6058 Willow Oak)*, built about 1886. There is little to be seen today of the once-busy Eastville Station. The brick storehouse beside the tracks, its front facade now completely sealed up, housed the Eastville Station Post Office until 1969. The house at 6138 James Street is an **Old Hotel**. This portion of town was from 1640 until the early 1800s within the bounds of Gingaskin, the only Indian reservation on the Eastern Shore of Virginia, and the road here leads eastward into Indiantown Neck *(see page 120)*.

*Beyond Eastville by Car

Eastville sits in the center of one of the most historic sections of the Eastern Shore, surrounded on almost all sides by some of the finest old homes in Virginia. Some of them can be seen from the public roads.

West of Eastville lies **Savage Neck** *(Turn west on Savage Neck Road #634, .5 mile south of the Courthouse Green; all roads in the neck are dead-ends, and you must retrace your route to this point; it is 5.5 miles to the furthest point in the neck)*. The neck is named for Thomas Savage, who was a lad of 13 when he arrived in Jamestown in 1608. He was promptly traded to the Indians as a hostage in an exchange of children to insure peace. Savage lived for years with the tribe of Powhatan, counting among his friends the princess Pocahontas. He learned the Indian language, and thus became a valued interpreter for the English. When he reached manhood Savage opened up trade with the Indians of the Eastern Shore and quickly became a favorite of their "Laughing King." About 1620 the Indian king gave Savage this large tract of land, and he settled on it, the first permanent white settler on the Eastern Shore. His descendants are numerous on the Shore today, one of America's oldest families.

Savage Neck is principally farmland, with handsome old houses tucked here and there around the edges. The only view of the Chesapeake is from **Smith's Beach** *(From #634 turn right on Smith Beach Road #666 after 2 miles; 1.7 miles to end)*, a continuous row of modest beach cottages facing the bay. Not one but two of these homes were originally railroad stations further up the peninsula: The former **Weirwood Railroad Station** is at 16301 Smith Beach Road, the old **Nassawadox Railroad Station** at 16201 Smith Beach Road. The road ends in a peaceful vista overlooking "The Gulf," once known as Savage's Creek.

Kirwan Hall *(From Savage Neck Road #634, 2 miles below Smith Beach Road, turn left on #705; .4 mile to gate)* is the "new" house in this neck of the woods, dating only from about 1800; it has five sections, and is pleasantly situated on Cherrystone Creek. Just beyond it is **Pleasant Prospect** *(On the left .4 mile below Kirwan Hall)*, a Savage family plantation dating from about 1750. Thomas Savage himself probably lived at Point Farm, at the end of the main neck road; the house standing there now is not particularly old by Eastern Shore standards.

North of Eastville stands **Bethel A.M.E. Church** on the site of the first Eastern Shore sermon preached by an ordained black minister, in 1865; the congregation was organized the following year and this building, the third on the site, was erected in 1901 and contains over 100 windows. Just beyond it is the entrance to **Old Town Neck** *(Turn west from Business Route 13 north of town, opposite Northampton High School, on Old Town Neck Road #630; it is 2.9 miles from this intersection to the end of the neck, and you must retrace your route to this point)*. The neck is named for the old Indian town that once stood on its north bank, now completely eroded away under the waters of Mattawoman Creek. In the same year that he gave Savage Neck to Thomas Savage, the "Laughing King" gave this land to Sir George Yeardley, Governor of Virginia. From Hungars Wharf, at the end of the neck, ships once sailed regularly to Europe and the West Indies.

At 2.7 miles down the neck stands **Ferry House** *(3209 Old Town Neck Drive)*, built in the late 1700s for the accommodation of passengers awaiting transportation across the bay from Hungars Wharf. In those days of sail, a regular schedule could hardly be maintained, and many well-heeled travelers spent the night here waiting for "contrary winds" to change.

ONANCOCK WHARF

8 ONANCOCK

Port Town for Three Centuries

*From Route 13 turn west in Onley on Route #179
and travel 1 mile to town limit.*

Onancock, pronounced *O-nan´cock*, is arguably the loveliest town
on the Eastern Shore of Virginia.

Nearby Accomac boasts more historic architecture, and any number of towns on the Shore offer equal views of the water. But Onancock
joins these two assets as no other community on the peninsula. This is
a 300-year-old town, beautifully situated on the waters of Onancock
Creek, and it is one of the Shore's most pleasant places.

History

*In the language of the Indians, Onancock means "Foggy Place,"
and there was an Indian town near here when Europeans first ventured into the area. In 1680 the Virginia Assembly authorized the
creation of a port town in each county, and Onancock is one of five
towns in Virginia that survive from that legislative directive, antedating the famous Williamsburg by 19 years. The site for Accomack
County's new town was the small peninsula at the head of
Onancock Creek where four or five Indian families lived. Daniel
Jenifer was paid 540 pounds of tobacco for "laying out the towne,"*

and Port Scarburgh was born, named for Charles Scarburgh from whom the land was purchased. In time the new Port Scarburgh became known as Onancock, a flourishing town now for more than 300 years.

Once established, Onancock Towne grew slowly. From 1680 until 1693 the county court was located here, and there was an Anglican church. In the early years Quakers lived in Onancock, and the town was home to the Presbyterian pioneer Francis Makemie. But no permanent church was established until Francis Asbury, the Methodist bishop, preached here in 1788 and a Methodist congregation was founded.

It was from Onancock that the combatants in the last battle of the American Revolution sailed. In November 1782, a full year after the surrender of the British at Yorktown, a Marylander named Zedekiah Whaley put into Onancock seeking aid against the Tory ships that were still marauding up and down the Chesapeake, and which had just been sighted at the entrance of Onancock Creek. Colonel John Cropper and 25 of his men from the Accomack militia volunteered to lend a hand, and they set sail from Onancock on board Whaley's fleet of barges. On November 30, 1782, the very day that the articles of peace were signed in Europe, the "Battle of the Barges" took place in Kedge's Straits above Smith Island in Maryland. At the first sign of battle all the American barges fled except Whaley's "Protector," which thereupon bore the brunt of the battle. When an ammunition chest aboard the "Protector" exploded, members of the crew who were not killed outright were thrown overboard, or jumped into the water with clothes ablaze. The British easily had the better of the engagement, and among those who died was Commodore Whaley. Cropper, though defeated, arranged an exchange of prisoners, and the Americans put back into Onancock with 25 drowned or killed, 29 wounded, and only 11 unscathed. Whaley was buried in Onancock, and in Maryland an official government investigation of the cowardice of the other American commanders was launched.

By the beginning of the 19th century Onancock was outgrowing its original boundaries and pushing eastward. In 1826 a post office was established, and in 1832 a ferry to Norfolk. A number of homes in town today date from the first half of the 1800s. When the Union army occupied the peninsula during the Civil War, they singled out Onancock as the place that had "concocted more mischief . . . in the way of blockade running and disloyalty" than any other community on the Shore.

After the Civil War, Onancock became one of the major stops for the colorful steamboats that ferried both passengers and freight up and down the Chesapeake. This direct link with the larger cities of Virginia and Maryland boosted the town's prosperity and growth, and much of the town dates from this period. The town was incorporated in 1882. Two years later the railroad lines missed

Onancock by about two miles, but the town, which lies four miles inland from the bay, benefitted from its presence and became even more important as a commercial center and port.

With a population of 1,434, Onancock is today the second largest community on the Eastern Shore of Virginia. Though almost all commerce is by land on the Shore today, the old wharf at the head of the creek is still in use and, more than three centuries after its founding, the town around it a sought-after address.

A Walking Tour of Onancock

This walking tour begins and ends at Ker Place, on Market Street in the center of town next to the Methodist church. Parking downtown is ample. The walking tour covers a total distance of about 2.5 miles, but can be shortened by referring to the map.

Homes on the walking tour are private residences not generally open to the visitors. Public restrooms are located in the Town Hall on North Street and at the Wharf.

Ker Place [1], pronounced "Car," was named for John S. Ker, who began its construction in 1799. It is one of the finest old homes on the Shore, a formal, dignified mansion in brick, and in it the Eastern Shore of Virginia Historical Society houses its headquarters and museum. Exhibits include rooms furnished to selected historical periods, representative costumes, portraits, and many other items of Eastern Shore interest, but the best part of the museum is handsome Ker Place itself, replete with ornate mantels and woodwork. (Open daily 9:00-4:00 except Sundays, Mondays and holidays; admission charged.)

From Ker Place turn right (west) down Market Street. There are homes and churches of note between Ker Place and downtown, but they are described later.

Downtown Onancock, though no longer the regional shopping mecca it once was, remains intact and vibrant, having survived fire and the inevitable move of many businesses to the highway. The facade of the **Roseland Theatre** [2] *(48 Market Street)* remains unchanged since the building opened in 1951 with a showing of "Quebec," starring John Barrymore Jr. The **Bank** [3] *(44 Market Street)* next door dates from 1894 and is the oldest commercial structure in downtown Onancock, now housing a pharmacy. The large **Lilliston Building** [4] *(38-40 Market Street)* dates from 1936. On the opposite side of the street stands the old **Waples Store** [5] *(63-65 Market Street)*, built in 1906, and the restaurant on the corner occupies the old **Rogers Hardware Store** [6] *(57 Market Street)*, built in 1916.

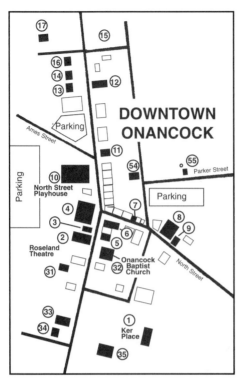

DOWNTOWN
ONANCOCK

North Street marks the eastern boundary of the original town plan of 1680. Restored and reopened after the lapse of almost a century is the **Charlotte Hotel** [7] *(7 North Street)*, which dates from 1907. Visible up the street beyond it is the **Town Office** [8] *(15 North Street)* and just beyond it, turning its back to downtown, an old **Doctor's Office** [9] *(17 North Street)*; here practiced Dr. John W. Robertson [1887-1981], beloved town physician and amateur photographer who birthed many local citizens and captured much of his native Shore on film.

The commercial structures on the right as you continue on Market were built of brick, according to a new town ordinance, after a disastrous fire wiped out almost the entire block in 1899. The **North Street Playhouse** [10] *(34 Market Street)* has come full circle; erected as a moviehouse in 1914 (the town's first "talkies" were shown here in 1929), it was superseded by the Roseland in 1951, became a store, and was enlarged and slightly relocated before it once again became a theatre, home of the North Street Players, in 2001. In 1935, when the **Post Office** [11] *(35 Market Street)* was being built on the site of an old hotel, considerable excitement surrounded the workers' excavation of six human skulls, a skeleton, and a wooden box 10 feet long, whose purpose still remains unexplained. The frame store still in use at 23 Market Street was originally **Mrs. Merrill's Millinery Shop** [12], c. 1900.

Beyond the business district you pass into Onancock's oldest residential area, and walk on streets laid out more than 300 years ago. The oldest part of the **Finney House** [13] *(18 Market Street)* dates from the 1700s; according to a local tradition, an Indian chief is buried under its dining room. Handsome gingerbread adorns the **George Fosque House** [14] *(16 Market Street)*, built in 1882. A long block past North Street is the **Town Square** [15], center of the original town and up through the early 1800s Onancock's "downtown." The larger of the monuments in the square is to Confederate General Edmund Bagwell of Onancock [1840-1876]. The old town hall which was built on the square in 1878 now stands across the street as **Taylor House** [16] *(14*

Market Street), since 1920 a private residence.

Down South Street stands **Scott Hall** [17], Onancock's oldest home. It dates from 1779 and is equipped with exceptionally thick walls, alcoves as hiding places, and trap doors for escape. The house is rumored to have a "ghostly presence" that makes three doors of a certain room open at once on their own accord. Behind the house, better reached from the lane adjacent to 10 Market Street, is its cemetery, dating back to 1775; Commodore Whaley of the Battle of the Barges lies buried here.

Old **Cokesbury Chapel** [18] was built in 1854, the second building of a congregation that functioned from 1788 until 1996. In its burial ground lie three ministers, including the Reverend William Lee [1767?-1841], who often sailed from Onancock to preach to the outlying islands and "necks" of the Chesapeake; at his death he is said to have left behind a barrelful of certificates from marriages he had performed. Just a few yards behind Cokesbury stands the 19th-century **25 King Street** [19], in whose front yard once stood Bascom's Chapel, a rival congregation that split from Cokesbury in 1850; the two churches were so near that they could hear one another at worship. Between this house and the Wharf no fewer than four homes date from before the Civil War; the oldest of them is probably **15 King Street** [20], the back part of which may date from the 1790s, and from which can be seen the North Branch of Onancock Creek.

The large gray house opposite Cokesbury Church is the **Stephen Hopkins House** [21] *(8 Market Street)*, built about 1860 by the founder of the firm that did much of the shipping and importing from the Onancock wharf. By the second quarter of the 19th century, Hopkins owned a shipyard on the creek behind his house, and the vessels built there sailed regularly to Norfolk, Baltimore, and even the West Indies. More recently this was the home of Virginia Hopkins Phillips [1891-1993], who lived her entire life—born and raised, lived and died—in this house, for which she was celebrated by The Guinness Book of Records (1995) as the world's "Most Durable Resident."

Two doors beyond the church stands **Holden** [22] *(9 Market Street)*, the earliest part of which dates from before the Civil War. On the edge of the lawn is a bronze marker to Francis Makemie, one of the earliest Presbyterian preachers in America. Makemie came to Virginia from Ireland in 1683, settled in Onancock in 1687, and married Naomi Anderson, whose family lived at this site, or very close to it. Trained for the ministry, Makemie also distinguished himself as a successful businessman for some years until, in 1699, he registered as required by law as a dissenting minister (the second person in Virginia to do so) and once again took up the practice of preaching. In 1706 he organized the first American Presbytery in Philadelphia, and in 1707 he was acquitted of the charge or preaching without a license in a New York trial that is still cited as a landmark in the evolution of religious freedom in America. Makemie's father-in-law William Anderson was the first person to purchase a lot in Onancock Towne—possibly this one—in 1682.

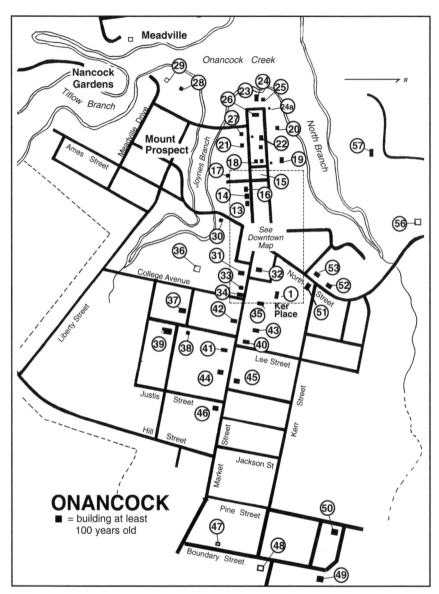

Market Street ends at the **Town Wharf** [23], and here you can see why Onancock's location was a choice one. At this point Onancock Creek splits into two branches (actually three; the third is hidden just beyond the land to the south), and the water is still navigable four miles from Chesapeake Bay. Though still active—it is here that the passenger ferry for Tangier docks—the wharf is today not nearly the busy place it was in former years. In the 1890s the Eastern Shore Steamboat Company had trips in and out of here several times a week. By the 1920s there was daily steamer service from Onancock to Baltimore, although passengers often had to share the voyage with such produce as barrels of potatoes and crates and baskets of onions and strawberries. Many old homes in town share identical doors, stair rails, and other features because the steamers that docked here—*Maggie, Eastern Shore, Pianketank, Pocomoke*— brought in the latest styles from manufacturers in the big city. On the regular run the steamers would sail straight to Baltimore, then home via Crisfield the next day, and it was not unusual for barrels of fresh white potatoes to accumulate in great numbers on the wharf before their return, even though some steamers could carry as many as 3,500 barrels each trip. The last steamers docked in Onancock in 1935, but the wharf has never been totally idle, because the fuel oil and gasoline imported here has been coming in by barge and tanker since 1933.

Hopkins & Brothers Store [24], established in 1842 by Stephen Hopkins, is now a Virginia Historic Landmark. It was moved to this site at the wharf (from the spot marked [24a] on the map) in 1966. Next to it stands the small **Ticket Office** [25] and waiting room once used by steamboat passengers. Overlooking it all from across the street is the **Alicia Hopkins House** [26] *(1 Market Street)*, a handsome variation on the standard Eastern Shore "big house, little house, colonnade, kitchen" design, dating from the early 19th century.

From the wharf Mount Prospect Bridge crosses Joynes Branch, or Middle Branch, to that part of town called Mount Prospect, settled in the late 1800s and annexed to Onancock in the 1950s. From the bridge notice **Ingleside** [27] *(4 Market Street)*, which only from the back reveals its age (c. 1840). The original **Mount Prospect** [28] *(8 Mount Prospect Avenue)* is the late 19th-century home on the right across the bridge, set back in its extensive lawns. From Mount Prospect Avenue turn right on Meadville Drive, where at the end of the street the **Bristow House** [29] *(1 Meadville Drive)* enjoys a good view of the creek; though parts of this house are more recent, the basic structure was ordered from Sears and Roebuck and assembled from pre-marked parts in 1926. Just below the house the road drops to where once Bristow's Bridge crossed Titlow (or South) Branch and linked the town to the old estate Meadville. The bridge fell into ruin and was dismantled in the early 20th century. From this landing you can look across to Meadville and Nancock Gardens, two communities which are geographically and historically related to the Town of Onancock but which are, without Bristow's Bridge, several miles distant by car.

From Meadville Drive you may wish to wander aside to the end of Ames Street, where there is a lovely view of Titlow Branch, but the shorter route back to downtown, via Division Street and Crescent Drive, crosses Ames Bridge, where there are good views towards the wharf on the left and the Onancock School on the right. At the end of the bridge stands **Harmon House** [30] *(3 Ames Street)*, the large section of which dates from the middle 1800s, the small from the late 1700s. Once past it, either continue straight to Market Street or cross the public parking lot (with its magnificent oak) to the **Waples House** [31] *(58

Market Street) opposite the Baptist church. Even the outbuildings of this handsome home were the "latest word" in architecture when erected at the turn of the twentieth century.

Onancock Baptist Church [32] was founded and built in 1855, but the oldest section of the building is now obscured by the front part erected in 1891. **Holy Trinity Episcopal Church** [33], a "country Gothic" structure built in 1886, has what may be the most elegant interior of any church on the Eastern Shore of Virginia; its Second Empire style **Rectory** [34] *(68 Market Street)* on the corner dates from 1890. **Market Street United Methodist Church** [35], descended from Cokesbury's rival Bascom's Chapel, was erected in 1882, significantly altered in 1898, and restored in 1977; its sanctuary, in the Victorian style, is on the second floor.

The old **Onancock School** [36] *(6 College Avenue)* was built in 1921 and enjoys a lovely view of Ames Bridge and Joynes Branch. It is the third school on the same site; two private schools preceded it, and the cornerstone of one of them is still visible in the present foundation. The building awaits restoration as a local cultural center, but already houses a number of art galleries and studios. A public walkway across the grounds down to the creek begins at the sidewalk at the property's edge.

Harbor Breeze [37] *(8 Joynes Street)* dates from the early 1900s and was built by the owner of the company that made Old Dutch Cleanser. **Holly House** [38] *(7 Holly Street)* was erected in 1861 in what was then the outskirts of town. Note its unusual configuration of window panes. Less elegant but unusually large is its neighbor (across the side street), **9 Holly Street** [39], erected in 1889.

Facing Holly Street on Market is **Naomi Makemie Presbyterian Church** [40], founded 1883, erected 1896, and named for the Onancock native who was the wife of Francis Makemie; she and her husband are named in the windows that face Market Street. Diagonally across the corner from it stands **Sans Souci** [41] *(80 Market Street)*, the front part of which was added in the 1880s to a smaller back part that dates from the 1850s. From here back to the beginning point of the tour Market Street is lined with admirable old houses, among them **Harmanson House** [42] *(74 Market Street)* in whose parlor was found, when it was restored, a 1904 wallpaper that has since been reproduced for sale on the current market. Across from it stands the **Quinby House** [43] *(85 Market Street)*, erected on what was then a 3-acre lot in 1865 by attorney Upshur B. Quinby; after Quinby committed suicide in a wing at the back of the house in 1898, the family had that part of the house removed.

Onancock by Car

The Town of Onancock covers almost a full square mile, which makes some of its sights beyond the range of a leisurely walking tour.

The **Colonial Manor Inn** [44] *(84 Market Street)* was built in the 1880s, and has offered room and board (now bed-and-breakfast) since

1939. Across the street stands the **Dentist Office** [45] *(97 Market Street)* of Dr. John Ross, erected in 1920, and on the corner diagonally across from that the **Ralston House** [46] *(96 Market Street)*, built in 1883 and largely unchanged, inside and out, since that time.

Boundary Avenue once marked the eastern end of the modern town, and leads to an old African American neighborhood. Here, just off Market Street, stands the **Old Blacksmith Shop** [47] *(Adjacent to 3 Boundary Avenue)* of Samuel D. Outlaw [1901-1994], now restored as a little museum to his labors. The building facing Kerr Street is the former **Black School** [48] *(6 Boundary Avenue)*, built in 1938. **Bethel A.M.E. Church** [49] *(40 Boundary Avenue)* dates from 1868 and was moved to this site in 1902; near it stands **St. John's Baptist Church** [50] *(2 Church Street)*, erected in 1885.

Kerr Street parallels Market Street on the north, and is also lined with attractive homes, especially at its western end. It ends on North Street where two bed-and-breakfasts face one another: the **Inn at Onancock** [51] *(30 North Street)*, built in 1886, and the **Spinning Wheel** [52] *(31 North Street)*, a "folk Victorian." Down the street to the left at **25 North Street** [53] is a charming split-level house dating from the 1840s; its only near cousin on the Eastern Shore is The Glade in Accomac.

A short block up King Street is a new shop occupying the **Old Power Plant** [54] *(44 King Street)*, erected in 1910. Around the corner from it is the town's **Old Water Works** [55] *(3 Parker Street)*, complete with a brick cistern in the back yard.

By water, if not by land, many of the homes on Onancock Creek west of town are related to the town. The creek is wide and lovely and has always been used as a setting for comfortable homes. To see the north bank of the creek, follow North Street out of town past **The Hermitage** [56], a retirement home established by the United Methodist Church in 1966, and turn left on Hermitage Road #1028, which will deposit you at the gate of **Cokesbury** [57]. This rambling old house of several sections was begun about 1806; on the grounds are a tiny one-room schoolhouse, where the family children were taught in the early 1800s, and an ancient cork tree, rare in these parts.

To see the south bank of Onancock Creek, take Hill Street #718 out of town, or from Mount Prospect follow Liberty Street to its intersection with Hill Street by the town cemetery and turn right. It will take a few miles to reach by car points that are, by water, only a few yards from the heart of town.

Nancock Gardens *(When #718 turns left towards Pungoteague, .5 mile south of Onancock, keep straight on Cashville Road #638, then turn right on Nancock Gardens Road #747, a total distance of 1.5 miles from Market Street)*. This is a modern section of Onancock, lying outside the town limits. The homes here are all recent, with very pretty views of Titlow Branch. **Meadville (Turn right on Locust Grove Road #778 a third of a mile beyond the road to Nancock Gardens)* has even newer homes on the grounds of an old house of that name which was built about 1811 by Colonel John Finney. The old house itself can only be glimpsed from the end of its long private lane; at the end of the public road are more glimpses of Onancock Creek and the Town Wharf from between the modern houses. At the corner of the road to Meadville stands the **Oliver House** *(25151 Locust Grove Road)*, the oldest part dating from 1822, moved to this location from Route 13 in 1974.

Having ventured this far south out of Onancock, you have already started on the tour of the Lower Accomack Bayside (see Chapter 14).

THE CONFEDERATE MONUMENT, PARKSLEY

9 PARKSLEY

Victoriana on the Railroad

*From Route 13 turn west on Route #176 at the traf-
fic signal at Fisher's Corner, 18 miles below
Maryland, 48 miles above the Bridge-Tunnel.*

Parksley is a nice place to live, but you probably wouldn't want to
visit there. Not unless, that is, you are one of those who can appreciate
the virtues of small town America, of which virtues Parksley has more
than its share.

History
*Parksley is a planned community, a rarity on the Eastern Shore
of Virginia. The town father was Henry R. Bennett [1849-1940], a
traveling salesman from Delaware who, when the railroad was being
built in 1884, envisioned the possibility of a thriving town at this
point. With friends and relatives Bennett formed the Parksley Land
Improvement Company, purchased 160 acres from farmer
Benjamin Parks, and laid out a completely new town around the
railroad.*

Henry Bennett did everything in his power to make his little town a model community. He wrote into its charter a clause to the effect that if alcoholic beverages were ever sold on any lot in town, that lot would revert to the Company (then did not live to see a state-owned liquor store that operated on the street that bears his name). All stores and businesses were gathered into a commercial district in the center of town near the railroad. Blocks of land were set apart for schools and parks, and acres for churches. Streets, well before the advent of the automobile, were made wide and laid out in regular patterns. In line with the attitudes of that day, blacks were segregated into their own section on the southern edge of town, where one street was named for abolitionist William Lloyd Garrison. Not everyone appreciated such efforts, however. Benjamin Parks, the original resident, soon quit his house in town for a new farm on the Seaside.

Parksley was planned and settled by northerners—Bennett's associates were from Dover, Philadelphia, and Boston—and even the street names seem a little foreign to the Eastern Shore of Virginia. Dunne, Patton, and Cassatt were named for railroad executives, the last of them for Alexander Cassatt, brother of artist Mary Cassatt. Several streets were named for members of Bennett's family—Catherine for his mother, Jones and Maxwell for brothers-in-law. Two streets were named for Mary Cooke, a fiancee who died before she could marry Bennett. When Bennett finally did marry a New Yorker named Phoebe Bell, someone asked her what she thought of Mary Cooke's streets; replied Phoebe, "She got the streets, I got the man."

As Bennett had foreseen, Parksley grew rapidly, and within a short time was one of the major towns on the peninsula. When it incorporated in 1904 (and the town fathers drew the boundaries so as to exclude the black section, known today as Whitesville, it boasted a hotel, banks, numerous stores and businesses, a school, several churches, and a local newspaper. The town was by then one of the most up-to-date places around, its homes admired for the latest in architecture and style, its people prosperous and well-traveled. Parksley was the first town on the Shore whose homes were lit by electricity, and one of the first places on the peninsula to see automobiles, indoor bathrooms, and permanent waves. From 1922 to 1927 it hosted a semi-pro team that played in the Eastern Shore Baseball League, making it, some say, the smallest town in the world with a team in organized professional baseball.

Parksley has never ceased to grow, and now after a century boasts a population just short of 1,000. It is the closest thing the Eastern Shore of Virginia offers to a Victorian town. Large handsome houses line its tree-shaded streets, and though Victorian styles were always used with restraint on the Shore, many of Parksley's older homes are admirable examples of the Victorian railroad era (Mary Street near the railroad offers a nice cluster of them). The *downtown section on Dunne Avenue is still vibrant and busy, but has lost much of its older facade; in the bank at 18501 Dunne can be seen a large mural by a local artist depicting downtown Parksley as it appeared in 1920.*

Parksley is small enough to be seen afoot, or from the car. Parking downtown is ample and free. Almost like a scene from an earlier era, Parksley is the kind of place where kids gather to play baseball in the schoolyard, and families chat at evening on the front porch swing. Not the most exciting place in the world to see, but— as Henry Bennett wanted it to be—a very nice place to live.

The **Eastern Shore of Virginia Railway Museum** [1] stands on the site of Parksley's old railroad station, but this building is from Hopeton, three miles up the tracks, moved to this location and restored in 1988. There are three rooms inside, the center one the agent's office, separating what were originally segregated waiting rooms for black and white passengers. A collection of railroad cars, part of the exhibits, sits on adjacent tracks. Entrance into the museum is through an old produce building facing Dunn Street. *(Open 10:30-4:00 Tuesday thru Saturday, Sundays 1:00-4:00. Admission by donation.)*

Most of the old buildings in downtown Parksley were built after a devastating fire destroyed much of the commercial district in 1896; it took 50 masons twelve months to build what the locals called "the brick block." Prominent among the old buildings is the **H. T. Mason Department Store** [2] *(18455 Dunne Avenue)*, at the northern end of the range of stores on Dunne Avenue, and the adjacent **Parksley National Bank** [3] *(18465 Dunne Avenue)*, erected in 1904. Behind the bank is the **Old Post Office** [4] *(24277 Cooke Street)* of 1928, which replaced an older post office then operating out of the charming **Old Bank** [5] *(18477 Dunne Avenue)*, now a store though the word "bank" is still visible in its slate roof. The large 3-story **D. H. Johnson Building** [6] *(18487-9 Dunne Avenue)* was originally a general store that sold groceries and clothes.

On Bennett Street stands the old **Opera House** [7] *(24276 Bennett Street)*, its western facade sporting a fading Coca-Cola mural. The adjacent hardware store was originally the **Parksley Coal & Supply Company** [8] *(24270 Bennett Street)*, built in 1905. The **Royal Theatre** [9] *(24262 Bennett Street)*, its marquis recently restored, operated from 1938 to 1959.

The tallest building in town is the **Matthews Building** [10] *(18554 Cassatt Avenue)*, built in 1919 as a farmers' supply and storage company but later a shirt factory that in its time turned out as many as 2,500 shirts a day. Around the corner stands **Benjamin Parks House** [11] *(24205 Bennett Street)*, home of the man who lived here when Parksley was still farmland. When still a farmhouse, it stood some blocks away on Catherine Street. Parks himself moved it to this location when the town was established, only to abandon it when he decided he did

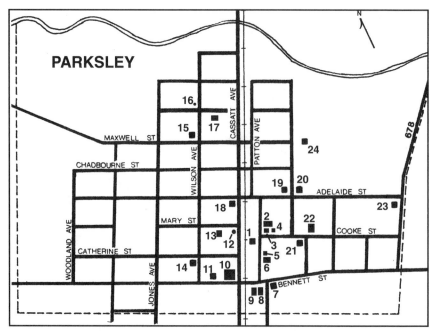

PARKSLEY

not like town life. With the exception of Williams Ordinary (see below), this is the oldest house in town.

Across the tracks from the museum stands the **Confederate Monument** [12] *(Corner of Cassatt and Mary)*. Throughout the South, such monuments usually adorn the county seat; Accomack County's monument to southern Civil War veterans stands in this town founded by Yankees two decades after the War. Henry Bennett lobbied vigorously to get the county to move the county seat from Accomac to Parksley, but a referendum defeated his efforts. This monument is the town's consolation prize. Two doors behind it stands a handsome Victorian house called **Homeplace** [13] *(24234 Mary Street)*, one of many graceful homes in this part of town.

Grace United Methodist Church [14], founded in 1892, is one of the largest congregations on the Eastern Shore of Virginia; this building dates from 1977, the third on the same site. **Williams Ordinary** [15] *(24311 Maxwell Street)* is both old and new, typical of many old Eastern Shore homes but curiously different here in Victorian Parksley. The two smaller sections date from as early as 1835 and were moved to this site from several miles east of town; the largest section was built in 1977. The corner of Wilson and Callen is supposedly the highest point of land in Parksley; here, on a lot now vacant, stood **Chadbourne Cottage** [16], home of Elizabeth S. Chadbourne, Secretary-Treasurer of the Parksley Land Improvement Company and, after Bennett, the moving force in the founding of the town. Wealthy, imperious, eccentric, and short on tact, this Bostonian career woman dismayed and delighted the locals in a day when most women stayed at home and left business completely to the menfolk. The **John Herbert Hopkins House** [17] *(24334 Callen Street)* is like no other in town; Hopkins, owner of the Royal Theatre, had it built to a design that he saw and admired at the New York World's Fair in 1939.

Though once virtually every house in town had one, only at the Blake House *(18464 Cassatt Avenue)* does the old **Hitching Post** [18] remain. Across the tracks on Adelaide at Browne Avenue is the **Sledge House** [19] *(18446 Browne Street)*, a lovely Victorian cottage that was the home of J. T. Sledge, one of two physicians in town and the first mayor. Opposite it, **Parksley Baptist Church** [20] antedates the town itself, having been organized in 1878 in the nearby village of Lee Mont. The congregation moved to Parksley soon after the coming of the railroad, and erected this building in 1897.

On Cooke Street stands the old **Parksley Hotel** [21] *(24316 Cooke Street)*, built in 1919. Just beyond it is the **First Railroad Station** [22] *(24331 Cooke Street)*, now an apartment building, erected in 1884 and one of only two such buildings left on the Shore. The **Byrd House** [23] *(24476 Adelaide Street)* was built about 1918 by a local physician, but was for forty years a funeral home.

Henry and Phoebe Bennett lived at **Bellwood** [24] *(18367 Browne Street)*, which Bennett built soon after the town was established. Bennett lived here permanently only after 1904, by which time he was totally blind. Sightlessness proved no impediment to him, and at the age of 90 he was still traveling up and down the Shore selling fire extinguishers. When bus or train could not take him where he wanted to go, he would hitch-hike, and the old man with the white cane by the side of the road was for many years a beloved Eastern Shore landmark. Henry Bennett died at 91 in 1940.

Whitesville, Parksley's African American neighborhood (south of Bennett Street), once had its own businesses, school, and churches. The quonset-hut building on Willis Street, just off Staunton Avenue, was built as the **Park Theatre**, one of the few black moviehouses on the Eastern Shore; it operated from 1948 until the early 1960s. The **Whitesville School** *(23459 Leslie Trent Road)* was built in 1925 not by the county but by the citizens of Whitesville themselves, chief among them merchant Robert H. Hall [1872-1935]. It stands on a street named for an educator who graduated from it.

Adams United Methodist Church *(23532 Lee Mont Road)* was founded 1878 by Rev. J. K. Adams; its building was erected in 1928 with lumber from an earlier Whitesville school building.

THE WACHAPREAGUE WATERFRONT

10 WACHAPREAGUE
The Fisherman's Enduring Resort

From Route 13 turn east on Route #180 at the traffic signal just north of Keller and travel 5 miles

Wachapreague enjoys a reputation disproportionate to its off-the-beaten-path location and its small size (population 291). Once the haunt of wealthy Yankee sportsmen, governors, film stars, even a former President, it is today a quiet place. Yet the fish are still biting at Wachapreague, and a surprising number of visitors still seek out the pleasant little village for vacation and relaxation.

History
The water at Wachapreague is Wachapreague Channel, and it winds through the wetlands out to the Atlantic between Parramore and Cedar Islands, the easiest natural access to high ground from the ocean between Cape Charles and Chincoteague. The first to recognize the site's assets were the Machipongo Indians, whose stone arrowheads and axe handles have been unearthed in the soil here. Wachapreague's first mention in the pages of history dates from 1656, when the Indian "emperor" Wachiwampe encouraged his people to live here, but English settlers laid permanent claim to the site a scant seven years later.

For two centuries Wachapreague was just another Eastern Shore farm, or "plantation," that backed up to its own landing on the water. The place was garrisoned during the American Revolution, the War of 1812, and the Civil War, but the only enemy to venture up the channel was a British gunboat which local marksmen turned back during the War of 1812. In the early 1800s, as the little village of Locust Mount arose just east of the site around a cluster of small stores, Wachapreague was still little more than a single farmhouse (17 Brooklyn Avenue) and its surrounding fields.

In 1872 the owner of the property sold 39 acres south of the house to the Powell brothers—George, John, and Henry—who promptly built a wharf and began to ship local produce, especially potatoes, to northern markets. "Powellton" blossomed quickly into a prosperous and busy village, eclipsing Locust Mount, then doubled in size when, in imitation of the Powells, Thomas F. Floyd purchased the adjacent 25 acres for development in 1882. When the community applied for a post office there was already a Powellton in Brunswick County, so the new post office, and the town, took the name Wachapreague in 1884. In that same year the steamboat "Tuckahoe" began plying between Wachapreague and New York City.

John Powell was the first to recognize Wachapreague's potential as a vacation spot, and he built a small hotel across the street from the store that he and his brothers owned at the wharf. In 1902, A. H. Gordon Mears [1861-1944] took a big gamble and erected a much larger 4-story, 30-room hotel costing $30,000. Local skeptics predicted its swift demise, but Mears advertised his Hotel Wachapreague in northern newspapers and national sporting magazines, and more than proved them wrong. Hotel Wachapreague soon won a wide renown, and for many years was a popular destination for visitors from the North, who would come down by train to nearby Keller, where Mears had carriages waiting to conduct them straight to his hotel. His business flourished, and the town with it.

In 1902 Wachapreague was incorporated, and its population and activity were steadily increasing. Mears built a department store on Main Street, whose immense freight elevator was as big an attraction among the locals as his hotel was among the sportsmen. By 1929 Wachapreague had 12 stores, five fishing companies, four oyster shucking plants, a restaurant, an ice cream parlor, a bank, a movie theatre, a pool hall, an ice plant, a service station, a dairy farm, and of course a renowned hotel where the dining was first class and the clientele up-scale. Within the town limits lived 585 people, and the population of the entire neighborhood was about 800.

Depression, storm, and fire hit the town hard in the 1930s, and over the next three decades its once-busy downtown declined almost to the point of disappearing. Movies, department stores, and *famous visitors were already a thing of the past when the Hotel Wachapreague burned in 1978, seemingly spelling the end. Yet Wachapreague has retained its popularity among fishermen, and still continues as a vacation destination. Though the town's downtown is much diminished, its residential sections remain largely unaltered. The handsome old homes of an earlier era are now increasingly admired, restored, and purchased as seasonal or vacation homes. Not a big place, nor the commercially active place that it once was, Wachapreague is nonetheless both enduring and endearing to the visitors who are still drawn to it.*

While Wachapreague can quickly be seen from your car, it is also a pleasant place for walking. It is small and contained, and this suggested itinerary can easily be covered on foot.

The late lamented **Hotel Wachapreague** [1] stood at the end of Main Street overlooking the water, the site, on the corner of Main and Atlantic Avenue, empty but well maintained today. The business continues in its direct descendants, the Wachapreague Motel (1962) and the Island House Restaurant. The boats at the waterfront include the largest private charter fishing fleet in Virginia. The **Wachapreague Marina** [2] is the oldest in town.

Atlantic Avenue parallels the waterfront, not all of which is tidy. Half a block north of the hotel site look for a metal cable sunk into a groove that crosses the street; this is the simple but effective mechanism by which **Parker's Marine Railway** [3] hauls boats ashore for repairs. Just beyond it on the right is the **Coast Guard Dock and Headquarters** [4] that replaced the Parramore Beach Station, which closed in 1994. The **Carnival Grounds** [5] have been the site of an annual fireman's carnival since 1952 (the fireman have purchased, but not yet occupied, a new site for the carnival on Finney Road). The new **Town Marina** [6] on the right and, on the left at the corner at Riverview Avenue, the newest building of the **Virginia Institute of Marine Science Laboratory** [7] were both built in 1995. V.I.M.S. has operated in Wachapreague continuously since 1959, pursuing important studies of the production, habits, life-cycles, and diseases of plants and animals, especially the shellfish, of the region. Its several buildings include **Owens House** [8] *(1 Liberty Street)*, built in 1938 by an executive of the Reese candy company. In front of it Atlantic Avenue becomes the private drive of the **Smith House** [9] *(4 Atlantic Avenue)*, originally the home of Captain John Richardson, enlarged into a summer home and hunting lodge in 1942.

From Liberty Street turn left down Brooklyn Avenue. From the corner where this street crosses Riverview Avenue are visible two houses, **1 Riverview Avenue** [10] and **26 Brooklyn Avenue** [11], which were moved to Wachapreague from the Barrier Islands. At **17 Brooklyn Avenue** [12] stands the "mansion house" of the farm on which most of Wachapreague was built. This is the second house on this site, erected in 1860 to replace the original (c. 1740) which burned.

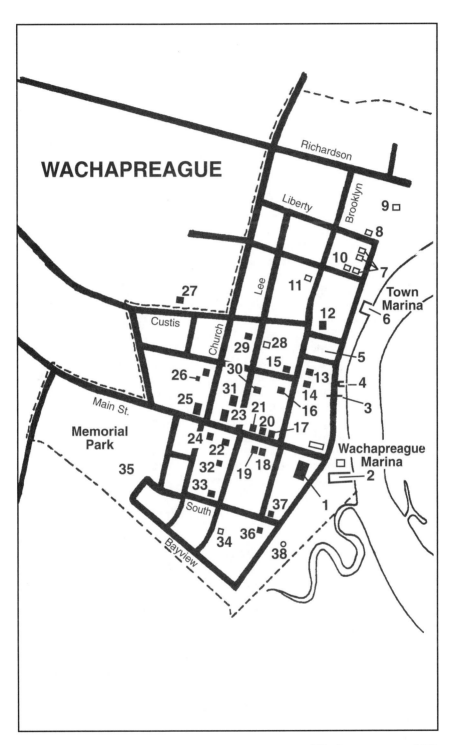

WACHAPREAGUE

In the side yard is buried Levin Teackle [1717-1794], who built the original house, but the Indian artifacts that have turned up on this property over the years are proof that Teackle was hardly the first resident of Wachapreague.

Four admirable homes cluster around the corner of Brooklyn and Powelton. **Burton House** [13] *(11 Brooklyn Avenue)* was built in 1883 and bears the name of W. Heber Burton, at one time the mayor of Wachapreague; the gazebo at the back contains beams and railings from the Hotel Wachapreague. Next door is **9 Brooklyn Avenue** [14], built in the early 1880s. Across the street stand **10 Brooklyn Avenue** [15], looking deceptively small on the outside though the ceilings on the lower floor are 10 feet high, and the **Levin Core House** [16] *(8 Brooklyn Avenue)*, a handsome home of the 1880s said to have been built by a Coast Guardsman, hence its style.

The corner of Main and High Street is still "downtown," though today's buildings constitute fewer than a quarter of the businesses that once lined the street here. The **Corner Grocery** [17] *(9 Main Street)* dates from 1879, the **Ray Nock Store** [18] *(14 Main Street)* opposite it from the early twentieth century. Main Street west of downtown is lined with handsome old homes. The **Ewell Stevens House** [19] *(10 Main Street)* dates from about 1882, the **Eva Stevens House** [20] *(17 Main Street)* from 1883, and at one time housed a still that supplied "moonshine" to the faucet in the kitchen sink; the little building in the back yard once stood at road's edge and housed a store. The **Post Office** [21] *(15 Main Street)* was built in 1920 as the Wachapreague Banking Company. The handsome **LeCato House** [22] *(16 Main Street)* was built about 1890 and was once the home of George W. LeCato, physician and state senator.

Lovely **Powelton Presbyterian Church** [23] was built in 1881, the first church in town. Across the street stands the **Gordon Mears House** [24] *(22 Main Street)*, built about 1885, home of the founder of the Hotel Wachapreague. **Ocean View United Methodist Church** [25] was built in 1935 to replace a building of 1902 that burned; the 1882 cornerstone of the congregation's original building can be found behind the shrubs at the corner.

Turn up Church Street to see the **Oldest House in Wachapreague** [26], now located in the backyard of 10 Powelton Avenue; this was undoubtedly a tenant house on the old Teackle plantation. From the corner of Church and Custis can be seen an old **Double House** [27] *(22317 Custis Street)* of the early- or mid-19th century. The house at 13 Lee Street was originally the **Pilgrim Holiness Church** [28], erected 1907. **At 10 Lee Street** [29] lived Isaac "Ike" Phillips [1858-1954], best known of the Wachapreague's carvers, who made decoys by the hundreds and sold them for $12 a dozen. The charming **Fanny Jones House** [30] *(7 Lee Street)* has been authentically restored. **2 Lee Street** [31] is large because it was once a guest house known as the Channel Bass Inn.

South of Main stands **1 Center Street** [32], a small house of undetermined age but undoubtedly one of the oldest in town. The whimsically restored **Phillips House** [33] *(7 Center Street)* dates from about 1887. Look past South Street for **14 Center Street** [34], the center portion of which is a small cottage that originally stood on Cedar Island. At the western end of South Street is the **Herbert S. Powell Memorial Park** [35], named for an educator who lived at 26 Main; among the trees on the knoll behind the pavilion is an old burial ground whose tombstones date back to 1771. At the eastern end of South Street stand two originally identical houses probably built by the Powell Brothers in 1872 as "model" or rental homes; **2 South Street** [36] is the least changed, but **12 High Street** [37] is of essentially the same design, complete to the "semi-outside" chimney on one end. At the very end of South Street is a **Scenic Overlook** [38] from which to admire the distant view across the marshes. To the left in the distance are cabins on Cedar Island, to the right is larger and wooded Parramore Island. The body of water between the mainland and Parramore Island is shallow Bradford's Bay. Wachapreague Channel winds to the ocean just to the left (north) of it, with the result that from this vantage point boats entering and leaving Wachapreague seem to plow through the marshes.

Locust Mount, the first village in this neighborhood, lies beyond the range of a leisurely walk, a half mile west of town. It is today an African American community dominated by the spire of **Grace Methodist Church** (1910). Opposite it, facing Custis Street, is the old **Jacob Bell Store** *(31378 Drummondtown Road)*, dating from about 1820; the old "double house" up the street is the **Callahan House** *(31342 Drummondtown Road)*, at one time the home of Methodist circuit-rider Griffin Callahan.

(For a fuller description of Wachapreague's history and sites, see *Wachapreague, Virginia: Then and Now* by Kirk Mariner, published by Miona Publications.)

LOCUSTVILLE ACADEMY

11 THE LOWER SEASIDE

Blood on the doorstep,
the oldest Sunday School,
and sights and smells of the sea

For two-thirds of the length of the Shore, from the Bridge-Tunnel north to Accomac, Seaside Road parallels Route 13, a pleasant alternative to the traffic and ugliness of the highway. It is good two-lane road, an officially designated "Virginia By-Way," and unless you have the misfortune to get stuck behind a school bus or an occasional piece of slow-moving farm machinery, you can travel almost as quickly here as on Route 13. And in place of service stations and shops, you can enjoy the view of pleasant rural countryside.

Despite its name, Seaside Road never offers a view of the sea, though if it's water you want, you're never far from it. Some of the

Shore's most picturesque harbors and landings are in this region, and this guide will be careful to direct you to them. There is a good deal of historic architecture visible from Seaside Road, and the fishing town of Wachapreague, described in its own Chapter 10, lies on this route as well.

Like all the Seaside tours in this book, this one works its way from south to north, beginning at the Chesapeake Bay Bridge-Tunnel and ending at Accomac, 51 miles distant. If you venture down every suggested road, you'll add another 35 miles to your route. Restaurants, even gas stations, are few and far between on this tour, but in case of hunger or emergency Route 13 lies always just to the left, sometimes less than a mile away.

Most of your tour will follow Seaside Road #600, which intersects Route 13 immediately north of the Bridge-Tunnel at the Sunset Beach Inn.

KIPTOPEAKE, where your tour begins, is the southernmost locale on the Delmarva Peninsula. When John S. Wise, politician-turned-writer, built his dream house here in the late 1800s, he named it Kiptopeake for the Accomack Indian, brother of the "Laughing King," who greeted Captain John Smith in these parts in 1608. Though Wise's house no longer stands (it was demolished to make room for the Administration Building of the Bridge-Tunnel), guests at the Sunset Beach Inn are free to use his own private beach on Chesapeake Bay. The Inn is also headquarters for the annual **Eastern Shore Birding Festival** (for information, call 757-787-2460), and the annual **Harvest Festival**, both held in October *(see pages 12-13)*.

Eastern Shore of Virginia National Wildlife Refuge *(Entrance on Seaside Road #600, just east of Route 13)* is well worth turning aside to see. The Refuge occupies the former Cape Charles Air Force Base, which was before that Fort John Custis, before that a Coastal Defense Artillery site, and originally a quarantine station. Begin at the excellent Visitor Center, then take the Butterfly Trail that connects with a half-mile walking trail that leads you around, through, and atop one of the bunkers left behind by the military. From a 60-foot high scenic overlook you get a spectacular vista over the cape out to the ocean between Smith Island and Fisherman Island—but not the Bridge-Tunnel, which from this point is obscured by the trees. At the foot of the overlook lies a small family cemetery, the oldest grave of which dates from 1856, and a short walk beyond that an up-close overlook of the marshes. Two other views are available from the Wise Point boat ramp. And of course Nature is almost certain to supply glimpses of waterfowl and other birds who use this final resting place before venturing southward over the broad waters of the Chesapeake. The Refuge is open to the public sunrise to sunset year round; Visitor Center open 9:00 a.m. to 4:00 p.m. daily April through November.

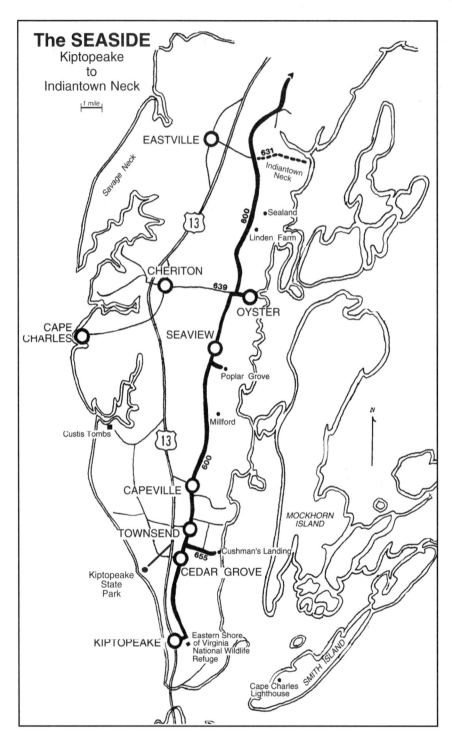

The SEASIDE
Kiptopeake
to
Indiantown Neck

1 mile

EASTVILLE

Savage Neck

631

Indiantown
Neck

13
US

600

•Sealand

Linden Farm

CHERITON

639

OYSTER

CAPE
CHARLES

SEAVIEW

•
Poplar Grove

N

•
Millford

Custis Tombs

13
US

600

CAPEVILLE

MOCKHORN
ISLAND

TOWNSEND

Cushman's Landing

655

CEDAR GROVE

Kiptopeake
State
Park

•

KIPTOPEAKE

•
Eastern Shore
of Virginia
National Wildlife
Refuge

•
Cape Charles
Lighthouse

SMITH ISLAND

CEDAR GROVE (*2.5 miles north of Kiptopeake*) is the first of three little villages in a row, hardly more than a cluster of homes around an intersection. Below the village, on the left just beyond Jones Cove Drive, stands the **Old Hopewell School** (*30248 Seaside Road*), the most southerly on the Delmarva Peninsula, which ceased to function in 1922. Half a mile beyond the village, Magotha Road #655 takes you 1 mile down to **Cushman's Landing**, which offers an extensive view across Magothy Bay to Mockhorn Island. From here you can see in the distance, four miles away, the steel-towered Cape Charles Lighthouse on Smith Island.

TOWNSEND, pronounced "Town's End," lies less than a mile above Cedar Grove, its post office located in an old bank.

CAPEVILLE, the third village in as many miles, is announced by the old **Capeville School** (1919) on the left. Though it looks much like Cedar Grove and Townsend, it is considerably older. The village's commerce has moved completely to the highway, half a mile to the west. The Methodist church, on Capeville Road #683 towards Route 13, was established in 1795.

Millford (*On the right 2.7 miles above Capeville*) sits back from the road among a grove of trees, one brick end of it facing the road; this handsome old home was built about 1775. **Poplar Grove** (*On the right 3.8 miles above Capeville*), erected 1783, can be viewed more closely from the end of Poplar Grove Lane #690.

> *From Poplar Grove it is 2 miles north, through the small village of Seaview, to Sunnyside Road #639, where your road stops for a turn either left to Cheriton or right to Oyster. Follow #639 right .3 miles into Oyster.*

OYSTER is an authentic fishing village clustered around a small harbor, complete with watermen in rubber boots, flocks of seagulls alighting on post and pier, roads and landings of shell, and seafood that can be purchased dockside. The smells of the sea, pleasant and otherwise, assault you here. If the tide is in, you may find it an attractive place; at low tide, we make no promises.

Oyster's homes are mostly modest and unpretentious, some of them ferried here from the Barrier Islands when those communities were evacuated in the early 1900s. Both parts of **Travis Chapel**, the little Methodist church, were moved to Oyster, the front part from Seaside Road, the back part from Hog Island. Beside it (*6428 Sunnyside Road*) and across the street from it (*6417 Sunnyside Road*) stand houses that came from Hog Island, the latter of which is adjacent to Oyster's one-room **Post Office**, which ceased to function in 2001.

The best access to **Oyster Slip**, as the harbor is called, is from the public boat landing at the end of Crumb Hill Road #1802. The older home facing the harbor here is the **Elkanah Cobb House**. The large and handsome building visible, but not accessible, from this road is **Cobb Island Station**, erected by the Coast Guard on nearby Cobb Island in 1936, moved to this site in 1998. The facility is currently operated as a learning and group center by World Healing Institute, and is open to those participating in its programs and events. *(Entrance gate half a mile above Oyster at 21025 Seaside Road; for information call 331-1925).*

> *From Oyster return to Seaside Road #600 and turn right.*

Two miles above Oyster, **Linden Farm** *(19259 Seaside Road)* sits back from the road on the right, an old white brick house dating from about 1750. **Sealand**, just above it on the right, is not so easily seen from the road; it dates from about 1800.

*Indiantown Neck *(Turn right on Indiantown Road #631 4.4 miles above Oyster)* was the site of the only Indian reservation on the Eastern Shore of Virginia, created in 1640 as white settlements began to encroach on Indian lands. Here in the scattered village they called Gingaskin, the peaceful Eastern Shore Indians, who never went to war against the white man, gradually wasted away. By the late 1700s they were reduced to a tribe of about 30 people, and white planters looked hungrily at their uncultivated fields. In 1813 the land was surveyed, divided into lots, and deeded directly to the individual members of the tribe who, as was hoped, thereupon sold their holdings and lost their land. The Indians were by then a heterogeneous mixture of native, black, and white blood, and had largely ceased to be of concern to the white population.

All that is left of this sad slice of history is the name Indiantown Neck, which is today farmland, and one historical marker in Eastville, a mile to the west. On the right stands **Eyre Rectory** *(6520 Indiantown Road)*, built in 1853. At the end of the road, a mile down the neck from Seaside Road, is a community recreational park. The Union Army camped in this vicinity when it occupied the Shore during the Civil War.

> *At 1.6 miles above Indiantown Neck, Seaside Road veers sharply left; be careful not to proceed down Indian Village Road #622.*

About two miles above Indiantown Neck, facing Cherrydale Drive, is **Homeplace** *(15189 Seaside Road)*, said to date from the 1700s. Box Tree Drive #627 leads less than a mile down to a small landing and pier on *Box Tree Creek; just north of it, set back in the field on the right, stands **Myrtle Grove**, which dates from about 1790. There's not much to see at *Webb's Island *(Turn right on Webb Island Drive*

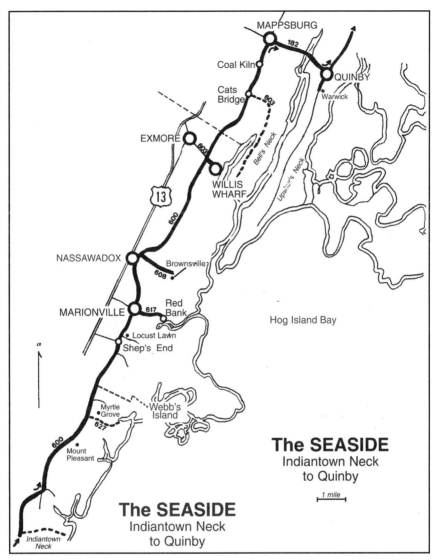

MAPPSBURG

Coal Kiln

Cats
Bridge

QUINBY

Warwick

EXMORE

Bell's Neck

Upshur's Neck

WILLIS
WHARF

US 13

NASSAWADOX

Brownsville

608

MARIONVILLE

617

Red
Bank

Hog Island Bay

Locust Lawn

Shep's End

Myrtle
Grove

Webb's
Island

627

600

Mount
Pleasant

The SEASIDE
Indiantown Neck
to Quinby

1 mile

The SEASIDE
Indiantown Neck
to Quinby

Indiantown
Neck

#629), but it is an island, sort of, separated from the mainland by a tiny gut. The road is public for the first mile, then privately owned, and at the junction the owners have set up a toll booth (25¢) to help with the upkeep of their shell road. The oldest house here was built in the late 19th century at a different site, but deposited at its present location *(10093 Webb Island Drive)* by the great Storm of 1933. Just off Seaside Road on Goshen Drive #621 stands the abandoned *****Taylor Memorial Baptist Church** (1913). **Locust Lawn**, a large farmhouse dating from the 1780s, stands on the right just beyond the village of Shep's End, adjacent to Locust Lawn Drive #621.

MARIONVILLE *(Intersection of Seaside Road and Red Bank*

Road #617) is hardly more than a church and a few houses, but two of its buildings are noteworthy. On the left just as the church comes into view is old **Birdsnest Tavern** (9332 Seaside Road), source of the name of the nearby village on Route 13. For many years when this house was a tavern, the road in front of it was often flooded during rainy weather, and locals used to spin yarns about the travails of those who attempted to pass through this "Deep Blue Sea." The church itself is **Red Bank Baptist Church**, founded in 1783 by Elijah Baker, pioneer of the Baptist faith on the Eastern Shore; this building was erected in 1899, the congregation's fourth. **Red Bank** (Turn right on Red Bank Road #617 and travel 1 mile to water) offers a pretty view of Red Bank Creek meandering peacefully through the marshes out to Hog Island Bay. The first two houses on Red Bank Court, where the road turns sharply left, were moved here from Hog Island.

NASSAWADOX. Above Marionville, Seaside Road winds westward into Nassawadox, where Route 13 is only a block away to the left. This is the oldest part of the town, and one of the houses here was originally **Nassawadox Methodist Church** (7813 Seaside Road), erected in 1908 and closed in 1928. On Mill Street stands the old **Nassawadox Sawmill**, now restored, a part of the extensive operations of the Nassawadox Lumber Company, founded in 1898, for many years the town's most important industry.

Brownsville (Turn right on Brownsville Road #608 at northern town limits and travel 1 mile) is the headquarters of the Virginia Coast Reserve, the project of The Nature Conservancy that owns and oversees the Barrier Islands. Check in here (9:00-4:30 Monday-Friday) for a self-guided walk out to the hammocks overlooking Hog Island Bay. (For Barrier Islands see Chapter 4).

> Four miles above Nassawadox your road stops at Willis Wharf Road #603 in front of Epworth United Methodist Church. To the left lies Exmore and Route 13, but your route lies to the right.

WILLIS WHARF. The main road into Willis Wharf is conspicuously neat, the homes and yards bright and cheery if not grand. At the waterfront the road turns sharply right, and this part of town is a bit less tidy. Willis Wharf is another of those places that turn to the sea for its livelihood, with a somewhat mixed result.

This was Downings Wharf in the early 1800s, renamed after Edward Willis moved here in the 1850s. The old **E. L. Willis Store** [1], built at that time, still stands on the corner. The large houses that face the water were built by the families who at various times ran the seafood companies along the waterfront.

Eighteen of the houses that once stood on Hog Island were moved to Willis Wharf when the island was evacuated in the 1930s and 1940s. The first to arrive was **Hog Island House** [2] (13175 Parting Creek

Road); next door to it now is the island's **M e t h o d i s t Parsonage** [3] *(13167 Parting Creek Road).* The old **Broadwater Post Office** [4] *(13057 Terry Lane)* was moved to this site in 1945; at the end of the lane stands the **George Doughty House** [5] *(13052 Terry Lane),* also from the island.

The best view of Willis Wharf is from the **Observation Deck** [6] south of the bridge. In this section the old house **Greenville** [7] hides behind a larger new one at 5280 Willis Wharf Road; its one brick end, dating from the 1700s, is said to have been built from bricks used as ballast for a ship arriving from England. At the very end of the road on Hog Island Lane, is the section of town known as **Little Hog Island** where no fewer than six of the eight houses [8-13] were moved from Hog Island.

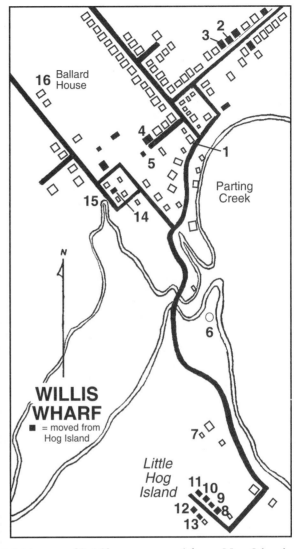

13015 Ballard Drive [14] is yet another house moved from Hog Island, and across the street from it is **Ballard Pond Park** [15], fronting a lovely but somewhat hidden pond. At the top of the hill stands **Ballard House** [16] *(12527 Ballard Drive),* built in 1908.

From Willis Wharf return to Seaside Road via Ballard Drive or Willis Wharf Road and turn right on Seaside Road #600.

For several miles north of Willis Wharf the road is lined with small settlements with intriguing names. You'll know you've passed through **Bacon Hill** once you reach **Mt. Calvary Baptist Church** on the left; just above it the road passes, without notice, into Accomack County. At **Cat's Bridge** *(2.8 miles above Willis Wharf Road)* you can turn right on Bell's Neck Road #603 for *__Bell's Neck__, a lonely stretch 3.3 miles long, at the end of which is a distant view of Willis Wharf across the waters of Parting Creek; 37595 Bell's Neck Road is another Hog Island house, floated to this site in the 1930s. Five miles above Willis Wharf your road stops at Hawk's Nest or **Mappsburg**, no larger than the previous settlements, but considerably older. Before you turn here look ahead and to the left for **Garrison Bed and Breakfast**; its shady location was a revered Methodist site from 1787 until 1927, for here stood old Garrisons Chapel; this house was built in 1931, after the church was moved to Painter *(see page 19)*.

> *At Mappsburg turn east on Route #182 (Quinby Bridge Road) and travel 2.3 miles to Quinby.*

QUINBY lies on the east side of the Machipongo River, the only "river" on the Eastern Shore of Virginia though it is in fact simply another tidal creek. The bridge was a toll bridge in the early 1900s. Quinby, another fishing village, is named for the family of Upshur B. Quinby, who lived nearby in the 1880s. The main part of the house at 20270 Quinby Bridge Road, on the right just before the stop sign, was once the **Old Store** that stood facing the intersection; in its time it served also as pool hall and skating rink. Turn right on Upshur's Neck Road #605 to see the village. **Smith's Chapel**, in the center of town, was built in 1896. Four doors south of it is **Atlantic View** *(35511 Upshur's Neck Road)*, dating from the late 1700s, which housed the village's first post office in 1896. **Quinby Harbor**, at the end of Harbor Point Road #606, was once known as "Besold's Gut" and is not a natural harbor; before it was dredged in 1931 local watermen anchored their boats out in Upshur Bay and trudged ashore over the marsh. Overlooking the harbor is **Fisherman's Lodge** *(20210 Harbor Point Road)*, built in the 1930s and once again catering to sports fishermen.

In Quinby stand four homes once located on Hog Island, as well as a number of other buildings constructed in part with lumber from that community. Half a mile below the village stands **Warwick** *(20071 Warwick Drive)*, barely visible from the road but worthy of note for its story as well as its antiquity. Here lived another branch of the Upshurs, one of the Shore's most prominent families. The brick portion of the house, the oldest part, dates perhaps from the 1600s, and may have been only the "kitchen" of a larger home which was burned by the British during the Revolution.

Rachel Revell Upshur, who lived at Warwick, is the subject of one of the Shore's favorite folktales. One night after a nightmare warning her not to leave the house, she went outside to see after her husband

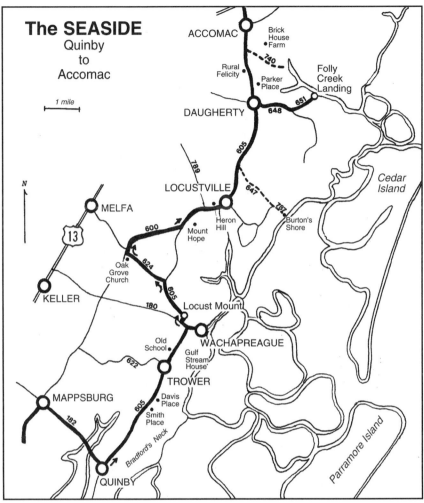

The SEASIDE
Quinby
to
Accomac

1 mile

N

ACCOMAC
Brick House Farm
Rural Felicity
Parker Place
740
Folly Creek Landing
651
DAUGHERTY
648
605
789
LOCUSTVILLE
647
Cedar Island
MELFA
600
Heron Hill
Mount Hope
Burton's Shore
624
Oak Grove Church
605
KELLER
180
Locust Mount
WACHAPREAGUE
Old School
Gulf Stream House
622
TROWER
MAPPSBURG
Davis Place
605
Smith Place
182
Bradford's Neck
QUINBY
Parramore Island

Abel, and was bitten by a rabid fox. As she was rushed back into the house, her foot bled on the doorstep. She developed hydrophobia, and on Christmas night 1749 was deliberately smothered by her servants in her featherbed, the merciful way to "put people out of their misery" in those days. To this day Rachel's blood reappears on the doorstep when it rains, and the tales of her occasional visits to and antics in the house persist. Her grave lies near the house, its unusual tombstone long since overturned by the roots of a large tree.

From Quinby proceed north out of town on Bradford's Neck Road #605.

Above Quinby the road passes through **Bradford's Neck**, where the water is always on your right beyond a border of trees. On the right

1.8 miles above Quinby stands **Smith Place** *(33457 Bradfords Neck Road)*, a house of three sections dating from the early 1800s. Just above it is **Davis Place** *(33341 Bradfords Neck Road)*, dating from before 1850. At the intersection known as Trower stands the **Abel J. Bell House** *(33006 Bradfords Neck Road)*, a typical "double house" of the 19th century. The old **Trower School** *(32496 Bradfords Neck Road)* is now a private home.

WACHAPREAGUE *(4 miles above Quinby; turn right on Route #180)*, the "Little City by the Sea," is one of the Shore's most popular fishing villages. It is described in detail in Chapter 10.

> *To continue your tour of the Lower Seaside, turn left when your road ends at Route #180, then right again on Drummondtown Road #605.*
>
> *If continuing the tour from Wachapreague, turn right on Drummondtown Road, which can be reached from Main Street, Custis Street, or Richardson Avenue.*
>
> *Just beyond Wachapreague cemetery, 1 mile above Locust Mount, turn left on Pickpenny Road #624 and travel 1.2 miles to rejoin Seaside Road #600.*

Oak Grove United Methodist Church *(Seaside Road at Pickpenny Road)* is not by any means the most ancient church on the Shore, but it is one of the most beloved. Its fame lies in its Sunday School, said to be the oldest in continuous existence in America.

In 1785, William Elliott, a Methodist who lived in Bradford's Neck, began teaching the children on his plantation, slave and free, to read so that they could read the Bible. Soon Elliott and his assistants were teaching all the children for miles around, the only education then available locally, and it occurred on Sunday afternoons.

In 1818 Elliott moved his "Sunday School" to Burton's Chapel, a Methodist church which stood near Locust Mount. There he operated it until his death in 1836, after which it became a regular part of congregational life at Burton's Chapel. When the chapel burned in 1870, the Methodists replaced it with this building on this site, renaming it Oak Grove. The Sunday School continues today, more than two centuries after its formation.

When erected in 1871, Oak Grove Chapel was "the latest word" in modernity, its congregation one of the most progressive on the Shore, and its location right in the center of its constituency. Thirteen years later the railroad came, members moved westward into Melfa, and the church declined to a small number of people.

Except for the addition of stained glass windows around the turn of the century, Oak Grove is not substantially changed from 1871. *(See illustration on title page.)* In the adjacent burial ground lies Rev. John Wesley A. Elliott, grandson of the Sunday School's founder.

From Oak Grove turn north (right) on Seaside Road #600 and travel 1.9 miles to Drummondtown Road #605; turn left and continue north.

Mount Hope *(29015 Drummondtown Road)* sits back from the road on the right almost immediately after your turn, a five-section house, the oldest portion of which dates from about 1840. A mile beyond it on the left is the even older **Heron Hill** *(28412 Drummondtown Road)*, almost hidden by its surrounding trees; this attractive house was built by James Ashby soon after 1795.

LOCUSTVILLE. Three miles above Oak Grove Church, your road crosses the wide marshes of Finney Creek and lands you in Locustville. Pause to look closely at this peaceful little village; this is the Eastern Shore much as it might have looked prior to the Civil War.

Locustville took shape in the early 1800s and was a stop on the old stagecoach line that ran up the Seaside Road from Eastville into Maryland. The homes here were modest ones, the stop not nearly so important as the next one up the road at the county seat. Still Locustville could boast a tavern, a store, a church, and a school. Remarkably, all of them still stand here today, and with the exception of the church, all of them still occupy their original buildings.

In the center of the village stands **Locustville General Store** [1] *(28251 Drummondtown Road)*, erected in 1844, one of the Shore's most renowned old-fashioned country stores. The stagecoach would probably have stopped two doors south at the **Locustville Hotel** [2] *(28269 Drummondtown Road)*, which dates from about 1820. Between the hotel and the store, set back from the road, is **29689 Burton's Shore Road** [3], dating from the 1830s; across from the hotel is **28268 Drummondtown Road** [4], the largest section of which sports the same kind of woodwork under the eaves that adorns the store, suggesting that it too may date from the 1840s. Opposite the store stands a little **Double House** [5] *(28246 Drummondtown Road)* which dates probably from the 1820s. Next door **28234 Drummondtown Road** [6] is a handsome "big house, little house, colonnade, kitchen" in the traditional Eastern Shore style, but only a recent aspirant to that rank; the "big house" is modern, the rest an authentic old double house. Perhaps older than them all is **29710 Burton's Shore Road** [7], the small house on the corner beyond the store; though hiding behind a lovely Victorian porch, it may date from as early as the 1700s.

The **Swanger House** [8] *(28186 Drummondtown Road)*, north of the center of the village, was built by the owner of the general store between 1830 and 1860. Next to it is **Wynne Tref** [9] *(28168 Drummondtown Road)*, dating probably from the 1820s, and next to

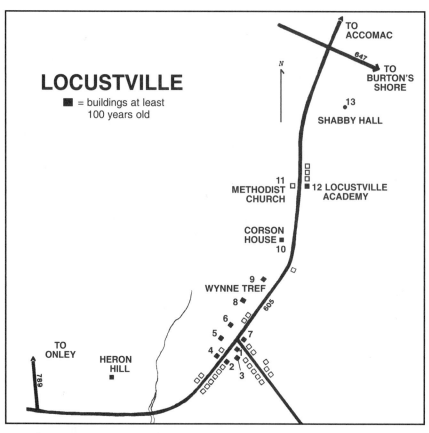

LOCUSTVILLE

■ = buildings at least 100 years old

N

TO ACCOMAC

647

TO BURTON'S SHORE

.13

SHABBY HALL

11
METHODIST
CHURCH

■ 12 LOCUSTVILLE
ACADEMY

CORSON
HOUSE ■
10

9
WYNNE TREF

8

605

6

5

7

4

1

2

3

789

TO
ONLEY

HERON
HILL
■

it is **Corson House** [10] *(28102 Drummondtown Road)*, from the 1840s.

On the northern edge of the village stands **Locustville United Methodist Church** [11], built in 1923; the congregation was founded in 1784, and no longer functions. Opposite it **Locustville Academy** [12] is the only survivor of the dozen or more schools of higher learning that dotted the Shore in the mid-1800s. The academy opened in 1859 and offered classes for boys and girls who planned to enter college or business professions. Among the subjects taught were reading, writing, arithmetic, philosophy, Greek, Latin, and piano. Girls studied on the first floor, boys on the second, and everyone carried a report card home every week. Except for a brief interruption during the Civil War, the Academy operated continuously until 1879, after which the building became the property of the Accomack County School Board. Today it is owned by the Society for the Preservation of Locustville Academy, which maintains a small museum inside. The Academy is open to the public on the last weekend in October and during Garden Week. *(For entry at other times, call 787-2460).*

Shabby Hall [13] is, alas, no longer standing in Locustville, but the

128   The Lower Seaside

map indicates where once stood a handsome little house erected about 1800, with a story that won it a place in "Ripley's Believe It or Not." According to the local tradition, it was at one time owned by a handsome bachelor who went to Baltimore in search of a wife. There he wooed a pretty girl with talk of his southern plantation, married her in a whirlwind courtship, and brought her to Locustville. Upon first seeing her new home she remarked, "Southern plantation, humph! Shabby Hall!" Nonetheless they lived there happily the rest of their lives. In the early 1970s, Shabby Hall was dismantled, transported to a new location across Chesapeake Bay, and re-erected. It stands today at 951 Bowie Shop Road in Calvert County, Maryland.

Just beyond Locustville is ***Burton's Shore** (Turn right on Burton's Shore Road #647, then left on Seagull Lane #787, a total distance of 1.7 miles to water), in the old days a favorite place for picnics and bathing. The view here looks across Burton's Bay to Cedar Island, where in the distance to the north can be glimpsed the abandoned Coast Guard station.

DAUGHERTY (On Drummondtown Road #605, 2.5 miles above Locustville) is pronounced "Darty." **St. Luke's A.M.E. Church** was established in 1872. **Clarke Presbyterian Church**, to the right on Custis Neck Road #648, preserves two buildings, the older built in 1894, the newer in 1922. **Gable Cottage** (24060 Custis Neck Road) dates from about 1840. **Folly Creek Landing** (Continue out of the village on Custis Neck Road #648, then left on Folly Creek Road #651, a total distance of 2.2 miles to water) offers an attractive view of the marshes, Folly Creek, and Joynes Neck; there is a public boat ramp here, with ample parking for boat users.

Above Daugherty, Seaside Road leads into Accomac, but not before passing two more old homes. **Parker Place**, on the right .5 mile above the village, dates from the late 1700s. On the left .75 mile further stands the late 19th-century **Rural Felicity**. In the fields behind this house the local Confederate militia established Camp Wise at the outbreak of the Civil War. When the Union Army took possession of the Shore in November 1861, they found the campsite abandoned and occupied it; it was renamed Camp Wilkes.

Your last chance to get a glimpse of the water on this tour lies one mile down Oysterhouse Road #740 (.9 mile to water), where wide and shallow ***Folly Creek** winds through the marshes. Set back in the field on the left is **Brick House Farm**, a handsome house erected about 1750.

Seaside Road ends at Front Street in Accomac, completing your tour of the Lower Seaside.

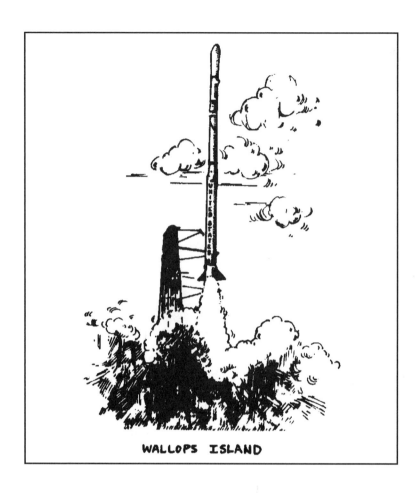

WALLOPS ISLAND

12 THE UPPER SEASIDE

A boy in an iron coffin,
a rocket base to outer space,
and the Eastern Shore's favorite ghost town

In the early 1800s there was a single daily stagecoach to and from the Eastern Shore of Virginia, and part of the route it traveled was the Seaside Road north out of Accomac towards Maryland. This tour follows that part of the old stagecoach route.

What were once the largest towns and most important stops on the line have long since faded into inconsequential little hamlets that hardly merit a road sign today. Except for an occasional old mansion, more occasional in this section than further south, this part of the Shore is modest and unpretentious. Despite its name, the Seaside Road never ventures close to the sea, so if you want to view the water you'll have to take a side trip.

The modern world thrusts itself abruptly into this otherwise quiet corner of the Shore. At Wallops Island there is a NASA installation from which rockets have put satellites into orbit around the earth. Chincoteague Island (see Chapter 2) is a modern vacation resort visited by hordes of tourists every summer. Further north is a housing development whose buildings on the wetlands became a celebrated ecological issue.

This tour travels from south to north, beginning on Route 13 at Zion Baptist Church, 3.5 miles above the town of Accomac. It ends at Franklin City in the northeasternmost corner of Accomack County, right on the Maryland border. On this route it is 23 miles from Route 13 to Maryland, and those passing through Virginia on their way to the Maryland and Delaware beaches will find the Seaside Road a less traveled alternative to the main highway. The total tour, with all suggested roads and options, covers more than 60 miles.

Despite its several modern names, #679 from Route 13 north to Maryland has been known since the 1600s as the Seaside Road. At Zion Baptist Church, 3.5 miles north of Accomac, #679 is known as Fox Grove Road, but it changes almost immediately to Metompkin Road. Except for side trips, #679 will remain your route throughout this tour.

Zion Baptist Church juxtaposes two buildings, a new brick one built in 1917 and, across the road from it, an older frame building of 1852.

METOMPKIN is the name of the small black settlement that clusters around the road a mile north of Zion Church. The name is Indian, and the small Metompkin tribe that lived near here migrated to this neighborhood after white settlement forced them out of Accomac. By 1705 their tribe was "much decreased of late by the Small Pox, that was carried thither." Today only their name survives, gracing a local church, a magisterial district, a bank, an island, and this unremarkable hamlet. A mile beyond, in "Mutton Hunk," stands **Calm Retreat** *(18552 Metompkin Road)* on the left, a low frame house in four sections, the oldest part of which was built in the early 1800s. Just beyond it on the right is a modern house *(18507 Metompkin Road)* framed by a pond on the site of old **Savage's Mill**, also established in the early 1800s.

Gargatha Neck *(Turn right on Gargatha Landing Road #680, 2.7 miles north of Zion Church)* takes its name from "Gargaphia," the local plantation owned by Mrs. Ann Toft [1643-1687?], one of the

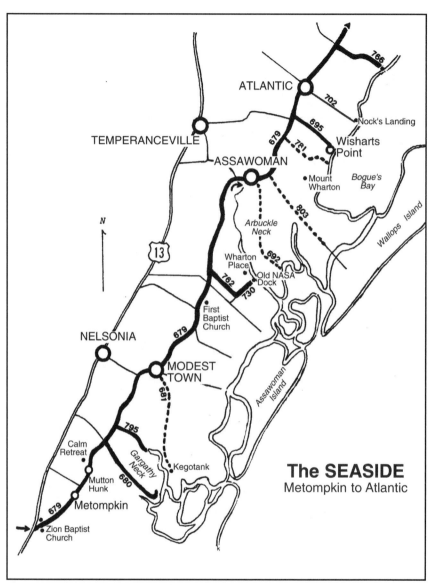

The SEASIDE
Metompkin to Atlantic

most mysterious women of early Eastern Shore history. Nothing is known of her prior to 1664 when she settled down near here with three small daughters, miles from the nearest neighbors, and proceeded to establish a plantation that was soon one of the largest and richest on the Shore. Col. Edmund Scarburgh, a powerful and avaricious neighbor, fell very much under the spell of her charms, but in the 1670s she married Daniel Jenifer. Sometime after 1687 she "just slipped out of the story as mysteriously as she had entered it." Her great-grandson, Daniel of St. Thomas Jenifer, was one of Maryland's signers of the

Federal Constitution in the next century.

Today all that is left of Toft's Gargaphia is the name Gargatha, or Gargathy. It is 1.7 miles down the neck from Metompkin Road, and the road ends at a landing with a peaceful and extensive view of Gargathy Creek near its mouth. Across the marshes can be seen hunting lodges on Metompkin Island, and further north the NASA installations on Wallops Island. ***Mitchell Drive** #795, half a mile further north on Metompkin Road, leads 1 mile down to a more inland view of Gargathy Creek.

MODEST TOWN *(4.5 miles north of Zion Church)*. In Modest Town, so the story goes, the old stage used to stop in front of a boarding house run by two very prim and proper ladies. Nearby Nelsonia on the Middle Road (Route 13) was called Helltown; this place, by comparison, took on a gentler name. In the early 1800s this was one of the largest towns on the peninsula; today you can zip through it almost before you know it, though it deserves attention.

Modest Town Baptist Church was founded in 1829; this building dates from 1922. In the cemetery across the street *(Fifth row from the southern end)* is the gravestone, but not the grave, of **"the Boy in the Iron Coffin."** William Taylor White [1837-1852] was a student in Washington, D.C., when he died and was buried there in 1852. When the cemetery in which he was buried was later re-located, his grave was inadvertently left behind, and a century and a half later, in 2005, construction workers replacing a gas line discovered an unmarked grave containing an iron coffin with a glass window, the body inside remarkably well-preserved because the coffin was air-tight. The coffin was sent to the Smithsonian Institution, where after a two-year study that was chronicled on TV's "History Detectives" its occupant was identified, through DNA, as this teenaged native of Acomack County. Though this stone honors him here, his body remains at the Smithsonian. The melancholy verse on the back of the stone is from his brief obituary in a Washington newspaper in January 1852.

***Kegotank** (Turn right on Kegotank Road #681 and travel 2 miles to water)* is a corruption of "Kickotank," the name of the Indians who lived in this vicinity. When Henry Norwood was marooned on the nearby coast after a winter storm in 1649-50, he found refuge with the Kickotanks, who treated him kindly and directed him southward towards his destination; his first-hand description of life among the Eastern Shore Indians is the most extensive that has survived from the 17th century. All there is to see at Kegotank today is a nice view, with a pier and a ramp for boats. In the center of the village opposite the store is 16386 Metompkin Road, which is probably the old **Modest Town Ordinary** or inn. **Tanyard House** *(16369 Metompkin Road)* is the quaint little house of several sections on the corner, the oldest part of which, in the "saltbox" style so rare in this region, dates from the early 1700s.

First Baptist Church *(On the right 2 miles above Modest Town)* was established in 1875, one of the earliest African American congregations on the Shore; there is a tradition that its first building was made out of logs. Turn right on the second road beyond it to the **Old NASA Dock***(Turn right on Pettit Road #762, then left on Pierce Taylor Road #730, a total distance of 1.2 miles to water)*. Before the bridge to Wallops Island was built, a car ferry shuffled workers back and forth across Assawoman Creek from this point. The installations on Wallops Island can be seen from here. From Pettit Road look across the fields to the north for **Wharton Place** *(13485 Wharton Drive)*, one of the Shore's premier and most storied old homes, built about 1800 by an architect imported from Philadelphia. Despite its importance, you will have to settle for distant views of it, or even less depending upon which crops have been planted.

Three and a half miles above Modest Town, #679 changes from Metompkin Road to Atlantic Road.

ASSAWOMAN *(5.5 miles above Modest Town)*, pronounced *Ass-a-wah'mon*, is an Indian name found on local creeks and bays as far north as Delaware. This little village has been settled continuously since the 1600s. Where the road crosses the creek at the southern edge of the village, the Reverend Francis Makemie, the pioneer of American Presbyterianism, built a mill in 1701. The Anglican church that once stood near the millpond is long gone, but the Episcopal church in Jenkins Bridge still owns a silver communion cup made for it in London in 1749.

The little house on the right at the top of the hill is **Arbuckle Place** *(12213 Atlantic Road)*, built in 1774 *(see illustration, page 7)*, a Virginia Historic Landmark. One of its residents was Alexander Stockley, grandfather of Rachel Donelson Jackson, the celebrated (or notorious) wife of President Andrew Jackson. Wallops Island itself lies just off the mainland here, and two roads lead down from the village towards it. The better view is from ***Arbuckle Neck** (Turn right on Arbuckle Neck Road #692)*, where the road ends abruptly on Oyster Bay after 2 miles. All you can see from the other road is the bridge to the island *(Turn right on Wallops Island Road #803, 1 mile to gate; public not admitted)*. The Main Base and Visitor Center of the NASA installation lie several miles up Seaside Road. At the intersection stand **Assawoman United Methodist Church** (1901) and the old **Assawoman School** (1889), the only "one room" school house still standing on its original site on the Eastern Shore of Virginia.

Leaving Assawoman you can glimpse **Mount Wharton** *(see illustration, page 8)* on the right, at the end of the long lane that bears its name; this home was built prior to 1772 by the Whartons of Wharton Place. ***Bogue's Bay** (Turn right on Taylor Farm Road #781, 1 mile above Assawoman)* is a small body of water separating Wallops Island from the mainland; the road to it winds for 1.3 miles through farms which enjoy a pleasing vista across the water. A wider view is from

Wishart's Point (*Turn right on Wisharts Point Road #695 at the southern edge of Atlantic; 1.3 miles to water*), the southern jumping-off-place for Chincoteague Island before the causeway was built from the mainland. During the 1890s there was a ferry from here to Chincoteague, and a hotel which has since been floated over to the island. In 1947 a harbor was dredged here, and the following year the Wishart's Point Yacht Club was established. The buildings of the Yacht Club are today an unsightly ruin, but the view across Bogue's Bay to Chincoteague and Wallops Island is a fine one.

ATLANTIC (*7 miles above Modest Town*) is trim, pleasant, and at first glance utterly unremarkable. Its well-kept houses and lawns cluster about Atlantic Road amid some of the best farmland on the Shore, giving little or no evidence of the fact that this village has been settled since the early 1800s. **Atlantic Baptist Church** and **Atlantic United Methodist Church** command the center of the village, prosperous congregations and friendly rivals in buildings that date from 1920 and 1922 respectively. The most noteworthy house in town is the **John S. Parsons Place** (*9588 Atlantic Road*), a late 19th-century home. Just off Atlantic Road is **Marshall Manufacturing Company** (*32489 Nock's Landing Road*), one of the few places in the Chesapeake region that make crab-pots; the wire-mesh crab-pots stacked here are as likely to end up in New Jersey or Texas as in Chesapeake Bay, for this is the source of most of the pots used to catch crabs up and down the East Coast. A mile north of town Wright's Road #766 leads 1.4 miles down to water and a popular seafood restaurant.

A mile and a half above Atlantic your road stops at Route #175. Turn right here and travel 2.3 miles to the Visitor Center of:

WALLOPS ISLAND. On July 4, 1945, the first rocket blasted off from Wallops Island, and since that time this has been one of the few places on the Eastern Shore of Virginia recognized nationwide. Today Wallops Island, officially Wallops Flight Facility of the Goddard Space Flight Center, is owned and operated by the National Aeronautics and Space Administration (NASA), and plays a vital role in the nation's space program.

There are two portions of the facility: (1) the Main Base on the mainland, on your left as you approach the Visitor Center, and (2) Wallops Island itself, three miles to the south off the mainland near Assawoman, where the launch complex is located. Only the Visitor Center is open to the public.

Wallops Island was named for John Wallop, who first laid claim to it in 1672. For many years prior to World War II, when the Federal government took it over as a Naval Ordnance Station, the island was a popular gunning and fishing area, and like neighboring Assateague Island had a herd of wild ponies. Nineteen earth satellites have been

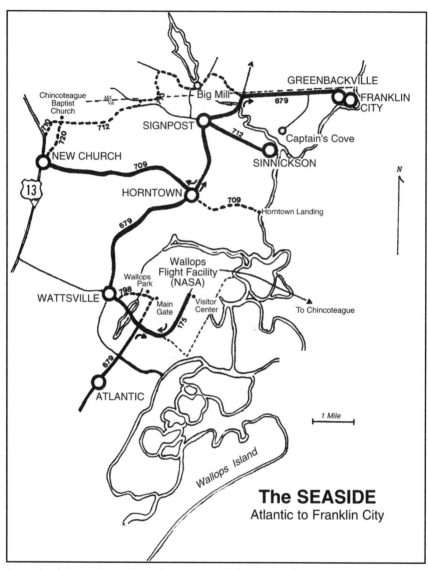

The SEASIDE
Atlantic to Franklin City

launched from this island, but most of the work done here today is concerned with components and systems development, aeronautical and meteorological research, tracking and data acquisition, and assistance to other government agencies domestic and foreign.

The Visitor Center *(Open 10:00-4:00 seven days a week from July 4 through Labor Day, Thursday through Monday for the rest of the year except December-February, then Monday through Friday; closed all Federal holidays except Memorial Day, Labor Day, and July 4; no admission charge)* will delight the space enthusiast: rockets displayed outside, satellite and rocket models inside, history of flight exhibits, videos and films, even a piece of moon rock. In addition there are puppet shows, spacesuit demonstrations, and model rocket launchings at various times and seasons. The center is interesting and well-staffed; a gift shop and refreshment area are adjacent.

The *Main Base *(When returning from the Visitor Center turn right on Atlantic Road #798 and travel .7 mile)* occupies the facilities of old Chincoteague Naval Air Station, and is better seen from the road than from the Main Gate, which you may not enter. Much of the old navy housing that once stood within the station has been dispersed across the Shore; an obvious collection of it hugs the road just south of the Main Gate.

(Note: Tours of the Main Base and Island for schools and civic groups, and occasionally for the general public, may be arranged in advance. For all information concerning Wallops, contact NASA Visitor Center, GSFC Wallops Flight Facility, Wallops Island, VA 23337, telephone 757-824-2298.)

> *From the Wallops Visitor Center it is 6 miles to Chincoteague Island, the Shore's premier tourist attraction (see Chapter 2). To continue the tour of the Upper Seaside, retrace your route on #175 for 3.4 miles to Wattsville.*

WATTSVILLE takes its name from the family of James Watt, who settled here around 1714. Just east of the village you cross Wallops Millpond, created about 1788, the largest on the Eastern Shore of Virginia. *Wallops Park *(Turn right on Mill Dam Road #798 just over the millpond, or from the Main Gate of Wallops head west on #798; park lies immediately left of abandoned housing)*, Accomack's first county-owned park, offers a walking trail through the woods in addition to the more visible recreational facilities.

> *In Wattsville turn right on #679, which for the remainder of your tour will be known as Fleming Road, and continue north.*

HORNTOWN *(3.7 miles above Wattsville)* is not only fading, it is actually disappearing piece by piece. Once one of the largest communities on the Shore, a major stop on the old stage line and one of only three villages with a post office in 1793, it is today a shadow of its former self, and its old homes and buildings sag with the passing of every year. In the center of town is the old **Methodist Church**, built in 1858, closed in 1994, and now used as a community center. **Horntown Baptist Church**, on Justice Road, was built in 1897. The original house in Horntown, which was demolished in 1970, was old Shepherd's Inn, established about 1730 on the site of today's post office. At *Horntown Landing *(1.7 miles down Justice Road #709 to water)* islanders from Chincoteague would land on shopping trips to the mainland, back when their community was still small and remote and Horntown was the regional metropolis. A better view across Chincoteague Bay to the island is from **Corbin Hall** *(Turn right half a mile beyond the village; 1.6 miles to road's end)*, a new development on an old estate of that name; the big house at the end of the lane occupies the site of the original Corbin Hall, which burned in 2000.

SINNICKSON *(At 2 miles above Horntown, turn right on Red Hills Road #712, just as village of Signpost comes into view; 2 miles to water)* is named for R. B. Sinnickson, a Cincinnati millionaire who in 1886 purchased the little village of Nashville, which already enjoyed status as a local resort because of its pleasant location on Chincoteague Bay. In the 1890s crowds as large as 3,000 gathered here to enjoy the water; a small hotel offered guests regular connections by land to Pocomoke City and by water to Chincoteague Island. In 1906 Sinnickson sold out at a 500% profit, and the new owners installed a merry-go-round and a motion-picture show. Sinnickson faded as better resorts became accessible; the last business here was a restaurant that closed in 1962. Today its view is still a good one, across Swan's Gut Creek where it meets Chincoteague Bay, but the waterfront is dilapidated and unsightly. Look for the stone **Julian Hines House**, set back in the woods behind 36519 Red Hills Road, now abandoned. The oldest house in Sinnickson is undoubtedly the small one at 36467 Red Hill's Road.

SIGNPOST *(2 miles above Horntown)* is named for a directional sign that once stood in the fork of the road here. When a post office was established in 1898, the government disallowed the name Signpost, so postmaster Columbus Davis invented the name Silva. The little store that once held the post office now stands in a backyard on the left opposite **Signpost United Methodist Church** (1902). Above the village **Sinnickson House** *(2621 Fleming Road)*, built by R. B. Sinnickson soon after his entry into this area in 1886, is remarkable chiefly for its size. Just beyond it, the road crosses **Swan's Gut Creek**; look to the right here for modern homes hugging the shore in Captain's Cove and, in the further distance, Chincoteague and the lighthouse on Assateague Island, eight miles away.

> *2 miles above Signpost, Fleming Road passes into Maryland, becoming Route 12. From this point it is a distance of 12 miles to Snow Hill, and an additional 24 miles, via U.S. Routes 113 and 50, to Ocean City.*
> *The Upper Seaside tour turns right towards Greenbackville on State Line Road #679, the left shoulder of which forms the Maryland-Virginia boundary.*

***Captain's Cove** (Main gate on the right after .3 mile) has been on your right since crossing Swan's Gut Creek, a residential and recreational development begun in 1969 on three old historic tracts of Eastern Shore farmland, forest, and marsh. Planned to contain 5,000 building lots, many with water access, canals and docks, swimming pools and recreational facilities, Captain's Cove was widely advertised up and down the East Coast, but its early growth was thwarted by what was then a new word on the Eastern Shore—ecology—after the initial developers ran afoul of both the law by dredging the marshlands to create canals. There are today about 850 homes in the development, and a year-round population approaching 500, making "the Cove" one of the larger "towns" on Virginia's Eastern Shore, though it has no official status as such.

At the site of today's Pro Shop (3370 Captain's Corridor) stood the ancient estate **Pharsalia**, birthplace of Warner Mifflin [1745-1798], one of the foremost abolitionists of his time, whose constant gadflying nudged Quaker congregations into an anti-slavery stance, and even persuaded the Virginia legislature to soften its slavery laws. Mifflin enjoyed a view across Chincoteague Bay that is best seen today from the **Marina Club**. Captain's Corridor, officially a private road "for members only," circles through the development and re-connects with State Line Road #679 about half a mile beyond the main gate. **2310 Captain's Corridor**, a farmhouse dating from about 1915, is the only remaining house antedating the development.

GREENBACKVILLE and **FRANKLIN CITY** cling to the last available piece of land on the Eastern Shore of Virginia at the end of State Line Road #679, two villages on an improbable site sharing an interesting history.

Greenbackville took shape in the late 1860s when there was an influx of would-be watermen anxious to "make a killing" by harvesting the oysters of Chincoteague Bay. Matthias Lindsay, who lived in what is now Captain's Cove, agreed to sell them land on which to live, at $100 of government greenback money for every acre of the almost worthless marshland. "One hundred dollars an acre," exclaimed Henry Pope, who lived alone on those marshes. "That shouldn't be called land—that should be called greenback," and thus he named the town.

Ten years later Judge John R. Franklin, who lived across the line in Maryland, persuaded the railroad to extend its line down to his property just east of the new village, and there on an even marshier spot he created Franklin City, an entire community planned from scratch. The railroad opened up Chincoteague Island, five miles across the open water, to swifter shipping of its produce to northern markets, and Greenbackville and Franklin City thrived as the shipping point. The depletion of oysters from Chincoteague Bay and the opening of a causeway to the island in 1922 doomed such prosperity, and the two villages went into slow decline. After a storm swept high tides through the streets in 1962, Franklin City was abandoned altogether and spent a number of years as a "ghost town;" a few of its remaining homes have been reclaimed.

The Canal *(Turn right on Harbor Drive #3006)* is what the townsfolk have always called their government-created harbor, dredged in 1939. **Union United Methodist Church**, built in 1895, stands in the center of town on Stockton Avenue, a street once lined with shops and stores, even a movie theatre. Behind it the **Old School** *(39148 School Street)*, long since abandoned, still oversees the village.

At **The Crossing**, Bayfront Street intersects Franklin City Road #3005, and this was the boundary between the two villages. From here to water's edge the old railroad bed lies on your right, while on your left Franklin City was once a continuous row of homes, shops, stores, and other buildings, house squeezed in upon house on the 25-foot lots that Franklin sold for $25. Although the railroad tracks were built up, houses were not, and sat right on the marsh, even on stilts out in the bay. All that is left today is five old houses, including some that turn their backs to the road, plus the old abandoned **Red Men's Hall**. The only original building still standing at the wharf is the railroad's **Old Freight Station**, at the very end of the road projecting out over the water, which may date from as early as 1876. Today two new houses rise high above the marsh, including the **Bay Watch Inn** at the corner of the long-deserted Clinton Street.

> The tour of the upper Accomack Seaside ends at Franklin City, which is 10 miles from Route 13. You have two options for getting out of this far corner of Accomack County:

> (1) Most direct route: Retrace route on #679 to Horntown, turn right on Horntown Road #709 and rejoin Route 13 at New Church, a total distance of 10 miles.

> *(2) More scenic route: The following extension of the tour will also take you back to New Church via a more winding route. Retrace route on State Line Road #679 to Maryland boundary just beyond Captain's Cove entrance, and continue straight across Fleming Road on Swancut Road. After 1.7 miles turn left to:

Big Mill Pond. You're in Maryland now, just barely, where an old mill dam backs up the waters of Swan's Gut Creek into peaceful, lovely Big Mill pond. The village of Welbourne once clustered around the pond, complete with homes, mill, and the obligatory country store with post office. Today only two houses overlook the pond.

> Cross the millpond and continue straight, turning left on Payne Road.

As you turn left, **Remson United Methodist Church** is visible to the right, a quarter mile across the fields. Dating from at least the early 1800s, it originally stood near Big Mill Pond, but was moved to its present site and enlarged in 1916.

At .7 miles, just before the curve, Payne Road passes back into Virginia from Maryland, one of several places on local roads where neither state has bothered to indicate the state boundary.

> *One mile from the curve turn left on Outten Road #725, then right on Signpost Road #712.*

Chincoteague Baptist Church *(On the right after 2.3 miles)* is the third oldest Baptist congregation on the Eastern Shore of Virginia, founded 1786; this building, dating from 1858, is an excellent example of the typical Eastern Shore country church of the ante-bellum period, improved during the prosperous 1890s.

> *From Chincoteague Baptist Church there are two opportunities to turn left, on Kelly Road #720 in front of the church, or on Davis Road #710 just beyond it. Either will take you to New Church and Route 13, and the end of this tour.*

CHESCONESSEX WHARF

13   THE UPPER ACCOMACK BAYSIDE

In the footsteps of a Presbyterian,
a White Rabbit and a root cellar,
and the ghost of villages past

Into this area the Chesapeake Bay thrusts its presence again and again, and it is a brooding presence. In the Bayside of upper Accomack County, the marshes and the dry land seem locked in combat. Back roads wander through lonely stretches that are alternately dry and marshy, past isolated homes perched on precarious spots where the two combatants have seemingly reached a compromise.

Perhaps because of its terrain, this section of the Shore has never been rich or especially prosperous. Handsome old homes are fewer here, because fewer people were able to build substantially. Savor instead a maze of back roads (this is the Shore at its widest point) and a host of quiet and lonely landings on the bay and its tributaries. Still, it is historic ground, and as you travel the main Bayside Road you may well conjure up the spirits of some of the Shore's most famous and colorful figures.

Like the other Bayside tours in this book, this one works from north to south. It begins on Route 13 at the Maryland boundary, meanders through the confusing back roads, and issues finally out at Onancock, where you can continue the tour of the lower Accomack Bayside. Because it is a long tour, with eating places and rest stops few and far between, there are two suggested points for ending it early by skipping back to Route 13. The total distance traveled, if you visit every suggested nook and cranny, will be about 94 miles. It's a long, slow tour, but well worth it.

Your tour begins on Route 13 at the Virginia-Maryland boundary, 1.7 miles above New Church. From Route 13 take Holland Road #705 to the west.

Before leaving the highway check out the historical marker at the state boundary, and look eastward towards the cemetery. Here stood the old **Marrying Tree**, where local couples were married in Maryland according to Maryland law without venturing more than a few feet from Virginia—some while still seated in their buggies. Still visible, though the tree is gone, is the boundary stone set in 1883, when the original line laid in 1668 was resurveyed.

The first four "places" you will see on this tour are villages that have vanished, once-thriving little communities now completely indistinguishable from the surrounding countryside. **Wagram** *(Turn right on Dunn's Swamp Road #707, a few yards to bridge)* grew up around a millpond established here on Pitts Creek late in the 1700s. Named for a Napoleonic victory of 1809, the village thrived for the better part of a century, straddling the state line (a line across the road just beyond the bridge marks the Maryland boundary). Today the mill is gone, the millpond drained, and not a single house remains. **Miona** *(Continue on #705 to its intersection with Pitts Creek Road #709, then turn right)* once boasted church, store, school, and a number of houses at this intersection. Only **Pittsville United Methodist Church** (1910) remains, visible in the distance across the field. **Pitts Wharf** *(Follow #709 3.2 miles to end at water, turning right on Bell Road #804 at very end)* was settled by and named for Robert Pitt, mariner, in 1663; many Native American artifacts have been found in this vicinity, and this may be the site of the Pocomoke Indian village indicated on John Smith's map of 1612. The water here is Pocomoke River, and on the other side is the small village of Shelltown, Maryland, 27 miles distant by road. There was a brief Civil War skirmish here on August 3, 1861, when local southerners repelled a landing by about 300 Union soldiers. When steamboats stopped here later in the 1800s this was a busy place, with wharves, stores, houses, and a post office. Surveying this scene is **Pitts Creek House** *(25282 Pitts Creek Road)*; though it is the newest section of this house that is most visible, the oldest section was built by Robert Pitt III in the late 1600s, and another "new" section by a later owner in the mid-1700s.

BULLBEGGER *(Retrace route on #709, turn right on Bullbegger Road #701)* consists of exactly four houses and a bridge over Bullbegger Creek, all that is left of the once larger village whose name means "bugbear" or "hobgoblin." At 1.7 miles south of the bridge the old home now named **Bullbegger Creek** *(6220 Bullbegger*

The BAYSIDE
Maryland to Guilford

Road) looms back in the field on the right, and just past its gate is a small family burial plot where former residents Thorogood and Julianna Dix lie buried. Julianna died mysteriously five days before Christmas in 1861. As she was sitting in her rocking chair in the big house, a shot rang out, crashed through the window, splintered off part of the chair, and struck and killed her instantly. Her tombstone reads, "It was not sickness that hurried me away from here. It was my enemies and the Balls, and my enemies without cause"—or perhaps not "Balls" but "Bulls," depending upon how you read it. The tradition has long persisted that the inscription thus indicts as her murderer some unidentified person named Bull, a common family name in these parts, but the who and why of her death have never been satisfactorily explained.

JENKINS BRIDGE *(Follow Bullbegger Road to Jenkins Bridge Road #703 and turn right, after making sharp left at #774).* The bridge at Jenkins Bridge crosses Holden's Creek, and preserves the name of Thomas Jenkinson, who settled here in 1699. **Emmanuel Episcopal Church**, facing the bridge, is one of the Shore's loveliest; originally erected in Temperanceville in 1860, it was moved to this site in 1887. Just beyond the bridge on the right is **Waveland** *(8288*

Jenkins Bridge Road), built about 1770, home of Anne Makemie Holden [1700?-1788], daughter of the Reverend Francis Makemie. On the grounds of this house was once a steamboat wharf.

> *Turn right on Saxis Road #695, which will be your route for the next several miles.*

The Makemie Monument *(Turn right on Monument Road #699 and travel 1.4 mile to end).* Here on a quiet grassy spot overlooking Holden's Creek lived one of the most important men ever to call the Eastern Shore of Virginia his home. The Reverend Francis Makemie [1658?-1708] was born in Ireland and came to America in 1683, settling first in Onancock, where he married local girl Naomi Anderson. Although trained for the Presbyterian ministry, Makemie ventured first into a number of business enterprises before, in 1699, registering as a dissenting minister. Most of his ministerial career took place off the Virginia Shore, and it climaxed in 1706 when he organized the first American Presbytery in Philadelphia. The following year he was acquitted of the charge of preaching without a license in New York, a trial that is still cited as a landmark in the evolution of religious liberty in America.

In 1698 Naomi Makemie inherited this land from her father, and it was here that she and her husband lived for the last ten years of his life. Francis, Naomi, and her father William Anderson are among those buried somewhere nearby. The Makemie farm ultimately passed to Anne Makemie, who married George Holden, for whom the small creek adjacent is named.

Late in the 1800s local Presbyterians began a movement to acquire the site as a permanent memorial to Makemie. On May 14, 1908, a larger-than-lifesize statue of Makemie was dedicated, copy of a Philadelphia original by renowned sculptor Alexander Stirling Calder [1870-1945], and to mark the event the railroad changed the name of its nearest station from Bloomtown to Makemie Park. After many years of vandalism the statue was removed to Makemie Presbyterian Church in Accomac in 1984 *(see page 74)*. It was replaced by this bronze replica, cast by local sculptors William and David Turner, in 2000.

A short distance beyond the road to the monument grounds, on the left in the tiny village of Grotons, stands **Pocomoke United Methodist Church** (1858), a trim example of the Shore's many small country churches. One-third mile beyond it on the left is the **Grotons Holiness Church** (1917), now abandoned and used as a barn.

SANFORD *(1.5 miles beyond Monument Road)* is a late 19th-century town, its oldest homes hugging the ridge on the right paralleling the road on the northern edge of town. Sanford offers two opportunities to see the waters of Pocomoke Sound. **Flag Pond** *(Turn right on Flag Pond Road #770 at the edge of the village)*, once a popular bathing and picnic spot, is by far the prettier view. At *Shad Landing *(Turn right on Shad Landing Road #719 in center of village)* an abandoned seafood factory hogs an otherwise wide view; a local store here housed a post office named Dreka from 1891 to 1911.

Over the years there have been eight stores in Sanford, but today only the **Sanford General Store** *(23644 Saxis Road)* is still in operation. On the southern edge of town, adjacent to 23276 Saxis Road, is a decrepit store which was originally built as the **Sanford Charity School**. Just beyond the village the road turns a sharp right and heads across wetlands once known as the **Freeschool Marsh,** so named because in 1712 Samuel Sandford, a wealthy London merchant who had lived on the Shore (and for whom the village of Sanford is named), bequeathed its use and profits for the schooling of poor boys in upper Accomack County. For over a century the marsh was so used, and when in 1873 it was sold the final proceeds helped to build this building.

*The Hammocks *(Turn left on Hammock Road #788 a mile below the village)* was in its time a thriving village of almost 100 people who lived in houses clustered around a steamboat wharf. When the steamboat began docking elsewhere it quickly declined, and today it is a lonely place with only a pier and a ramp. The extensive view to the south is across Messongo Creek to Chesapeake Bay and the desolate Michael Marsh; the view to the west is of Saxis, the larger place to which the steamboat moved in 1903.

SAXIS *(3 miles beyond Sanford)* is not the most picturesque town on the Shore, nor the most historic, nor the most renowned, but it ought to be seen. Here is a place for those who cherish authenticity, a real, live seafood village well off the beaten path with not an iota of tourism, and rarely a visitor. Not many people get this far when they visit the Shore, but those who do see the real thing.

Strictly speaking Saxis is not an island, for it is connected to the mainland by Freeschool Marsh (since 1957 known as the Saxis Marsh Waterfowl Refuge, a state facility). Yet its remoteness has made it functionally, if not officially an island, and its modern name derives from Sykes' Island, named for Robert Sykes, who owned the land but never lived here.

It was William Anderson, Makemie's father-in-law, who introduced what was to be the chief industry for 150 years: cattle. Anderson established a tenant farmer on the island to raise cattle, prepare dried beef, hides, butter, and cheese for half the profits. By 1800 there were 35 people on the island, and cattle was still the chief industry. By the mid-1800s the island population had grown to village-size, and in 1851 the Methodists evangelized the community with a series of camp meetings and established a Sunday School which was the first school of any sort on the island. Sykes' Island was still so remote that the only communication or trade with the mainland Eastern Shore was by boat.

In the last quarter of the nineteenth century a growing population squeezed out all possibility of farming or raising cattle, and the islanders turned to the water for their livelihood. The result was a period of rapid growth in which the town as it is today took shape. A corduroy road was built across the marshes to the mainland (the present route dates from 1888) and the price of a building lot soared to an unbelievable $150 an acre. In 1896 Sykes officially became Saxis, and a few years later the Baltimore steamboats began stopping at a new wharf located out in the Sound completely detached from land. By the early 1900s the southern end of the island had become the chief landing place for the islanders' boats. The town was incorporated in 1959 and is now home to 367 citizens.

Today's main road through Saxis is, appropriately, Saxis Road, though most of the side lanes are named for members of the local volunteer fire department. The little house on the right at 20303 Saxis Road began life in 1884 as **Rechabite Hall**, a meeting lodge for a temperance and benevolent society. Around the corner on the left, Saxis Volunteer Fire Department occupies the **Saxis School**, fifth and last school house on the island, built in 1949 and used as such until 1970. In front of it stood, until 1940, Saxis Baptist Church, its cemetery still visible. **Saxis United Methodist Church** was established after the camp meeting in 1851; the present building replaces a much older one that burned in 2000. The island is predominantly Methodist, and this church has almost 200 members.

Saxis once had over a dozen stores. The **Crockett/Lewis Store** *(20101 Saxis Road)* stands just beyond the sharp right curve; built in 1915, it closed in 1968. Another abandoned store (1923) stands on the corner at Mary's Drive, diagonally across the street from the front yard where the local movie theatre once stood; the Evans Picture Parlor survived long enough to show "talkies" but closed in the early 1930s. **Saxis Wesleyan Church** *(20001 Saxis Road)* was founded by William Vickers in 1917, after he evangelized the island with services held in a portable tent. It is uncertain which is the oldest surviving house in town, but one candidate is **19460 Saxis Road**, though its front section is newer (late 19th-century).

At the end of the road lies **the Wharf**, a 600-foot addition to the island built by the W.P.A. in 1936, from which a public fishing pier affords a wide view from across Pocomoke Sound to the southernmost point of Maryland near Crisfield. The several small buildings here include "shedding pounds" where the molting crab can be monitored, then packed in grass and ice for shipping at just the right moment after shedding. Around the corner on Starling Creek Road lies the **Harbor of Refuge** (1965) where most of the village vessels are docked. Safely ashore, on the left as the road turns right, is the **Harvey A. Drewer** (1949), a "buyboat" capable of carrying 1,800 bushels of oysters, now awaiting restoration.

From Saxis retrace your route to the edge of Sanford and turn right on Belinda Road #692.

BELINDA. It is one mile from Sanford United Methodist Church to Halls Chapel Baptist Church, and passing through you will see a grand total of about a dozen houses. This is Belinda, or what is left of it, a little village that took shape in the 1890s. In 1895 the men of the village gathered around the pot-bellied stove in the general store trying to decide what to name the post office that was about to be established here. They settled on the name Belinda, after the most popular young belle of the community. Belinda the town faded away after the store burned, the post office closed, and most of the people moved away. Belinda the belle lived here until 1934, when she died in a fire that swept through her home.

Your road turns sharply right at **Halls Chapel Baptist Church**, erected 1886. Just beyond it is **Marsh Market** *(Where #692 turns sharply left keep straight down Marsh Market Road #698, .6 mile to water)*, yet another vanished town, in its time older and larger than Belinda. Land here sold for $200 an acre in the 1880s, though it was only marshland reached by roads of shell; the nearby waters were "alive with boats engaged in oystering," and the road to the water was lined with homes, stores, and a post office. Time and tide have carried away all remnants of this activity, the view is marred by litter, and only seagulls frequent the place.

The **Wessels Root Cellar** *(From Marsh Market Road turn right on Savannah Road #692, travel 1.4 miles to Wessels Farm Road #701, and turn left)*. Here in an out-of-the-way place on the grounds of a small white farmhouse *(10313 Wessels Farm Road)* is an unlikely treasure, its value attested by its official Virginia Historic Landmark status. Once a substantial colonial farm was located here, but all that is left is a brick outbuilding erected about 1770 for use as a root cellar and storage shed. Very few outbuildings of the colonial period have been preserved anywhere, and this one is remarkable for its detailed brickwork, its arched door, and its fine state of preservation. The storage shed, on the second floor, is accessible only from the back of the building.

> *Return to Savannah Road #692 and continue 1.3 miles to bridge over Messongo Creek.*

Messongo Creek and its marshes stab deeply inland here, and for more than a mile you skirt its edge. The battle between land and marsh seems to have been won temporarily by the marsh; there are three bridges to cross and not a house in sight until, just before the last bridge, the **Northam Place** *(26274 Savannah Road)*, built in the mid-1700s, stands on the right.

> *To cut short the tour of the Upper Accomack Bayside, continue left on Main Street #692 and follow through the Town of Hallwood to Route 13, a distance of 3.8 miles. To continue the tour, bear right on White's Crossing Road #690.*

The point at which your road crosses Messongo Creek is known, for reasons that no one can remember, as **Skin Point**. A short distance beyond the bridge, on the left, is the burial ground of **Messongo Primitive Baptist Church**, established in 1779.

Cattail Neck *(Turn right on Cattail Road #688)* is arguably the most desolate stretch of Virginia's Eastern Shore. The road winds for four miles through forests and fields that were once high, fertile farmland, but now seemingly sinking and turning into wetlands. The original **Shiloh Baptist Church** was a larger and prettier building erected in 1888; after it burned, the present tiny building was occupied in 1976. On the left stands a home which was once the **Shiloh School** *(13619 Cattail Road)*, which closed in 1906. Cattail Road turns a sharp left *(Avoid going straight down Dividing Road #686)* and ends in the little village of **Mearsville**, where no fewer than three old country stores are still standing: Gladding's Store *(26041 Gladding Road)*, Byrd's Store *(facing Gladding Road)*, and Mason's Store *(13325 Winterville Road)*.

At Mearsville turn right on Winterville Road #658.

***Muddy Creek** *(Turn right on Muddy Creek Road #683)* is aptly named, but the view of it is quite pretty. Less than a mile below is tiny Winterville and the road to **Guard Shore** *(Turn right on Guard Shore Road #684, 2.3 miles to water)*, a favorite bathing and docking area with one of the best views of the bay on the upper Bayside. To the left is Sandy Point, to the right Old Tree Island, as Guilford Creek and Muddy Creek join to meet the bay in this wide open space.

GUILFORD *(2.5 miles below Mearsville)* is an old village, settled by Quakers as early as 1683, but has little to show for its antiquity and former prominence. In its day Guilford had several stores, three private academies, two gristmills, and a steady influx of peddlers and "drummers." All are gone, and of the modest homes hugging the road here today few are old; even the main road through the village has been relocated in recent years.

At the northern edge of Guilford, as the road swings left and the village comes into view, look to the right down an unpaved lane next to an old farmhouse for **Mason House**. This dignified old ruin, a Virginia Historic Landmark, is a story-and-a-half brick farmhouse of the early 1700s, with admirable brickwork in a pre-Georgian style. It sits way back in the field, inaccessible to close examination. **Guilford United Methodist Church** *(On the left on Guilford Road #187)* is a new building dating from 1950, but Methodists have worshiped on this site since at least as early as 1795. In the center of the village on the right is **Boxwood Estate** *(15510 Winterville Road)*, which has survived from Guilford's earlier days in good style. Beyond it two old country stores stand abandoned at the intersection.

In Guilford turn right on Ann's Cove Road #682, keep straight past St. Thomas Road #675, and turn right on Ewell Road #675, .75 mile to water.

Guilford Wharf (*At end of Ewell Road #675*) is today only a landing with a pier, a ramp, and a peaceful view of Guilford Creek, but in the 1700s the creek was busy with commerce, and near here stood a public warehouse for the storage of tobacco before it was shipped. **Cals Hammock** (*Follow Ann's Cove Road #682, 1.25 miles to end*) offers a wider and lonelier view of Guilford Creek; the present landing on the creek is at the end of New Road.

> Retrace your route to St. Thomas Road #675 and turn right.

CLAM is the little village of homes a mile below Guilford; you'll know you've already passed through it when you reach **St. Thomas United Methodist Church** (1893) on the right. In **Parker's Landing**, after a left curve below the church, turn right on Justisville Road #675 (*Avoid going straight on St. Thomas Road #674*).

JUSTISVILLE is the tiny village half a mile further south where the road again turns sharply left amid a small cluster of homes; turn right here on Justisville Road #675 (*Avoid going straight on Wonney Rew Road #673*). **Muskeetoe Pointe** (*18071 Justisville Road*) is the current name for the house on the corner with the handsome gingerbread porch, built by Levin Crowson in 1905. 18060 Justisville Road was built in 1884 as part of the old **Crowsontown Methodist Church** and moved to this site in 1934 after the church closed. Until 1888 Justisville was known as Crowsontown, after the family who lived at **Tall Pines** (*18238 Justisville Road*) on the southern edge of the village; the Crowsons produced a distinguished line of educators and writers.

HUNTING CREEK (*At the end of Justisville Road turn right on Hopkins Road #669 and follow winding route into the village*). The village of Hunting Creek was also known as Hopkins, because John H. Hopkins, its first postmaster, named the post office after himself in the 1880s. When **Calvary United Methodist Church** was dedicated on July 5, 1888, the locals staged a parade to it from Lee Mont, the nearest village to the east, and established a great community feast which still continues, open to the public, on or near the Fourth of July every year. The road ends at a docking area and small harbor where the view is inland, up the creek, not out to the bay. Behind a fence at the landing stands the little **General Store** which once stood in the center of the village, opposite the town sign, until high tides swept through in 1970 and it was abandoned and moved to this spot. From the end of Martz Road can be seen in the distance, out towards the bay, the location of the old **Steamboat Wharf**, also known as Hez's Wharf, after Hezekiah Fitzgerald [1845-1910], who kept a store here; it was located well beyond the crabhouse visible from here.

From Hunting Creek retrace your route on #669, and after a sharp right turn keep straight on Johnsons Landing Road #670.

A mile and a half from the village the road ends again at **Johnson's Wharf**, which has a pretty view of Hunting Creek. Across the creek stands **Hills Farm**, a beautiful home erected in 1697 by Richard Hill. It is one of the very few houses on the Eastern Shore of Virginia dating from the 1600s, a small, elegant home as lovely inside as it is outside. Because Hills Farm stands at the end of a long private lane on the other side of the creek, this view of it from the rear across the water is your only chance to see it.

Retrace your route on #670 and turn right on Lee Mont Road #669, traveling 1.5 miles to Lee Mont.

LEE MONT was originally known as Woodstock, and had you passed this way over a century ago you would now be in one of the larger towns of the Virginia Eastern Shore. When the residents applied for a post office in 1878, officials in Washington pointed out that there was already a Woodstock, Virginia, in Shenandoah County, and insisted upon a different name. Southern sentiment was still strong in these parts, and in retaliation the locals named their post office, thus renam-

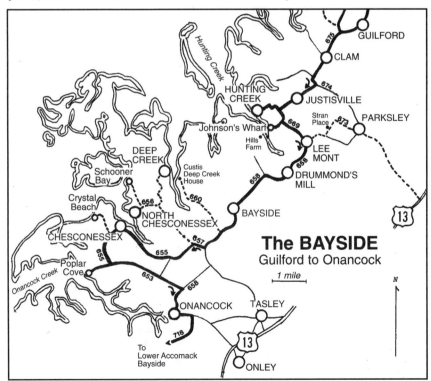

The BAYSIDE
Guilford to Onancock

ing their village, Lee Mont, after General Robert E. Lee.

Before the coming of the railroad Lee Mont was the metropolis of the upper Bayside. In 1881 it could boast 7 stores, a cabinet maker, a blacksmith, a carriage shop, a milliner, a mill, two physicians, and a sizeable population. There was a Methodist church, a Baptist church, and two places to get your liquor. The first free public school "bus" on the Shore traveled between this busy village and Wiseville to the south, a horse-drawn wagon shaded against sun and rain by a strip of canvas. Lee Mont started to fade when the railroad came through in 1884 and the new town of Parksley was created just 2 miles to the east.

Today Lee Mont does not appear especially old, but a careful look at some of its homes will reveal signs of their antiquity. In front of one of them stands the abandoned **Post Office**, a tiny room-size building. On the right after you turn right on Bayside Road #658 is the **Lewis Burial Ground**, not one of the oldest or most remarkable of such family plots on the Shore, but conveniently up close for examination. Some of the older vaults are above ground, as in many other such cemeteries on the Shore.

The ***Stran Place** *(Instead of turning on Bayside Road, continue through Lee Mont on #669, turn left on Hart Road #671)* is a handsome farm house dating from 1750 and still in use, about a mile outside the village towards Parksley.

> To cut short the tour of the upper Bayside, turn right on Airport Road #673 just beyond Stran Place to the Town of Parksley, from which you can make your way to Route 13 via Route #176 (Bennett Street).

> To continue the tour of the upper Bayside, turn right in Lee Mont on Bayside Road #658.

Drummond's Mill *(1 mile below Lee Mont on Bayside Road #658)*, its millpond visible on the left, was established in 1720 and continued in operation until August 25, 1937, when heavy rains swelled the waters behind the dam and washed the mill away. One of the last operating gristmills on the Eastern Shore of Virginia, it was the center of a little village known as Wiseville. **Drummond's Mill Farm** *(Just beyond millpond turn left on Drummonds Mill Road #661 and travel a few yards to gate)* was the home of the miller, by the standards of that time a "modest" dwelling for working people of moderate means. The oldest part of this "telescope" house dates from the 1750s, the largest part from 1820 *(see illustration, page 8)*. Across the road from it stood the old **Wiseville Store**, built by mill owner John Y. Bagwell in 1818; its foundations are still visible on the grounds of a modern home built in 1973 in the colonial style *(22234 Drummonds Mill Road)*. The post office housed in the store from 1897 to 1905 was known as Grape. Behind this property is **Bayly's Millpond**, which was at one time connected to Drummond's Millpond. Ayres Circle #772 has been called "the Road to Nowhere," for it simply circles around to Bayside Road; it follows, however, the route of the original Bayside Road through this neighborhood, circumventing the gristmill itself, which stood where today's road crosses the spillway from the pond.

Continue south on Bayside Road #658, turning left at its intersection with Doe Creek Road #661.

BAYSIDE is what the residents call the continuous row of homes, old and new, that line the Bayside Road for almost two miles on Bayside Road; one of the oldest and largest black communities on the Shore, it is known, among white non-residents, as "White Rabbit." At its southern end stands **Metropolitan Memorial United Methodist Church** (1889), opposite it the old **Bayside School** (c. 1913). *Custis Deep Creek House *(Just past the church turn right on Mink Farm Road #660 and follow 1.8 miles to end)* was erected in 1792 by Thomas Custis, and commands a beautiful view of Deep Creek. The public road ends just short of the front gate.

One mile below Metropolitan Church turn right on Deep Creek Road #657.

*DEEP CREEK *(At the end of #657, 3 miles from intersection)* was an active port as early as 1725, and is still active today. There is little to see here of historic interest, though there is a view of the wide creek itself at road's end.

*NORTH CHESCONESSEX *(At Leatherbury Church turn left on Northside Road #656 and travel .75 mile to the village)* is a small village with a pretty view of Chesconessex Creek. Another view of the water is from **Schooner Bay**, a modern development that lies a mile down Schooner Bay Road #802. As you retrace your route from the village, notice that **Leatherbury United Methodist Church** (1872), when viewed from behind, betrays the fact that it was constructed from several different buildings, one of which was the community schoolhouse (1912) that once stood across the road from it.

From Deep Creek Road #657 take Plantation Road #655 south to the village of Chesconessex, a distance of 2.5 miles from the intersection.

CHESCONESSEX is the Anglicized version of the Indian word "Chiconnessick," which means "place of blue birds." The village sits astride the wide and lovely Chesconessex Creek, by which it is divided into two completely different communities known as North and South Chesconessex; only a few hundred yards distant from one another by water, they are five miles distant by land, and have never been joined by a bridge. The first English settler here was John Wise [1616-1693], who in 1663 purchased the land on which South Chesconessex sits from the Indian king Ekeeks for six Dutch blankets. For over 200 years thereafter the Wises held sway from this neighborhood, establishing a numerous and distinguished line that included a governor, a member of Congress, several writers, and local Shore leaders in every generation.

A handsome gate on the right identifies **Clifton** *(17541 Plantation Road)*, ancestral home of the Wises. Two hundred years and six generations after John Wise I settled here Captain George Douglas Wise, owner of the property, died defending the Confederacy, and the estate passed out of Wise hands. The present house here dates only from the 1880s. A brick wall surrounds the **Wise Burial Ground**, on the south side of the road beyond Clifton; here are buried John Wise I through John Wise VI and their wives. Plaques in the wall honor others of the family, and read like a "Who's Who" of Eastern Shore gentry for three centuries.

South Chesconessex Wharf *(Turn right on Southside Road #649)* is today only a small pier and a boat ramp, but steamboats were docking here as early as 1868 when the wharf was much bigger. **Riverview United Methodist Church** (1910) preserves the name of a planned community attempted here early in this century. *****Crystal Beach** *(From Southside Road #655 turn right on Crystal Beach Road #782 and travel 1.5 miles)* is a private beach, but the road to it is public and provides glimpses of Chesapeake Bay.

At **Poplar Cove** *(Take #655 to end, turn right on Poplar Cove Road #653 and follow to water)* there is a wide and lovely view across Onancock Creek and out towards Chesapeake Bay. George Parker settled here in 1661, and not far from the 19th-century house right at the wharf are the tombs of George Parker V [1735-1784] and his wife Adah [1734-1766]. The large house visible across the cove is **Franconia**, built in 1853.

As you retrace your route, **Oatlands** *(17500 Poplar Cove Road)* is the large house that sits back from the road on the right about a mile from Poplar Cove. This was the site of the village of the Onancock Indians and their king Ekeeks. The house dates from the 1780s.

Continue on #653 until it ends at North Street #658, then turn right and end your tour of the Upper Accomack Bayside in one of two ways:

(1) Turn left on Market Street in Onancock and follow it 2 miles to Route 13, or

(2) After turning left on Market Street, turn right on Hill Street and begin the tour of the Lower Accomack Bayside.

ST. GEORGE'S EPISCOPAL CHURCH, PUNGOTEAGUE

14 THE LOWER ACCOMACK BAYSIDE

First drama, oldest church,
steamboat wharves and scenic creeks,
and a passage through Little Hell

In the Bayside region of Accomack County below Onancock the creeks are lovely and the Chesapeake Bay is very much in evidence. It is an area rich with local history, the center of which is the small village of Pungoteague, with its church dating from colonial times.

Your route through this region follows the Bayside Road south out of Onancock, but there are a number of interesting and pretty spots worth turning aside to see. The distance from Onancock to Belle Haven, the southern terminus of this tour, is less than 15 miles, but if you cover every nook and cranny suggested here, you'll travel well over 65 miles.

There are no restaurants or service stations in this area, so stock up before setting out. You may well find yourself at a quiet landing with not another soul in sight—but that's part of the charm of this part of the Shore, and you'll be glad you sought it out.

Your tour begins in Onancock where Hill Street #718 meets Market Street (Route #179). Turn on #718 and follow it out of town. For the first 2 miles out of Onancock you will be following a route described in Chapter 8 (See there for #638 and #778 to Nancock Gardens and Meadville).

At the intersection a mile out of Onancock, do not turn left towards Pungoteague on Savageville Road #718 unless you wish to shorten this tour by skipping the first part and rejoining it at "Locksville" (page 157).

FINNEY'S WHARF *(2 miles from Onancock turn right on Finney's Wharf Road #637)* was a stopping place for many of the steamboats on their way up the creek to Onancock. The road ends right at the driveway of the oldest house at the wharf; though much changed by modern additions, it dates from 1782. Opposite it stands **Creekside** *(24221 Finney's Wharf Road)*, a late 19th-century home enjoying a lovely view. Directly across the creek stands **Onley** (1843), once the home of Governor Henry A. Wise. The late 19th-century house set back from the road on the right before reaching the wharf is **Windward Hall** *(24269 Finney's Wharf Road)*, where in 1942 the first Mass was said in this area, and from which eventually came St. Peter's Roman Catholic Church in Onley. Back at the corner stands **Cricket Cottage** *(17187 Cashville Road)*, originally a public schoolhouse that functioned from 1875 to 1921.

*****BAILY'S NECK** is named for John Baily, who settled here in 1710. It is .7 miles down the neck to the gate of **Bailywicke** *(24311 Baily's Neck Drive)*, built by his great-great-great grandson in 1850. Baily's Neck Drive is two miles long and ends (last section unpaved) with views of Onancock Creek and Finney Creek amid the homes of new subdivisions.

CASHVILLE is the small scattered village of unpretentious homes 1.5 miles beyond Finney's Wharf Road. The first house on the right here is little **Chandler Place** *(15837 Cashville Road)*, dating from

1775, a perfect example of the Eastern Shore "double house" except that one of its units is turned at a right angle to the other. Turn right in Cashville for **Broadway Baptist Church** (1885). Two miles beyond it *(Turn right from Broadway Road #641 to East Point Road #767)* is **East Point**, a handsome community developed in the late 1940s, with a lovely view across Onancock Creek out into Chesapeake Bay. The boats docked in the marina on the inland side attest to the fact that East Point is a desirable address; among them you may see the vessels of the Virginia Marine Patrol, which dock here.

Half a mile beyond Cashville, **Andrew Chapel** (1877) and the old **Cashville School** (1923) mark the entrance to Slutkill Neck, and though there is little to see in the neck you may enjoy speculating about how the name Slutkill arose. No one knows for sure; one Eastern Shore historian states that there is a "vague and scurrilous tradition" that he

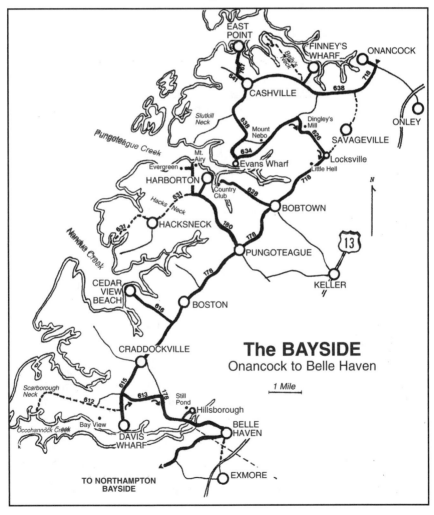

The BAYSIDE
Onancock to Belle Haven

1 Mile

modestly does not repeat. Though the locals have long invented stories to explain the name, early records find it often spelled Sleuthkill, or Sluitkill, or Slutgill, making it likely that Slutkill is a modern corruption of a much more innocent name, and all the story-telling in vain.

EVANS WHARF *(Follow #638 to end at water 2 miles below Andrew Chapel, taking care to avoid a right turn on Tarkill Road #717).* The road ends where once sidewheeler steamers docked at a prosperous and busy landing; today there is only a view across Pungoteague Creek, giving you glimpses of places still to come. Across the creek from left to right (east to west) are: the Eastern Shore Yacht and Country Club, the village of Harborton (.5 mile across the water, 11.5 miles distant by land), the three-sectioned old house Mt. Airy, and the Chesapeake itself. To the east on your side of the creek is **Fairfield**, a handsome estate whose gate you will pass in a few minutes.

> *From Evans Wharf retrace your route .3 miles to Mount Nebo Road #634 and turn right.*

*****Mount Nebo Baptist Church** *(16075 Omega Road)* stands just off your road to the left after 1.2 miles. Next to it is the **Mount Nebo School**, built in 1914 by the black community, later a part of the public school system.

> *After 2.5 miles turn right on Dingley's Mill Road #626 and follow it 1.5 miles to Bobtown Road #718, where you will turn right.*

At .4 miles down Dingley's Mill Road your route crosses a tiny stream amid a swamp. This is the headwaters of Pungoteague Creek, and the site of **Dingley's Mill**, established in 1787 and a local landmark for a century afterwards. The large millpond was located in the woods to your left. The corner where your road meets Bobtown Road, and where those who have skipped the earliest part of this tour can rejoin the route southward, was once known as **Locksville.**

LITTLE HELL consists of exactly two houses half a mile below Locksville, a less than spectacular spot opposite Evergreen Lane. The more northerly of these homes *(27488 Bobtown Road)* occupies the spot where once a tavern stood. The story is that an old black preacher, widely known for his excessive sanctimoniousness, used to pass by regularly between his churches in Onancock and Pungoteague, and he always let it be known that he disapproved of the riotous activities at the tavern. One day the tavernfolk could take his criticism no longer, and they forcibly invited the preacher in. "Drink with us," they offered, and when he refused they held him and poured the liquor down his throat. "Dance for us," they insisted, and when he refused one of them produced a gun and shot bullets at his feet until he "danced." "Sing for us," they commanded, and when he would not someone twisted his arm until he "sang." And then they let him go.

When he arrived at his church in Pungoteague, the preacher preached an unusually forceful hellfire and brimstone sermon, and in it he told his flock: "I don't know what Hell is like, but I sure have been to Little Hell—and you'd better mend your ways if you don't want to go there." The name stuck, and long survives the tavern and its riotous activities.

Below Little Hell on the left is the **Revel's Millpond**, last remnant of the mill that was operating here at least as early as 1715, perhaps as early as the late 1600s.

BOBTOWN *(On #718 2 miles below Locksville)*, once a thriving place, is now reduced to a few buildings next to Pungoteague Elementary School. On the left stands a home *(28507 Bobtown Road)* which was once the girls' dormitory of old **Margaret Academy**, erected in 1819 and originally located far back in the field behind the present site. In the days before free public education, many well-to-do Eastern Shore families educated their children at private schools. Margaret Academy, the most successful of them, was chartered in 1786 and opened in 1807. Among its graduates was Henry A. Wise, who became Governor of Virginia. It is said that at the Academy students were called upon to say a grace before each meal; on one such occasion Wise was asked to pray, and he arose from his chair, pondered a moment, then prayed in a loud voice:

> *Lord from above*
> *Send down his love*
> * As thick as thorn and thistles*
> *Upon the back*
> *Of Madame Hack*
> * For giving us no better victuals.*

During the Civil War, Union soldiers used and abused the Academy buildings, and the school went into decline. In 1892 it relocated in Onancock and continued in operation there until it was succeeded by the public high school. This old building is the only portion of the Academy still standing. The **Eastern Shore of Virginia Yacht and Country Club** *(Turn right on Country Club Road #628)* lies 1.5 miles down Yeo Neck. Although it is a private facility for members only, the view across Taylor Creek to Harborton is easily accessible, and quite fine.

Keep straight at Bobtown, though the number of your route changes from #718 to Route #178.

PUNGOTEAGUE *(On the Bayside Road 6.5 miles below Onancock)*. Its Indian name means "Place of Fine Sand," and it is one of the most historic spots on the peninsula. Here was performed the first drama on record in the New World. Here stands the oldest church on the Eastern Shore of Virginia. Here almost every other home is a century old or more.

Nicholas Waddilow, the first white settler here, obtained title to his land in 1655, and by 1664 the court of newly-formed Accomack County was meeting here in the home of his son-in-law. John Cole purchased this house in 1673 and converted it into a tavern. When later he moved to Accomac, the court followed him, but Pungoteague continued to grow because of the church that was by then standing on the northern edge of the village. By 1835 Pungoteague was a bustling place with two churches, a school, a tavern, a store, a tannery, a shoemaker, a blacksmith, a physician, and a population of 100. There were 20 homes in the village, a number of which are still standing, and trade on nearby Pungoteague Creek employed five "regular coasting vessels." In 1861 the Union army occupied the village, commandeering both churches for its use; when the soldiers left several years later, the two churches were in ruins.

Like so many other places on the Shore, Pungoteague declined after the railroad shifted the Shore's commercial activity towards the center of the peninsula. It is today a small village easily examined from your car, though St. George's Church deserves a closer inspection.

Approaching from the north, the site of **Fowkes Tavern** [1] is the first place you see, an ordinary house on the left with an historical marker in the front yard. On this spot on August 27, 1665, Pungoteague's citizens witnessed a performance of "Ye Beare and Ye Cubb," the first known dramatic production in America. It was written by William Darby, who directed and played the leading role, assisted by Cornelius Watkinson and Philip Howard. For their artistic efforts the three men were hauled before the court, whose justices ordered Darby held without bail until the next court session, when the actors were again to don their costumes and repeat the performance. When the play was presented a second time, the justices decided that nothing indecent had occurred, and they ordered John Martin, who had brought charges against the three actors, to pay all court costs, including the board for Darby while he was in jail.

Just beyond on the right stands **St. George's Episcopal Church** [2], the oldest church building on the Eastern Shore of Virginia. The first church was erected here about 1678; this building dates from about 1738. Today's church is only a portion of the original structure, which was an elegant building in the shape of a cross—or, as some of the less devout locals put it, the ace of clubs. The building contained molded columns, hand-carved woodwork, box pews, and a mahogany pulpit. Union soldiers used the building to stable their horses during the Civil War, and within a few years floors, galleries, and all interior woodwork were removed (probably burned for firewood), and one wing of the building was dismantled to provide bricks for a cookhouse. The building that the Episcopalians reclaimed about 1880 was an empty shell. Not

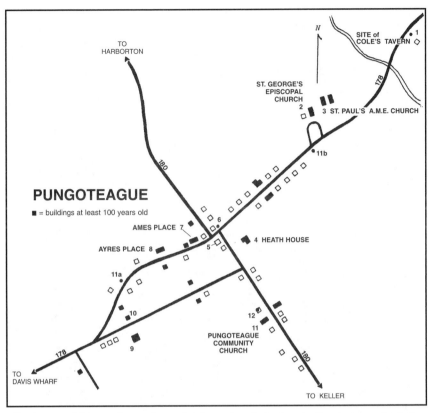

all of it could be salvaged, and what stands today is the transept of the original structure; an examination of the brickwork will show places where the original walls were patched in 1880. The church has been in continuous service since 1880, and today the congregation numbers about 100, who on occasion use the communion silver inscribed with the date 1734. The adjoining cemetery, though attractive, is not especially old, for prior to the late nineteenth century most well-to-do Eastern Shoremen were buried in family plots on their own estates. The oldest tombs are near the road; the most interesting stone is the cenotaph honoring Lt. Otho K. West [1838-1864], a Confederate who fell at the Battle of Petersburg and on whose monument is carved a broken sword.

St. Paul's A.M.E. Church [3] stands next door to St. George's, providing a graphic juxtaposition of the differences in affluence still current among the races on the Shore. This congregation was founded about 1870, this building erected in 1886. Next door stands the building of the Lone Star Masonic Lodge. On April 12, 1866, a black man named John Holden, accused of killing two women, was hanged just a few yards from the gate of St. George's, one of the few lynchings on record on the Eastern Shore of Virginia.

On the left at the main corner of the village is **Heath House** [4]

(15305 Pungoteague Road), named for the family who lived there during the Civil War. The oldest portion of the house (better seen from the rear) dates from the 1700s; the main portion was built about 1809, and contains no stairway between the two floors. The business, not the building of the **Village Store** [5] *(30285 Bobtown Road)* is now over a century old. Across the street, facing Pungoteague Road, stood **Pungoteague Tavern** [6], commercial center of the village until it burned in 1903.

Ames Place [7] *(30304 Bobtown Road)* dates from the early 19th century, and is said to have housed army officers when the Eastern Shore was under Union occupation during the Civil War. **Ayres Place** [8] *(30344 Bobtown Road)* was built by William Savage about 1815; since the house was modernized at the turn of the twentieth century only the northern brick end betrays its antiquity.

On the "back street" stands **Four Chimneys** [9] *(15226 Waterfield Street)*, dating from about 1830. Whoever built this home apparently started an architectural trend in the village, for more than half a dozen other 19th-century buildings in Pungoteague have copied, in some way or another, the pilasters that adorn the corners of the main house here. Across the street is the old **Methodist Parsonage** [10] built in the 1870s and sporting its own imitation of this feature.

Pungoteague Community Church [11] began as a Methodist church; this is the third Methodist building in the village (the map indicates two earlier sites at 11a and 11b), erected 1888. Next door is the old **Pungoteague School** [12] (1903). Several other homes in the village are now more than a century old, typical of late 19th-century architecture except for their various versions of the corner pilaster ornamentation peculiar to Pungoteague.

A mile west of the village stands **White Hall** *(29368 Harborton Road)*, visible back in the field on the left, a farmhouse dating from 1840 which surveys, at its back, a beautiful view of Nandua Creek.

> From Pungoteague turn west in the center of the village on Route #180 and travel 3 miles towards Harborton.

HARBORTON is a trim little village pleasantly situated on Pungoteague Creek, well worth turning aside to see. The first settler here, in 1678, was Robert Hutchinson, who had an important wharf at the western end of today's village. In 1858 James Hoffman, who owned the adjacent land to the east, established his own wharf and began selling building lots. Not to be outdone Raymond Hutchinson, great-great-grandson of the first settler, also sold lots, and the little town of Hoffman's Wharf began to take shape. By 1894, when the name was changed to Harborton, the town could boast several stores, a blacksmith, a schoolhouse, two churches, a factory for making fertilizer from fish products, and "a comfortable waiting room" where ticket-holders could await the arrival of the steamboat at the wharf. Among the many boats that docked at Harborton was the James Adams Floating Theatre, which played to audiences here from 1914 to 1939; Edna Ferber spent a week aboard this barge, and from her experiences came the musical *Show Boat*.

Today's Harborton Road follows the old Hutchinson-Hoffman boundary; at one time each family had its own road paralleling the other, separated by trees. Beyond **Harborton United Methodist Church** [1] (1894) stretches a handsome collection of "ship's carpenter" houses of the late 1800s, notable among them **Ross House** [2] *(28087 Harborton Road)*, overlooking the creek from the end of its own long lane, and **Harborton House** [3] *(28044 Harborton Road)*, erected in 1900. The little building opposite Harborton House was originally a **Lawyer's Office** [4] *(28045 Harborton Road)* in Keller.

The oldest house on the Hoffman (eastern) side of Harborton is the **Evans House** [5] *(28021 Harborton Road)*, erected by Capt. Egbert G. Evans in 1883; the village post office was once located in the little room to the right of the front porch, and the house once sported a

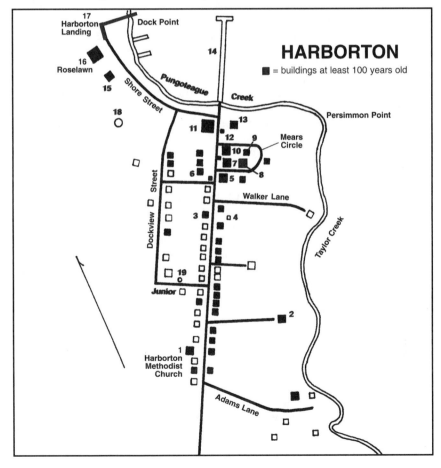

glass-enclosed cupola. Across from it on the Hutchinson (western) side stands the 1890 **William Hutchinson House** [6] *(28020 Harborton Road)*, with a red country store in the corner of the yard. **Rosemear** [7] *(28009 Harborton Road)*, with its handsome two-story front porch, was built in 1889; the adjacent little building was the village post office in the 1940s. Behind Rosemear is **Kelley House** [8] *(14376 Mears Circle)*, the first house in Harborton to have running water and a bathroom (1890). Around the circle are **Harbor Haven** [9] *(14314 Mears Circle)*, built in 1885, and the **Thomas Dize House** [10] *(28001 Harborton Road)*, from the 1890s.

Facing the wharf is the large building, built in 1892, that housed the firm of **Martin & Mason** [11] *(27484 Harborton Road)*, which used its own vessels to import lumber, coal, and building supplies via the wharf. The tiny building across the street from it is the old **Barber Shop** [12], adjacent to the handsomely situated **Walker House** [13] *(27485 Harborton Road)*, the oldest part of which dates from around 1850.

Most of the businesses of Harborton—ticket office, post office, stores, barroom, barrel factory, crab house, warehouses—were located at and actually on the **Wharf** [14]. The pier that occupies the site today is not nearly as wide as the old steamboat wharf, but approximately as long.

At water's edge the road turns left on Shore Street, where two admirable homes share the view across the creek: **Harbor Rose** [15] *(14262 Shore Street)*, built by Colie Hutchinson in 1905, and **Roselawn** [16] *(14250 Shore Street)*, built about 1887. Albro J. Morse, owner of the local fish factory, lived at Roselawn in a splendor rare for the Eastern Shore, with a fleet of carriages, a coachman, servants, a well-stocked wine cellar, and even a private schoolhouse on the grounds for his daughter.

The road ends at **Harborton Landing** [17], once known as "Dock Point," the site of the old Hutchinson Wharf, Morse's "fish factory," (1880-1917), and a short-lived car ferry to Deltaville on the Western Shore (1933-1934). Here is a public pier, boat ramp, toilet facilities, and a wide view of Pungoteague Creek. Half a mile to the west, behind its own pier on the south side of the creek, can be seen **Mount Airy**, a handsome old house, the largest section of which dates from 1849. Here, prior to the founding of Harborton, docked the steamboats, and here lived Smith K. Martin [1862-1951], founder of Martin & Mason and for many years the dominant figure in Harborton.

As you make your way back Shore Street, notice the old **Hutchinson Burial Ground** [18], just east of Harbor Rose, where graves date back to 1848, including that of William S. Hutchinson [1831-1852] who was "inhumanly assassinated in Baltimore." Dockview Street leads back to the main road via Junior Street, so named because on the lot where the post office stands today the Junior Order of the United American Mechanics erected a lodge hall which also housed the **Harborton School** until 1944. The cornerstone of the building is preserved next to the driveway at 14207 Junior Street [19].

*HACKS NECK** lies west of Harborton on Hacksneck Road #631, a total of 10 miles of public road through lonely rural countryside. This part of the tour is an option; the only way into and out of Hacks Neck is through Pungoteague.

Hacks Neck was named for Dr. George Hack [1621-1665], who settled here in 1652 after securing the land from the king of the Nassawadox Indians. A physician born in Germany, Hack also prospered from growing tobacco, cattle farming, and general trade. At his death his personal library included 22 books in German and Dutch, 54 in Latin, and 20 in English, in a day when books were a rarity on the Eastern Shore. His Czech-born brother-in-law was the more renowned Augustine Herrmann [1621?-1661] of New Amsterdam and Maryland.

Just west of Harborton stands **Evergreen United Methodist Church** (1868). From the end of Evergreen Road #632 can be glimpsed two noteworthy homes on Muir Path. **Pretty Byrd Cottage** is a Victorian gingerbread fantasy, but a modern structure; it sits on its own little island in the middle of its own little pond. Stately **Evergreen** *(13230 Muir's Path)*, built in 1766, stands at the end of the same road, its hip roof and tall chimneys atypical of Eastern Shore architecture.

Hacks Neck, the village, is a small cluster of homes two miles beyond the Harborton road. The **Old Store** on the corner dates from the late 1880s, almost facing another one across the street on the left; both at one time housed the local post office, as did part of the house at 12049 Hacks Neck Road, then at another location. From the corner it is a mile down to the waters of **Back Creek** *(At road's end, turn on Killmon Lane #759)*, where there are some small docks, a small seafood company that produces excellent crabmeat, and a pretty view. **29262 Mason Beach Road** is older than it appears, a back portion dating to the early 1800s long since obscured by early twentieth century construction.

A more restricted view of Back Creek can be had from the end of Back Creek Road #633 *(2.6 miles to water)*. **12492 Hacks Neck Road** was until 1935 the local schoolhouse for whites. **Mount Olive Church** *(13458 Hacks Neck Road)* has a cornerstone with two dates, 1897 for the African Methodist Episcopal congregation that first worshiped here, 1926 for the present Baptist congregation. The little two-story building next door was originally a shop that once stood in Harborton.

From Hacksneck or Harborton retrace your route to Pungoteague and turn right on Route #178, which quickly becomes Boston Road and which will be your route for the next several miles.

BOSTON is the name of the scattered black settlement hugging Bayside Road below Pungoteague, marked by **Holy Trinity Baptist Church** (1905) and **Shiloh Baptist Church** (1875) on the left. In 1913, Booker T. Washington spoke to a large crowd at Shiloh. In 1806 Abel West [1734-1816], who lived near here, freed all his slaves and provided for them and their descendants a 200-acre "place of refuge." The refuge was a little south of this area and was known as Guinea; in modern times the settlement has shifted slightly to the north and survives under a different name. At the corner of Fairview Road stands the **Boston School** *(32168 Boston Road)*; though built in 1920, it is a descendant of the school for freed slaves which James T. Martin, a local black resident, erected at his own expense in 1867.

CEDAR VIEW BEACH *(1 mile below Shiloh Baptist Church turn right on Cedar View Road #616)*. It is 1.8 miles down to Cedar View Beach, once Cedar View Wharf, an important landing point as early as 1652. The beach here, which is eroding away, is private, but the view is not. Directly across Nandua Creek stands the handsome home **Andua** (c. 1800).

CRADDOCKVILLE lies a mile below Cedar View Road, marked by the steeple of the Methodist church on the right. Route #178 turns left in front of the church; your route lies straight ahead on Craddockville Road #615 through the main part of the village.

DAVIS WHARF is a picturesque little community where the road ends at Occohannock Creek, with a store right by the dock. Across the creek is Morley's Wharf in Northampton County. To the east, not easily visible for its trees, is *Glebe Farm *(12074 Glebe Farm Road)*, built in the mid-1700s as a home for the rector of St. George's Church. The story is told of the Confederate soldier who sought refuge here after running the blockade during the Civil War; trapped by Federal troops, he hid under a pile of potatoes, and when the soldiers stuck their bayonets through the potatoes escaped death by a matter of inches.

*Scarburgh Neck *(Turn left on Scarburghs Neck Road #612 after leaving Davis Wharf)*. On the left but hardly visible as you head down this neck is **Bay View Farm** *(35350 Copes Drive)*, built in 1801. At road's end, 3 miles from the turn, there is a pleasant view across Tawes Creek. Another view is from **Occohannock-on-the-Bay**, a Methodist camping and retreat center *(1.3 miles from Scarburghs Neck Road)*. As you return from Davis Wharf or Scarburgh Neck, retrace your route 1.3 miles on #615, then turn right on Indian Trail Road #613. Here just beyond the corner, sitting back among the trees on the left, is the old **Craddockville School** (1902), used by white students until 1914, then by black students until 1947.

Indian Trail Road #61 rejoins Route #178, now known as Shield's Bridge Road, after 1.5 miles; turn right.

HILLSBOROUGH *(Turn left on Hillsborough Drive #810 after 1 mile)* is a neighborhood of new homes beautifully situated on Occohannock Creek. Chief among the houses here is **Still Pond** *(14004 Still Pond Lane)*, at street's end on the left. Named for the water over which you cross to get to Hillsborough, Still Pond was originally a farmhouse located almost 15 miles away until moved to this spot and restored. It was built about 1850.

Shields Bridge, just east of Hillsborough, crosses Occohannock Creek, considered by many to be the most beautiful stretch of water on the Eastern Shore. The steamboats once stopped here at a wharf established in 1876. The bridge was then a toll bridge; in the late 1880s the toll was 5 cents for pedestrians, 10 cents for horse and buggy. On the right just beyond the bridge stands **Rues Wharf** *(14190 Shields Bridge Road)*, a handsome home of the mid-19th century.

BELLE HAVEN. As soon as you cross Occohannock Creek you land in Belle Haven, though the village proper is still a mile away. This is an old town, on the skinniest portion of the peninsula; the distance from navigable water here on the Bayside to Willis Wharf on the Seaside is only about 3 miles. Belle Haven takes its name from an old house in which, by 1764, a tavern was in operation. In the village that took shape around the tavern there was, by 1826, a post office but no church, for religion seemed unable to take root here, and the early Methodists called Belle Haven the most ungodly place on the Shore. The town was over a century old when at last the Presbyterians broke the barrier in 1879.

Had the railroad touched Belle Haven, this would undoubtedly have become one of the larger towns on the Shore. Instead the tracks were laid a mile to the east, and Exmore became the local metropolis. Even so Belle Haven prospered, and when the town was incorporated in the 1880s the founding fathers drew the boundaries so widely that they created a "township" the size of a small city, more than a mile and a half square. Because the town never grew to fill them, these boundaries were soon forgotten, only to be rediscovered in 1967 when Belle Haven was attempting to establish a community water supply. At that time it was learned that, according to the old maps, Exmore's water tower was in fact located in Belle Haven. Today both towns share the same water supply.

Belle Haven is a town of stately homes, shaded streets, and neat lawns. Turn left on the Belle Haven Road to see **Belle Haven United Methodist Church** and **Belle Haven Presbyterian Church**, built in 1887 and 1879 respectively. Opposite the Presbyterian church stands one of the town's oldest homes *(35485 Belle Haven Road)*, dating from the early 1800s. On King Street stands the old **Belle Haven School** *(15293 King Street)*, built in 1924, now the Eastern Shore's Own, a local art center. Another early 19th-century home *(35577 Belle Haven Road)* stands just south of the post office, its neighbor the much more ornate **Kellam House** *(35603 Belle Haven Road)* from much later in the same century. The building of the **Idle Hour Theatre** dates only from 1950, but the business is the oldest continuous moviehouse on the Eastern Shore of Virginia, dating from 1920 and the days of vaudeville and silent films. On the corner opposite is a small marker commemorating an historic store building which operated here from 1835 to 1959.

On the south corner of Lee Street stood **St. Michael's Episcopal Church**, erected in 1849 only to be dismantled when it was learned that the denomination did not really have title to the land on which it stood. Today a small burial ground surrounded by a brick wall under a grove of trees marks the spot. Three doors south of it is a small **Sears and Roebuck House** *(36066 Belle Haven Road)*, built in the 1920s from parts ordered from the mail-order house. Easily the longest house in town, and probably the oldest, is **Wainhouse** *(2296 Belle Haven Road)*, on the left behind a white gate as you leave town headed for Exmore; the oldest section of this frame home dates from about 1824.

> *The tour of the Lower Accomack Bayside ends at the traffic light on Route 13 at Route #178 in Exmore, just beyond Belle Haven.*

> *The tour of the Northampton Bayside can begin in Belle Haven. To continue down the Bayside, turn on Lee Street and follow it out of town; this road joins Route #183 in Northampton County after 2 miles.*

HUNGARS EPISCOPAL CHURCH

15 THE NORTHAMPTON BAYSIDE

Silver Beach and Crystal Palace,
Anglican church and ancient inn,
and the Shore's only Cabinet officer

The Bayside in Northampton is filled with ancient homes, many of them among the oldest and finest on the Shore. One of the Shore's two colonial churches is located here, and not far from it lived the only Federal cabinet officer ever to hail from the Eastern Shore of Virginia.

On the Northampton Bayside, however, the water is often hard to find, the view across it too often impeded by a line of trees or a handsome old house. Still the water is all around, and this tour will sniff it out and take you to places where steamboats docked and colonial planters shipped tobacco overseas.

In actual distance covered north-to-south this is the shortest tour in the book, beginning at Exmore and spilling back onto Route 13 at Shadyside only 11 miles to the south. Yet many of its best sights are on one of the several "necks," each one of which is serviced by only one main road, forcing you to double back and running the total distance, if you cover it all, up to over 60 miles. It's a good area for leisurely meandering. Restaurants and rest rooms are not to be found, so be prepared.

This tour begins in one of two places:

(1) From Route 13: Turn west on Route #183 in Exmore, at the traffic light.

(2) From Belle Haven, continuing south after the tour of the Lower Accomack Bayside: Turn right (west) on Lee Street in the center of town; this road joins Route #183 after 1.2 miles, and the first site on the tour is just beyond that.

MORLEY'S WHARF *(Turn right on Morley Wharf Road #606, 2.8 miles from Exmore, half a mile beyond Ebenezer Baptist Church; road ends 1 mile from this turn).* This is the only really good view you'll get of lovely Occohannock Creek from Northampton County. In the late 1800s, when this was known as Read's Wharf, steamboats docked here regularly and there was a post office and a church. Today you can launch your boat or just admire the view across the water to Davis Wharf. Surveying the scene from the east, across its own private bridge, is **Ingleside**, constructed about 1786; a deed of 1897 divided this property straight through the house, giving each party who was to live there equal access to the center stairs.

*OCCOHANNOCK NECK. The village of **Wardtown**, at the intersection with #606 to the left, announces the beginning of Occohannock Neck, named for the creek on its northern border. The neck is basically farmland, remarkably free of old homes and buildings and offering not enough views of the water. It's 5.5 miles from Wardtown to the end of the neck, and the road is good, but this part of the tour is an option.

Before passing Wardtown look right down Grapeland Circle for **Grapeland**, a handsome old house built about 1825. A mile and a half beyond it turn right for **Johnson's Cove** *(Turn right on Concord Wharf Road #611, then left on Old Neck Road #612, 1.3 miles to water)*, surely one of the most private and peaceful vistas on the Eastern Shore, worthy of any camera.

The next village beyond Wardtown is **Jamesville**, scattered along the road past **Bethel United Methodist Church** (1883), most of its old stores now closed. From Jamesville, Saltworks Road *(Turn left on #615, 2.4 miles to water)* passes the old **Jamesville Black School** (1937) on its way to the **Salt Works**, said to be the spot where in colonial times seawater was dehydrated to produce salt. Nothing old remains, but where the road ends abruptly between two homes there is a wide and handsome view across Nassawadox Creek. Almost straight across is Bayford, less than half a mile away by water, 14 miles distant by car.

At the end of Occohannock Neck Road is **Silver Beach**, a community of modest beach houses right on Chesapeake Bay. The water is shallow and peaceful, the beach sandy and fast eroding, the view wide. There is a confusing configuration of roads in this neighborhood, but all of them except Downing Beach Drive #691 and Mackatouces Point Road #713 will give you some view of either Chesapeake Bay or Nassawadox Creek. The best view of the bay is from Kellam Drive #686.

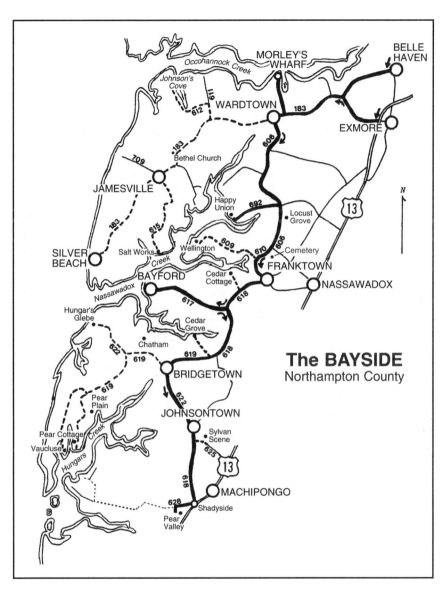

*In Wardtown turn south on Wardtown Road #606,
which will be your route for the next several miles.*

At the corner in Wardtown stands an L-shaped "big house-little house-colonnade-kitchen" house *(4356 Wardtown Road)*, and as you head south the old homes begin to make their appearance. On the left after one mile is an old three-section "telescope" house probably dating from the early 1800s. **Happy Union** *(Turn right on Happy Union Drive #692, 2.5 miles below Wardtown; 1.3 miles to end)* majestically surveys a wide and beautiful view of Nassawadox Creek; this three-section brick home was erected about 1774. **Locust Grove**, on the left a third of a mile south of the road to Happy Union, turns one brick end toward the road to show off its handsome gambrel roof; it was erected in 1828.

> *Keep straight when the name of your route changes to Short Street #610 at the intersection with Rogers Drive, 3.7 miles below Wardtown.*

Arthur Crudup Grave. Who'd have believed that "the Father of Rock and Roll" would be buried on the Eastern Shore? Yet the small cemetery on the left just below Rogers Drive contains the grave of Arthur "Big Boy" Crudup [1905-1974], small farmer, day laborer, and migrant worker boss who was also a self-taught musician and an important part of the Chicago blues scene of the 1930s. Crudup's 1946 Victor recording of "That's All Right, Mama" is said by some to have "essentially ignited the rock-and-roll revolution;" the song later became the first record of another Mississippi native, Elvis Presley, who credited Crudup with being a major inspiration for and influence on his own music. "When you hear Elvis Presley, you hearin' Big Boy Crudup," insisted blues performer Big Bill Broonzy. Despite an on-and-off performing and recording career that spanned several decades, Crudup never received the recognition or remuneration that was his due, and ended up on the Eastern Shore of Virginia in 1954 simply trying to support his large family. He recorded 64 songs and five LPs, performed with, among others, B. B. King and Bonnie Raitt, yet died a poor man in 1974, after suffering a stroke during a tour in Washington, D.C. His grave is located near the center of the cemetery, its large gray stone facing away from the road, two stones to the right of the "Mapp" stone that faces the road. Near it lie Crudup's mother Minnie, his wife Annie, and son James, one of several children who were, and are, performers in their own right.

> *Half a mile beyond the cemetery your route number becomes #609, but keep straight into Franktown, unless taking the optional side trip to Wellington.*

*Wellington *(Turn right on Wellington Neck Road #609; 1.7 miles to gate)* was erected in several stages, the earliest part in the mid-1700s. Handsomely situated on Nassawadox Creek, its lawns have been gradually eroding away with the passing years, and the water ventures ever closer to its back door.

FRANKTOWN *(Keep straight on #609; if coming from Wellington, turn right on Short Street #609)* is a quiet, almost quaint little village of about 30 homes lining a single road. When Quakers settled here in the 1600s, this region was known as Nassawadox; the

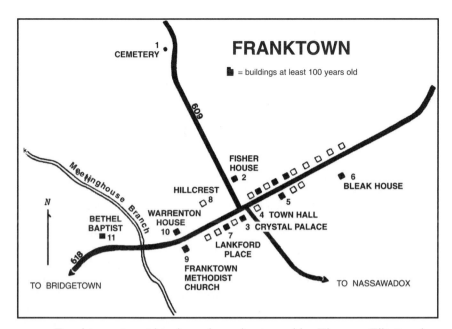

1 CEMETERY •

609

k

N

Meetinghouse Branch

618

BETHEL BAPTIST ■ 11

WARRENTON HOUSE 10 ■

HILLCREST □ 8

FISHER HOUSE ■ 2

□ □ ■ □ □ □ □ □

□ □

■ 5

□ 4 TOWN HALL

□ □ ■ □ □ 3 CRYSTAL PALACE

□ □ □ 7 LANKFORD PLACE

9 ■ FRANKTOWN METHODIST CHURCH

■ 6 BLEAK HOUSE

TO BRIDGETOWN

TO NASSAWADOX

name Franktown is said to have been bestowed by Thomas Elliott, who moved here in 1799, in honor of his son Franklin who died while still a child. The village took shape around 1800, centering upon a tavern in front of which the mail coach stopped three times a week on its trip down to Eastville. When the post office was established here in 1818, there were few others on the Shore, and this was a local metropolis. Like many another such community on the peninsula, Franktown declined after the railroad by-passed it, creating the new Nassawadox only a mile away. Today the community is completely residential, with no business or industry of any sort.

The first thing you will encounter is **Franktown Cemetery** [1], a quarter mile north of the village, established during an influenza epidemic in 1917-18. It is located near the site of an old tobacco warehouse of the early 1700s from which the local gentry shipped its cargo overseas. The first building on the left is **Fisher House** [2] *(9041 Wellington Neck Road)*, built in the early 1800s. It once served as a store, and the "hoist" by which large bundles were lifted to the second story storage room can still be seen on the end of the house nearest the road.

Crystal Palace [3] *(7465 Bayside Road)* commands the center of the village, a formal brick home unlike any other on the Eastern Shore of Virginia. John Smith began the construction of this house in 1849, presumably for his bride-to-be; when she eloped with another man, Smith moved in alone and remained a bachelor for the rest of his life. Henry A. Wise made a campaign speech here when he ran for governor in 1855; more recently this was the home of Judge Charles M. Lankford [1898-1977], for whom Route 13 is officially named the

Lankford Memorial Highway. Franktown has a **Town Hall** [4] *(7447 Bayside Road)* though it has no official town government. In its time this little building was a barber shop, a post office, and a sheriff's office. For many years the menfolk of the village used to gather in it to pass the time of day; forbidden by their wives to play cards, they discovered that they could play the same games using dominoes instead. Moved to this site in the 1940s, the building now serves principally as a polling place. Next to it stands **Stillmeadow** [5] *(7423 Bayside Road)*, built in 1895.

Four doors north of the Town Hall, **Bleak House** [6] *(7303 Bayside Road)* belies its name by standing comfortably in a big yard of shade trees, its size and manner reflecting the prosperity of the village in the years prior to the Civil War. Louis D. Heath erected this house in 1845.

In the shed that once stood behind the 19th-century vintage **Lankford House** [7] *(7497 Bayside Road)*, two doors south of Crystal Palace, Ira P. Lankford operated a small factory that bottled carbonated soft drinks; old bottles bearing Lankford's brand, and the name of Franktown, still turn up occasionally in local antique shops. Opposite it **Hillcrest** [8] *(7518 Bayside Road)*, built in 1924, occupies what was probably the site of the early tavern around which the village took shape.

Franktown United Methodist Church [9] dates from the 1790s, occupied this spot in 1843, and erected this building, the third, in 1894. The church is built on the site once occupied by a Quaker meetinghouse of log construction, which was abandoned by 1720. Across the street is **Warrenton House** [10] *(7542 Bayside Road)*, home of the family that operated a gristmill on the adjacent creek, which is known as Meetinghouse Branch. **Bethel Baptist Church** [11], erected in 1882, houses one of the largest black congregations on the Shore.

> *In Franktown turn right on Bayside Road #618 in front of Crystal Palace and continue south.*

Half a mile beyond Franktown, *****Cedar Cottage** *(Turn right on #616 and travel .5 mile)* nestles among the trees overlooking Warehouse Creek, a tiny, attractive house built by Thomas Jacob soon after 1790.

BAYFORD *(1 mile below Franktown turn right on Bayford Road #617)* is a tiny and charming little village at the point of Elliott's Neck, fewer than a dozen homes nicely situated on the waters of Nassawadox Creek. In the late 1800s Bayford was a popular bathing resort for the locals, and in 1887 the Bayford Oyster Company began a prosperous operation at this point.

The large home at the turn of the road is **Merton** *(6110 Bayford Road)*, built in 1895 after a much older house burned; this was the home of the family that gave its name to Elliott's Neck. Two of the village's oldest homes face each other: **Bayford Park** *(5558 Bayford Road)*, dating from about 1890, and **Foxcroft** *(5561 Bayford Road)*, an old farmhouse of about the same period. The **Bayford Store** *(5513 Bayford Road)* at the waterfront was for many years a local institution, but now no longer dispenses the candy bars, soft drinks, and chit-chat for which it was famous. On the adjacent building are marked the height of the tides of storms in 1933, 1962, and 1970. The view from here is a fine one, across the creek to Chesapeake Bay; to the right is Occohannock Neck and the tower of the Exmore radio station, to the left is Church Neck. All of the homes on the other side of Merton are of recent vintage, including **Cherokee Point Farm**, built in the traditional Eastern Shore style in the 1940s. Older is **Blenheim** *(6231 Bayford Road)*, on the left as you leave the village.

> *Retrace your route to Bayside Road #618 and turn right. Keep straight even though the number of your route changes to #619 at 1.3 miles below the Bayford road.*

*****Cedar Grove** *(Turn right on #695, 1.5 miles below Bayford road; .7 mile to gate)* is a large gambrel-roofed house of several sections built by Thomas Parramore early in the 1800s, situated on Church Creek. The public road ends right at the gate.

BRIDGETOWN *(On Bayside Road #619, 2.5 miles below the Bayford road)*. Faded little Bridgetown is the oldest village on the Eastern Shore of Virginia, continuously inhabited—just barely—since the 1660s. The marshes here are the headwaters of Hungars Creek, once navigable to this point. Bridgetown guards the entrance to Church Neck, which early filled up with settlers and where a church was erected in the 1640s. In the 1680s that church was moved here to the village, and it is for that reason alone that Bridgetown is noteworthy today.

Hungars Episcopal Church, on the left at the northern edge of the village, is the second church building on this site; it dates from the 1740s, and is the second oldest church building on the Virginia Shore, an admired piece of colonial architecture. Hungars was a prosperous church up until the American Revolution, then fell upon hard times, was abandoned, and suffered 30 years of neglect and vandalism. It was reopened in 1819, and has been in continuous use since that time. In 1850 the congregation, plagued with a building too often in need of repairs, voted to replace the structure. The following year they reversed that decision and decided to fix the old building once and for all. A major restoration followed, in which the front of the church was completely rebuilt, the building shortened by several feet, side doors eliminated, and a new roof put on. The workmanship was so skillful that it is virtually impossible to distinguish the "new" brickwork of the restoration from the old brickwork of the original. Today the church has a membership of over 100, and shares its rector with Christ Church in Eastville.

The other church in faded Bridgetown is **Shorter Chapel A.M.E. Church** (1886), on the right below the intersection. Just beyond it on the left is the home that was the old **Bridgetown School** *(10397 Bayside Road)*, built in the 1920s and used by local black students until 1953.

Church Neck *(Turn right on Church Neck Road #619)* lies west of Bridgetown, and takes its name from old Hungars. **Chatham** sits back in the field on the right, visible from the road as you leave Bridgetown; it was erected in 1818 by Major S. Pitts, who named it in honor of William Pitt, first Earl of Chatham and friend of the American cause during the Revolution. A vineyard-winery is now located on the property. **Hungars Glebe** *(Turn right on Glebe Road #622 and travel 1.3 miles to gate)* was the home of the rector of Hungars, the surrounding plantation the source of much of his livelihood. It may be one of the Shore's oldest homes; some say it was built as early as 1643.

It is 3.3 miles down to **Vaucluse** *(Return to Church Neck Road #619 and follow to end)*, an old home of great beauty and importance which you may not be able to see at certain seasons because of its surrounding trees. The largest section of this house was built about 1784, the second section about 1829. Here in 1790 was born Abel Parker Upshur, conservative politician who served as Secretary of the Navy and Secretary of State under President John Tyler. Upshur was killed in an explosion aboard the gunboat *Princeton* on the Potomac in 1844. On Sparrow Point Road stand two other old homes, **Pear Plain**, back in the field on the left, built in 1835 by Littleton Upshur, and **Pear Cottage** *(11576 Sparrow Point Road)*, on the right near the end of the road, the oldest part dating from perhaps as early as 1724.

> *In Bridgetown, Bayside Road becomes #622; keep straight on it, or turn right if coming from Church Neck.*

JOHNSONTOWN, a mile and a half below Bridgetown, is a tiny burg named for Johannes Johnson, who moved here in 1787. Johnson converted to Methodism after Bishop Francis Asbury visited his home in 1789, and the following year he gave the land for the church that still bears his name. The home he built became, in time, a tavern, a store, and a post office. From the yard of **Johnsons United Methodist Church** the whole of Johnson's little village can be seen. The church building, erected 1858, is the second on the site. The large house across the cemetery, facing a side road, is **Johnsontown Tavern** *(11284 Johnsontown Road)*, which Johnson built soon after 1787. A little off your main route south of the village stands *Sylvan Scene* *(Turn left on Sylvan Scene Road #625, .2 mile to gate)*, the largest portion of which was built prior to 1814 from materials of an even older house on this site. Its "kitchen" (second largest portion) was originally a slave quarters moved from another part of the estate. Here lived William Bullitt Fitzhugh, who enjoyed a national renown of sorts as the Sergeant-at-Arms of every national Democratic convention from 1928 to 1940. The next road to the left is Young Street #627, which takes you quickly to the gate of the **Barrier Islands Center** *(see page 21)*.

As your road rejoins Route 13 at Shadyside, 2 miles below Johnsontown, turn right on Wilsonia Neck Drive #628, then left on Pear Valley Lane #689 after half a mile.

The last "neck" on this tour is Wilsonia Neck, site of one of the earliest landmarks of the Eastern Shore of Virginia: **Pear Valley** *(see illustration, page 7)*. This tiny little house sits in the backyard of one farmhouse *(6390 Wilsonia Neck Road)*, and is best seen from the road adjacent to the neighboring farmhouse. Though not much to see in its present state—it is less than 20 feet long and 16 feet wide, and consists of only one room, with a loft above—Pear Valley is a rare antique, one of the oldest houses in Virginia that can be precisely dated from an inscription. In the center of the chimney, carved on a single brick, is the year 1672, when Teigue Harmon built the house. The house is typical of many other now-vanished homes of the late-17th century, and is owned by the Association for the Preservation of Virginia Antiquities,

Three miles further down the neck is a lovely view of *Hungars Creek *(Continue past Pear Valley Lane on Wilsonia Neck Road, turn right on Wilsonia Drive, then left on Wilsonia Harbor Lane)*, which looks across to Vaucluse Point on Church Neck.

Your tour of the Northampton Bayside ends at Shadyside on Route 13, 3 miles above Eastville.

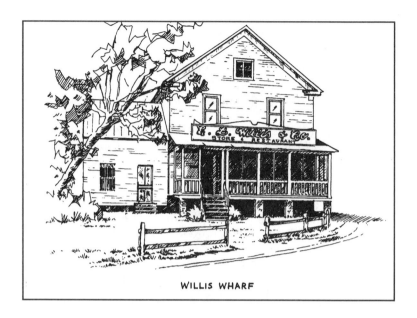

WILLIS WHARF

16   WHERE TO STAY, WHERE TO EAT

In many a guidebook the chapter on restaurants and hotels is the longest part of the book, or the most thumbed—or even the reason for buying the book in the first place.

This chapter is as brief as it is because tourism is not yet widespread on the Eastern Shore of Virginia, and the number of places to feed and house travelers remains relatively small. It's the price one pays for seeing an area still largely unspoiled.

For many years Chincoteague was the only exception. Chincoteague thrives on tourism, and in that one corner of the Shore there are many choices of where to stay and where to eat, and in season more than enough people to fill them. An upsurge in the number of people visiting the Shore has, in recent years, threatened to add more communities to the exception list, principally resurgent Cape Charles.

Yet it remains true that to see the Eastern Shore of Virginia as a whole it largely to move in an area largely devoid of tourism. Restaurants and motels do not abound on every corner, and you may have to seek out a place to eat or to stay, or plan ahead if you are touring the countryside. However, prices are reasonable, establishments are locally owned, places are generally not crowded, and local color is easily found.

On the Eastern Shore of Virginia one should not expect the fancy or the elegant. Restaurants tend toward the plain and down-home, with decor and atmosphere at a minimum. Understandably, many of the best restaurants feature seafood, and many of them offer not only good food but also plenty of it. Similarly, Eastern Shore motels rarely put on airs, "no frills" predominating over "luxury" lodgings. Eating and lodging establishments are not evenly spread across the peninsula. They tend to cluster around the main highway, though some are found in out-of-the-way spots, and some of the largest communities boast not a single place to eat or spend the night. Still, the Shore can accommodate you, with lodgings that range from basic economy motels to expensive inns, and restaurants that cover the spectrum from fast food carry-outs to dining rooms of distinction.

In this guidebook, all information about eating places, lodging, shops, and such is gathered here in this chapter. Here we single out the best of what the Shore has to offer, then list most, but by no means all, of the rest.

The telephone area code for the Eastern Shore of Virginia is 757.

RESTAURANTS

Fine Dining

Bizzotto's Gallery-Caffe, 41 Market Street, Onancock (787-3103)
Creative American cuisine in a handsome gallery; lunch and dinner
Charlotte Hotel & Restaurant, 7 North Street, Onancock (787-7400)
Fine dining in 33-seat dining room of downtown Onancock's new boutique hotel

The Shore's Best

AJ's on the Creek, 6585 Maddox Boulevard, Chincoteague (336-5888)
Seafood, pasta, veal steaks. Lunch and dinner, Saturday lounge until 1 a.m.
Aqua, 5 Marina Circle, Cape Charles (331-8660)
Innovative cuisine in elegant setting with stunning view; lighter fare upstairs at Cabana Bar (331-8670)
Bill's Seafood Restaurant, 4040 Main Street, Chincoteague (336-5831)
Good food and plenty of it; breakfast, lunch and dinner year-round
Eastville Inn, 16422 Courthouse Road, Eastville (678-9091)
Lunch and dinner in handsomely restored inn of the mid-1700s; local specialties and favorites; closed Monday-Tuesday
Harbor Grille, 203 Mason Avenue, Cape Charles (331-3005)
Good food in handsome setting in downtown Cape Charles
Inn and Garden Cafe, 145 Market Street, Onancock (787-8850)
Handsome dining room of B&B in restored house of 1880; limited hours, reservations recommended; its Sunday brunch is especially good
Flamenco European Restaurant, 4 North Street, Onancock (787-7780)
European cuisine served a la carte; bar and gift shop attached
Island House, 17 Atlantic Avenue, Wachapreague (787-4242)
Seafood, steaks, and a great view of the Wachapreague waterfront
Little Italy, 10227 Rogers Drive, Nassawadox (442-7831)
Seafood and vegetable lasagna, pasta, authentic Italian dishes
Mallards at the Wharf, 2 Market Street, Onancock (787-8558)
Overlooking the Onancock Wharf in historic building of 1842
Old Firehouse, 10 Peach Street, Cape Charles (331-4440)
Lunch and dinner in attractively restored building of old Cape Charles
Saigon Village Restaurant, 4069 Main Street, Chincoteague (336-7299)
Vietnamese and Thai dishes

Sting-Ray's Restaurant, Route 13, Capeville (331-2505)
*Decor and ambiance of a truck stop (some call it Chez Exxon), but
"Southern Living" magazine approves. Great food including renowned
chili. No waiters: order from the counter, then find a table*

Sunrise Grill, 25345 Lankford Highway, Onley (302-1275)
Extensive menu, huge portions; breakfast, lunch and dinner year-round

Village Restaurant, 6576 Maddox Boulevard, Chincoteague (336-5120)
*Good seafood with a nice view; steaks, chicken, and an enormous seafood
platter; reservations recommended*

Wright's Seafood Restaurant, Route #766 north of Atlantic (824-4012)
*Seafood, steaks, chicken, with view over waters to Chincoteague. Dinner
only till 9:00, year-round. Very popular locally.*

Different and Special

Bay Creek Railway, 202 Mason Avenue, Cape Charles (331-8770)
*Dinner excursion (or "pizza run") aboard a 1913 interurban railway car;
reservations required*

Behind the Racks, 5 North Street, Onancock (787-8805)
Wine bar, espresso; dinner Friday and Saturdays (reservations)

Double-Six, 16146 Main Ridge Road, Tangier (891-2410)
*The local watermen's hang-out famous for its hot oyster sandwich; once
pictured in "National Geographic"*

Exmore Diner, 4264 Main Street, Exmore (442-2313)
"Old-fashioned food at old-fashioned prices," breakfast anytime

Hilda Crockett's Chesapeake House, 16243 Main Ridge, Tangier (891-2331)
*Catering to the boatloads of visitors to the island, its enormous seafood
meals are served family style. Open daily April 15 thru October 15; reservations required*

Island Cafe, 4391 Main Street, Chincoteague (336-3141)
"The island's best breakfast"

Janet's General Store and Cafe, 49 King Street, Onancock (787-9495)
*Healthy food — soups, sandwiches, and more — in a country store setting;
breakfast and lunch only*

Machipongo Trading Company, 13037 Lankford Highway, Machipongo
(678-0005)
*Sandwiches, espresso, desserts, local books and art in what was once a ser-
vice station*

Tammy's and Johnny's, Route 13 north of Melfa (787-1122)
"Best fried chicken in Virginia," worth waiting for

Woody's Beach BBQ and **Fried Chicken Joint**, 6700 Maddox Boulevard,
Chincoteague (410-430-4429)
*"Serious smoking, serious attitude;" eat outside because there is no inside;
in season only*

Other Good Restaurants

Al's Cafe & Restaurant, 29106 Lankford Highway, Kiptopeake (331-1000)
Annie's, 24256 Bennett Street, Parksley (665-4990)
Blarney Stone Pub, 10 North Street, Onancock (302-0300)
Irish-style pub; lunch & dinner; live entertainment on weekends

Capt. Fish's Steaming Wharf, 3855 Main Street, Chincoteague (336-5528)
Good seafood right on the water; bar

Channel Marker Restaurant, 4409 Chambers Lane, Tangier (891-2220)
China Chefs, Four Corner Plaza, Onley (787-8711)
China Wok, 4086 Lankford Highway, Exmore (442-3300)
Chincoteague Inn, 6262 Marlin Street, Chincoteague (336-6110)
The island's oldest eating establishment; overlooking Chincoteague Bay

Clammee Hands, 2118 Harbor Drive, Greenbackville (824-0771)
Club Car Cafe, 18497 Dunne Avenue, Parksley (665-7822)
Coach House Tavern, 1 Clubhouse Way, Cape Charles (331-8630)
At the intersection of two signature golf courses in a gated community; gatekeeper will allow entrance for the restaurant
Daily Grind, 24399 Lankford Highway, Tasley (302-1212)
Don Valerio's Mexican Restaurant, 57 Market St., Onancock (787-3151);
19035 Lankford Highway, Eastville (678-0011);
29106 Lankford Highway, Melfa (789-5226)
Don's Seafood Restaurant, 4113 Main Street, Chincoteague (336-5715)
Breakfast, lunch, and dinner, seafood specialties; lounge, raw bar, dancing
Dragon House, 25086 Lankford Highway, Onley (787-7779)
El Maguey, 2638 Lankford Highway, Exmore (442-2900)
Popular locally for Mexican food
Etta's Channel Side Restaurant, 7452 East Side Rd., Chincoteague (336-5644)
Excellent crabcakes, great view of Assateague Channel
Fish Tales at the Marina, 15 Atlantic Avenue, Wachapreague (787-4110)
Fisherman's Corner Restaurant, 4119 Long Bridge Road, Tangier (891-2571)
Great Machipongo Clam Shack, 6468 Lankford Hwy., Nassawadox (442-3800)
Great seafood, eat in or carry out
Great Wall Chinese Restaurant, *Route 13, T's Corner (854-4558)*
Great Wall II, 6341 Maddox Boulevard, Chincoteague (336-5529)
Johnno's Bistro, 2526 Lankford Highway, Onley (789-3444)
J. H. West Seafood Restaurant, 4150 Townsend Road, Townsend (331-4420)
Kelly's Gingernut Pub, 133 Mason Avenue, Cape Charles
Irish-style pub in restored bank building of 1907
Ledo Pizza, 6477 Maddox Boulevard, Chincoteague (336-6597)
Pizza, pasta, Italian dishes
Los Tejones, 25318 Lankford Highway, Onley (787-7445)
Mallard's Sidewalk Cafe, 23410 Front Street, Accomac (787-7321)
Maria's Family Restaurant, 6506 Maddox Blvd., Chincoteague (336-5040)
Breakfast, lunch, and dinner; pizza and subs; carry-out and free delivery
Martha's Kitchen, 19396 Saxis Road, Saxis (709-1658)
Not even a sign out front! At road's end, last building on the left first door on the left facing the water
Mr. Baldy's Family Restaurant, 3441 Ridge Road, Chincoteague (336-1198)
Parksley Family Restaurant, 21013 Lankford Highway, Parksley (665-7450)
Pelican Pub, 32246 Lankford Highway, Kiptopeake (331-4229)
On the beach at Sunset Beach Resort at Bridge-Tunnel
Placa Garibaldi, 19083 Lankford Highway, Parksley (665-1296)
Ray's Shanty, 32157 Chincoteague Road west of Wattsville (824-3429)
Popular locally for seafood
Rock-n-Robins, 22512 Lankford Highway, Cape Charles (331-3601)
Lunch and dinner specials; pizza, nachos
Sage Diner, 25558 Lankford Highway, Onley (787-9341)
Sea Gull Pier Restaurant, South Island on the Bridge-Tunnel (757-464-4641)
Sea Shell Cafe, 7085 Maddox Boulevard, Chincoteague (336-6005)
Seaside Family Restaurant, 3435 Lankford Highway, Exmore (414-0175)
Shucker's Roadhouse, 20250 Fairgrounds Road, Onancock (787-7441)
Seafood, ribs, sandwiches until midnight; darts, pool, video games, live entertainment on weekends
Steamers Seafood Restaurant, 6251 Maddox Blvd., Chincoteague (336-5300)
All-you-can-eat crab and shrimp
Sunset Beach Resort, Route 13 at Bridge-Tunnel (331-1776)
The Bistro, 25 Market Street, Onancock (787-1180)
Excellent crab soup

That Mexican Place, 5030 Chicken City Road, Chincoteague (336-0010)
Yuk Yuk & Joe's, 15617 Courthouse Road, Eastville (678-7870)

Delis, Sandwiches, and Such

Dixieland, Lankford Highway, New Church (824-0914)
Good for You Naturally, 3257 Main Street, Exmore (442-4484)
   "Healthy yums," bakery, gifts; 10:00–3:00 only
Harley's Hidden Creek Deli, 6429 Maddox Blvd., Chincoteague (336-0039)
Highway Market, 4230 Lankford Highway, New Church (824-5002)
J & B Cold Cuts, 3571 Main Street, Chincoteague (336-5500)
Matthews Market, 14141 Lankford Highway, Mappsville (824-3061)
Ocean Deli, 33591 Chincoteague Road east of Wattsville (824-4111)
Onancock Deli, 170 Market Street, Onancock (787-7191)
Rayfield's Pharmacy, 2 Fig Street, Cape Charles (331-1212)
   Lunch counter
Sandy's Market, 9 Main Street, Wachapreague (787-4660)
Sanford General Store, 23644 Saxis Road, Sanford (824-9852)
Shore Treasures Market, 425 Mason Avenue, Cape Charles (331-1546)
Village General Store, 30285 Bobtown Road, Pungoteague (442-2124)
Yanni's Market, 15508 Courthouse Road, Eastville (678-7900)

In addition, many local convenience stores, including Shore Stop, Corner Mart, and Royal Farms, offer quick foods to go.

In a Hurry?

Bojangles, 26164 Lankford Highway, Onley (787-3300)
Burger King, Route 13, Onley (787-1896)
Capt. Zach's Seafood Carry-Out, 4422 Deep Hole, Chincoteague (336-3788)
Famous Pizza & Sub Shoppe, 6738 Maddox Blvd., Chincoteague (336-3301)
Hardee's, 22031 Lankford Highway, Cheriton (331-4029)
Hardee's, 3435 Lankford Highway, Exmore (442-2536)
Hardee's, 25048 Lankford Highway, Onley (787-8947)
Lorraine's Sandwich Shop, 4417 Chambers Lane, Tangier (891-2225)
McDonald's, 22492 Lankford Highway, Cape Charles (331-1855)
McDonald's, 7100 Maddox Boulevard, Chincoteague (336-3644)
McDonald's, 4183 Lankford Highway, Exmore (442-3534)
McDonald's, 25297 Lankford Highway, Onley (787-7888)
Paradiso Pizza, 9332 Lankford Highway, Temperanceville (824-9882)
Pizza Hut, 25092 Lankford Highway, Onley (787-3800)
Pizza Hut, 6471 Lankford Highway, T's Corner (824-5689)
Sea Star Gourmet Carryout, 4121 Main Street, Chincoteague (336-5442)
Sonic Drive-In, 7015 Lankford Highway, T's Corner (824-5500)
Starlight Pizzaria, 25363 Lankford Highway, Onley (787-7688)
Stuckey's, Route 13, Mappsville (824-3616)
Subway, 6743 Maddox Boulevard, Chincoteague (336-2480)
Subway, 4090 Lankford Highway, Exmore (442-0090)
Subway, 25076 Lankford Highway, Onley (787-1151)
Subway, Route 13, T's Corner (824-0094)
Taco Bell/KFC/Pizza Hut, 4112 Lankford Highway, Exmore (442-7827)
T's Corner, 6291 Lankford Highway, T's Corner (824-5935)
Veneto's Pizzaria, 227 Mason Avenue, Cape Charles (331-2275)
Waterfront Restaurant, 16125 Main Ridge Road, Tangier (891-2248)
Wendy's, 4116 Lankford Highway, Exmore (442-6997)
Wendy's, 25403 Lankford Highway, Onley (787-8598)
Wolff's Sandwich Shoppe, Atlantic Road, Atlantic (824-6466)

Coffee and Espresso

The Bear & Cub Coffee Shoppe, 30241 Bobtown Rd., Pungoteague (442-7222)
Local roasted coffees, espresso, gifts, local books and artworks

Book Bin, 25304 Lankford Highway, Onley (787-7866)
Coffee and espresso, books, stationery and toys

Cape Charles Coffee Company, 241 Mason Avenue, Cape Charles (331-1880)
Coffees, sandwiches, desserts in exquisitely restored historical building

Machipongo Trading Company, 13037 Lankford Hwy., Machipongo (678-0005)
Espresso, sandwiches, desserts, local books and art in what was once a service station

Main Street Shop & Coffeehouse, 4288 Main St., Chincoeague (336-6782)
Espresso, natural and gourmet foods in gallery setting

Specialty Dining: Ice Cream, Bakeries, and More

Becca's, 156 Market Street, Onancock (789-3686)
Smith Island cake, homemade soups, daily lunch specials; eat in, take out

Cape Charles Coffee Company, 241 Mason Avenue, Cape Charles (331-1880)
Sandwiches, coffee, desserts in exquisitely restored historical building

Channel Bass Inn, 6228 Church Street, Chincoteague (336-6148)
Afternoon tea with scones, trifle, and other desserts; serving days vary; reservations required

Corner Bakery, 36 Market Street, Onancock (787-4520)
Sinfully good donuts and pastries, known even off the Shore

Island Creamery, 6243 Maddox Boulevard, Chincoteague (336-6236)
Ice cream cakes, slushes, smoothies, yogurt

Kate's Kupboard II, Route 13, Belle Haven (442-7437)
Baked goods, pastries

Mister Whippy, 6201 Maddox Boulevard, Chincoteague (336-5122)

Muller's Ice Cream Parlor, 4034 Main Street, Chincoteague (336-3118)

Nostalgia, 59 Market Street, Onancock (787-7780)
Soups, breads, and desserts

Scoops Ice Cream Shoppe, 132 Market Street, Onancock (787-3230)
Ice cream, pizza, chili dogs, barbeque

Spanky's Place, 16200 Main Ridge Road, Tangier (891-2514)
Ice cream

Sugarbakers, 4095 Main Street, Chincoteague (336-3712)
Sandwiches, baked goods

Two Sisters, 718 Randolph Avenue, Cape Charles (331-2005)
Pastries, smoothies, cappuccino, fresh produce

Yellow Duck Bakery Cafe, 3312 Main Street, Exmore (442-5909)
Baked goods, desserts, coffee

HOTELS

Cape Charles Hotel, 235 Mason Avenue, Cape Charles (331-3130)
Restored 18-room hotel of 1884; private baths, cable TV; some rooms have views of harbor from second-story terrace; smoke free (www.capecharleshotel.com)

Charlotte Hotel, 7 North Street, Onancock (787-7400)
Restored hotel of 1907 now features eight guest rooms, 33-seat restaurant, full service bar; individual baths; smoke free; one room ADA accessible (www.thecharlottehotel.com)

INNS

Bay View Inn, 16408 West Ridge Road, Tangier (891-2396)
Bed-and-breakfast in admired island home of 1904; air-conditioned cottages, cable TV, private tours. Open year-round

Bay View Waterfront, 35350 Copes Drive, Davis Wharf (442-6963)
A "big house-little house-colonnade-kitchen" Shore home of 1800 overlooking Occohannock Creek; swimming pool, fishing, crabbing, deep water dock (www.BayViewWaterfrontBedandBreakfast.com)

Bay Watch B & B, 2053 Franklin City Road, Greenbackville (824-4114)
The newest house in the old "ghost town" of Franklin City is wrapped with decks with views of water on three sides (www.baywatchbandb.com)

Baywood B & B, 31400 Latimer's Bluff, Cape Charles (269-209-4406)
Balconies overlooking Chesapeake Bay; full breakfast plus "sunset hour" with light refreshments (www.thebaywood.com)

Cape Charles House, 645 Tazewell Avenue, Cape Charles (331-4920)
Bed-and-breakfast in a 1912 colonial revival home; cuisine by national cooking magazine author (www.capecharleshouse.com)

Cedar Gables, 6095 Hopkins Lane, Chincoteague (336-1096)
A modern home with vistas across the water; all rooms with jacuzzi, fireplace, waterfront deck, waterfront dining porch and private dock

Channel Bass Inn, 6228 Church Street, Chincoteague (336-6148)
Chincoteague's oldest "hotel" continues as elegant bed-and-breakfast in an island home of the 1890s. Spacious rooms, full breakfast, afternoon tea (www.channelbass-inn.com)

Cheriton House, 21191 N. Bayside Road, Cheriton (499-0658)
Century-old house in the heart of smalltown Cheriton; accommodates up to 10 guests (http://thecheritonhouse inn.com)

Chesapeake Charm, 202 Madison Avenue, Cape Charles (331-2676)
Bed-and-breakfast in a 1921 house three blocks from the beach; antiques and period furnishings, jacuzzi (www.chesapeakecharmbnb.com)

Chesapeake House, 16243 Main Ridge Road, Tangier (891-2331)
Two century-old houses across the street from one another; definitely not fancy, but seafood meals are renowned. April 15-October 15

Colonial Manor Inn, 84 Market Street, Onancock (787-3521)
Oldest of the Shore's inns, in operation continuously since the 1930s. Located in a stately late-19th century house (www.colonialmanorinn.com)

Creekside Inn, 37 King Street, Onancock (787-7578)
Three rooms in vintage waterfront house in the heart of Onancock; private baths, gourmet breakfast (wwwcreeksideinn.biz)

Fisherman's Lodge, 20210 Harbor Point Road, Quinby (442-7109)
Built in the 1930s and still catering to fishermen; sleeping quarters for 40; family breakfast, boxed lunches available (wwwfishermanslodge.com)

Garden and the Sea Inn, 4188 Nelson Road, New Church (824-0672)
Elegant European-style country inn in a house that began as a tavern in 1802. Bed-and-breakfast plus meals in gourmet dining room. April thru October (www.gardenandseainn.com)

Garrison Bed and Breakfast, 34000 Seaside Road, Painter (442-9446)
Four antique-filled guest rooms in a 1931 southern colonial home; shaded country setting, gazebo (www.garrisonbandb.com)

Gladstone House, 12108 Lincoln Avenue, Exmore (442-4614)
Brick Georgian-style house named for a local physician; Nautical Room and Doll House Room; decorated with antiques; (www.gladstonehouse.com)

Harborton House, 28044 Harborton Road, Harborton (442-6800)
Bed-and-breakfast in a "ship's carpenter" house c. 1900 with open porches on two stories; "casual but full of luxuries." (www.harbortonhouse.com)

Inn and Garden Cafe, 145 Market Street, Onancock (787-8850)
Four guest suites in large restored house of 1880; handsome dining room attached (www.theinnandgardencafe.com)

Inn at Onancock, 30 North Street, Onancock (789-7711)
Handsome Victorian c. 1900; 5 guest rooms, some with fireplaces, each in the style of a favorite worldwide destination; private baths, gourmet breakfast (www.innatonancock.com)

Inn at Poplar Corner, 4248 Main Street, Chincoteague (336-6115)
Modern mirror-image twin of its older neighbor Watson House B&B on opposite corner; air-conditioned, private baths, full breakfast, afternoon tea (www.poplarcorner.com)

Island Manor House, 4160 Main Street, Chincoteague (336-5436)
Two mid-1800s island homes joined by handsome sunroom; spa; antiques; breakfast and afternoon tea (www.islandmanor.com)

Kellogg House, 644 Monroe Avenue, Cape Charles (331-2767)
Bed-and-breakfast in a large 1924 colonial revival home; gourmet breakfast and afternoon refreshments (www.kelloghouse.com)

Miss Molly's Inn, 4141 Main Street, Chincoteague (336-6686)
Miss Molly Rowley was the daughter of the man who built this house in 1886. Marguerite Henry wrote part of "Misty of Chincoteague" here. Victorian decor, breakfast, and afternoon tea (www.missmollys-inn.com)

Montrose House, 20494 Market Street, Onancock (787-7088)
Bed-and-breakfast in a traditional Eastern Shore "big house-little h o u s e - colonnade-kitchen" dating from 1810; antiques, rose garden (www.bbon-line.com/va/montrose)

Nottingham Ridge, 28184 Nottingham Ridge Lane, Cape Charles (331-2212)
A birdwatcher's paradise on a high wooded ridge overlooking Chesapeake Bay view, private beach

Pickett's Harbor, 28288 Nottingham Ridge Lane, Cape Charles (331-2212)
Bed and breakfast in a quiet, wooded setting with fine Chesapeake Bay view, private beach (www.pickettsharbor.com)

Pretty Byrd Cottage, Muir Path, Hacks Neck (442-3375)
A Victorian gingerbread fantasy cottage sitting on its own island reached by a footbridge over its own pond

Seagate, 9 Tazewell Avenue, Cape Charles (331-2206)
A 1910 house elegantly restored, antique furnishings; near the beach; bed-and-breakfast plus afternoon tea; open year-round (www.seagatebb.com)

Spinning Wheel, 31 North Street, Onancock (787-7311)
1890s "folk Victorian" in the heart of town; antiques, private baths, full breakfast (www.1890spinningwheel.com)

Sunset Inn, 16650 Hog Ridge Road, Tangier (891-2535)
Bed-and-breakfast in an A-frame house close to isolated Tangier Beach; cottages available. Air conditioning. Open all year

Watson House, 4240 Main Street, Chincoteague (336-1564)
Turn-of-the-century Victorian furnished with antiques, air-conditioned rooms with private baths, full breakfast and afternoon tea (www.watson-house.com)

Windrush Farm, 5350 Willow Oak Road, Eastville (678-7725)
Comfortable accommodations in a mid-19th century farmhouse surrounded by beautiful gardens; great for walking tours, cycling; pets welcome

MOTELS

The Shore's Best

Best Western Chincoteague, 7105 Maddox Blvd., Chincoteague (336-6117)
52 units, large rooms with balconies or patios, pool; near bridge to Assateague; AAA rated

Best Western Eastern Shore Inn, 2543 Lankford Hwy., Exmore (442-7378)
44 units, 8 suites, cable TV, continental breakfast, internet; AAA rated

Comfort Inn, Route 13, Onley (787-7787)
80 units, color TV, pool; restaurants adjacent, award-winning staff

Comfort Suites, 4195 Main Street, Chincoteague (336-3700)
60 units with waterfront balconies and sitting area; free continental breakfast buffet; indoor heated pool and hot tub

Hampton Inn & Suites, 4179 Main Street, Chincoteague (336-1616)
59 units; waterfront balconies; free deluxe continental breakfast; indoor heated pool and hot tub

Hampton Inn & Suites, 4129 Lankford Highway, Exmore (442-7722)
86 units; hot breakfast, high speed internet, fitness center.

Holiday Inn Express & Suites, 3446 Lankford Highway, Exmore (442-5522)
Free hot breakfast, internet access, indoor heated pool, smoke free

Island Motor Inn, 4391 Main Street, Chincoteague (336-3141)
48 units, all rooms overlook water with balconies; observation deck and boardwalk; AAA rated

Kiptopeake Inn, 29106 Lankford Highway, Kiptopeake (331-1000)
103 units, cable TV, pool, internet

Quality Inn, 6273 Maddox Boulevard, Chincoteague (336-6565)
92 units, cable TV, pool, pet friendly, AAA rated

Refuge Motor Inn, 7058 Maddox Boulevard, Chincoteague (336-5511)
68 units near bridge to Assateague; pool, sauna, sun deck; AAA rated.

Rittenhouse Motor Lodge, 23054 Lankford Highway, Cheriton (331-2768)
13 units; small 1950s motel lovingly maintained amid grove of pines and gardens; cable TV, AC, but no phones!

Shore Stay Suites, 26406 Lankford Highway, Capeville (331-4090)
20 units; full-size kitchen & dining area in each unit; cable TV, internet; extended stay hotel catering to travelers, vacationers, fishermen

Sunset Beach Resort, Route 13 at the Bridge-Tunnel, Kiptopeake (331-1776)
82 units, pool, restaurant, observation tower, private beach on the Bay

Waterside Motor Inn, 3761 Main Street, Chincoteague (336-3434)
45 units, waterfront balconies; tennis court, pool, spa, jacuzzi, fishing pier

Best of the Rest

America's Best Value Inn, 6151 Maddox Blvd., Chincoteague (336-6562)
America's Best Value Inn, Route 13, Nassawadox (442-6363)
America's Best Value Inn, Route 13, Onley (787-8000)
Anchor Inn, 3791 Main Street, Chincoteague (336-6313)
Assateague Inn, 6570 Coach's Lane, Chincoteague (336-3738)
Birchwood Motel, 3650 Main Street, Chincoteague (336-6133)
Blue Heron Inn, 7020 Maddox Boulevard, Chincoteague (336-1900)
Captain's Quarters Motel, Route 13, Melfa (787-4545)
Chincoteague Inn Motel, 4417 Deep Hole Road, Chincoteague (336-6415)
Edgewood Motel, Route 13, Townsend (331-3632)
Lighthouse Inn, 4218 Main Street, Chincoteague (336-5091)
Sea Shell Motel, 3720 Willow Street, Chincoteague (336-6589)
Seahawk Motel, 6250 Maddox Boulevard, Chincoteague (336-6527)
Sunrise Motor Inn, 4491 Chicken City Road, Chincoteague (336-6671)
Wachapreague Inn, 1 Main Street, Wachapreague (787-2105)

Cottages, Apartments, Short-Term Rentals: Chincoteague

An Island Sun, 6175 Ocean Boulevard, Chincoteague (410-827-5635)
Apple Tree Apartments, 6185 Poplar Street, Chincoteague (703-360-4150)
Assateague View, 7569 East Side Drive, Chincoteague (760-492-8625)
Bay House, 3639 Main Street, Chincoteague (410-343-1495)
Bayside Retreat, 4215 Main Street, Chincoteague
Baywatch Cottage, 6140 Leonard Lane, Chincoteague (888-831-0300)
Chincoteague Cottage Company, 6299 Clark St., Chincoteague (336-5088)
Chincoteague Island Vacation Cottages, 4405 Deep Hole Road, Chincoteague (1-800-457-6643)
Chincoteague Resort Realty, 6378 Church St., Chincoteague (800-668-7863)
Dove Winds Cottages, 7023 Maddox Boulevard, Chincoteague (336-5667)
Eagle's View, 7151 Sheepshead Lane, Chincoteague (540-687-6923)
East Side Rentals, 7462 East Side Road, Chincoteague (336-5555)
Eastern Shore Retreats, 6759A Maddox Boulevard, Chincoteague (336-1088)
Eastern Shore Vacation Homes, 6207 Maddox Blvd., Chincoteague (1-866-339-6353)
Easy Does It Vacations, 3066 Main Street, Chincoteague (717-571-1765)
Grandview at Wildcat, 5064 Wildcat Lane, Chincoteague (301-657-3830)
Happiness House, 5047 DeMarco Lane, Chincoteague (336-6502)
Harbor Rentals, 6455 Maddox Boulevard, Chincoteague (336-5490)
Heron Woods Cottages, 6095 Hopkins Lane, Chincoteague (888-491-2944)
Holiday Cottages, 6113 Taylor Street, Chincoteague (336-6256)
Horseshoe Hideaway, 7129 Horsehoe Drive, Chincoteague (732-460-1176)
Island Getaways, 7038 Maddox Boulevard, Chincoteague (888-757-0100)
Island Haven, 6425 Pine Drive, Chincoteague (610-258-1983)
Island Pride Cottages, 4375 Chicken City Road, Chincoteague (336-6345)
Island Property Enterprises, 6395 Maddox Blvd, Chincoteague (336-3456)
Joshua B. Jones Homeplace, 3874 Main Street, Chincoteague (336-3456)
Kaliedoscope Kottages, 6250 Mumford Street, Chincoteague (336-0582)
Lott's Cottage, 5425 Deep Hole Road, Chincoteague (336-5773)
My Tern, 3878 Main Street, Chincoteague (336-1517)
Ocean East Rentals, 6363 Maddox Blvd., Chincoteague (866-406-3354)
Payton Place, 2569 Main Street, Chincoteague (336-3572)
Pier Pleasure, 7462 Pony Swim Lane, Chincoteague (410-721-0097)
Porter Properties Vacation Rentals, 6335 Jester St., Chincoteague (336-5036)
Sailer Moon, 3739 Main Street, Chincoteague (336-1236)
Snug Harbor, 7536 East Side Road, Chincoteague (336-6176)
Spinnaker, 5295 Hibiscus Drive, Chincoteague (484-905-5072)
Steve's Cottages, 6167 Taylor Street, Chincoteague (336-7474)
Sunshine Manor House, 5327 Main Street, Chincoteague (800-887-5486)
Uncle Joe's Cabins, 4477 Chicken City Road, Chincoteague (336-5107)
VIP Island Rentals, 6357 Maddox Boulevard, Chincoteague (336-7288)

Cottages, Apartments, Short-Term Rentals: Mainland

Alexander's Cottage, 507 Tazewell Avenue, Cape Charles (331-4679)
Almost Paradise, 4247 Kiptopeke Drive, Cape Charles (804-513-4004)
Archie's Place, 2 Brooklyn Avenue, Wachapreague (703-795-8169)
Bay Creek Resort Rentals, 3335 Stone Road, Cape Charles (331-8750)
Bay Dreaming, 108 Monroe Avenue, Cape Charles (434-960-6840)
Bay Lake Condominium, Washington Avenue, Cape Charles (331-1055)
Bay View Cottage, Smith Beach (276-346-3677)
Blue Heron Realty, 113 Mason Avenue, Cape Charles (331-4885)
Cape Charles Realty, 219 Mason Avenue, Cape Charles (331-4661)
Cape House, 309 Strawberry Street, Cape Charles (331-4275)
Captain's Corner, Wachapreague (787-2346)

Casual Cottages, 212 Monroe Avenue, Cape Charles (331-4679)
Chesapeake Properties, 7 Fig Street, Cape Charles (331-8100)
Coldwell Banker Harbour Realty, 235 Mason Ave., Cape Charles (331-3255)
Cozy Cottage, 540 Randolph Avenue, Cape Charles (331-4679)
Drummond Point Cottages, 10055 Craddock Neck Road, Craddockville (229-559-0181)
Eastern Shore Cottage, 10184 Sunset Point Road, Belle Haven (442-7349)
El Shaddai Vacation Rental, 15 Nectarine St., Cape Charles (301-248-1206)
Fisherman's Paradise, 2469 Stone Road, Cape Charles (252-229-2280)
Heartsworth Cottage, 19000 Hermitage Road, Onancock (789-5915)
   Accommodates six, deck and dock on Onancock Creek
Latimer's Bluff, Route 13 north of Cape Charles (331-2082)
Loblolly Haven, 15164 Russel Drive, Onancock (304-582-2443)
Matchotank Country Home, Onancock (787-3399)
Neptune Vacation Suite Apartments, 21033 Front Street, Onley (630-5193)
   Quirky, retro theme suites from vintage television shows
Parkside Cottages, 214 & 216 Strawberry Street, Cape Charles (331-4679)
Pearce's Waterfront Lodge, 20147 Mosher Lane, Quinby (442-7318)
Plum Porch Cotteages, 7 & 9 Plum Street, Cape Charles (999-4060)
Runaway, Silver Beach (410-860-0893)
Wachapreague Inn, 1 Main Street, Wachapreague (787-2105)
Wainhouse Guest House, 2296 Wainhose Road, Belle Haven (414-0324)
Watson Realty, 225 Mason Avenue, Cape Charles (331-4444)

Campgrounds
Cherrystone Campground, 1511 Townfields Road west of Cheriton (331-3063)
Inlet View Campground, 2272 Main Street, Chincoteague (336-5126)
Kiptopeake State Park, Route 13, 3 miles south of Bridge-Tunnel (331-2267)
Maddox Family Campground, 6742 Maddox Blvd., Chincoteague (336-3111)
Pine Grove Campground, 5283 Deep Hole Road, Chincoteague (336-5200)
Sunset Beach RV Resorts, Route 13 at Bridge-Tunnel, Kiptopeake (331-1776)
Tall Pines Harbor, 8107 Tall Pines Lane, Sanford (824-0777)
Tom's Cove Park, 8128 Beebe Road, Chincoteague (226-6498)

SOME OTHER LISTS TO AID THE VISITOR

Antiques
Antique Addicts, 3515 Main Street, Exmore (442-5100)
   70+ dealers antique mall
Bay Treasures, 3845 Main Street, Chincoteague (336-1747)
Blue Crow Antique Mall, 32124 Lankford Highway, Keller (442-4150)
   150+ dealers antique mall
By Chance Antiques, 14062 Lankford Highway, Machipongo (678-5999)
Cape Charles Station, 211 Mason Avenue, Cape Charles (331-2600)
Capeville Flea Market, Route 13, Capeville (331-4930)
Duck Duck Goose, 4134 Main Street, Chincoteague (336-3000)
Exmore Antique & Craft Emporium, 3304 Main Street, Exmore (414-0111)
   40+ dealers antique mall
Grace's Stock Exchange Antiques, 28526 Lankford Hwy., Melfa (787-1464)
Memory Lane, 4091 Main Street, Chincoteague (336-6560)
Old Diner Collectibles, Route 13 north of Parksley light (787-8608)
Shore Flea Market, 12085 Lankford Highway, Temperanceville (824-3300)
   Open weekends only
Silver Cricket, 4090 Main Street, Chincoteague (336-0515)
Timothy Smith Restorations, 37 Market Street, Onancock (787-3733)

Wachina Company, 12148 Bank Avenue, Exmore (414-0671)
Windsor House, 4290 Capeville Road, Capeville (331-4848)
Worcester House, Route 13, New Church (824-3847)

The Fall Antiques Show, held annually on the first weekend of November in the Exmore Moose Lodge, 15315 Merry Cat Lane, Belle Haven, is the oldest and largest on the Eastern Shore of Virginia, benefiting Shore Memorial Hospital. Watch for notices throughout the peninsula; admission charged.

Art Galleries

Anopheles Blues, 4362 Main Street, Chincoteague (336-7335)
Photographs and drawings of Chincoteague's land, sea, and skyscapes
Artisans Guild, 6 College Avenue (Room 107), Onancock
Juried featured artists (www.esartisans guild.org)
Bayside Arts Emporium, 4215 Main Street, Chincoteague (336-1031)
Paintings and prints by local artist Jenny Somers; decoys
Bizzotto's Gallery-Caffe, 41 Market Street, Onancock (787-3103)
Leather, glass, paintings, jewelry, pottery by American craftsmen
Cape Charles Art Co-Op, 2 Fig Street, Cape Charles (331-2433)
Local artists and artisans, jewelry
Clouds & Folly, 6123 Maddox Boulevard, Chincoteague (336-3739)
Paintings and fantasy furniture by artist Randolph Payne
Clay Werks, 4058 Main Street, Exmore (414-0567)
Tiles and mosaics
Crockett's Gallery, 39 Market Street, Onancock (787-2288)
Paintings by popular local artist Willie Crockett
Dan Lawrence Studio, 6 College Avenue (Room 103), Onancock (709-2626)
Paintings, pastels, drawings by local artist Dan Lawrence
Decoys, Decoys, Decoys, 4039 Main Street, Chincoteague (336-1402)
Vintage and contemporary handcarved decoys and waterfowl
Dragonfly Gallery, 6 College Avenue (Room 117), Onancock (710-8724)
Local artists' co-operative; paintings, pottery, sculpture, jewelry
Eastern Shore Art League Gallery, 6 College Avenue (Room 109), Onancock
Paintings, photograph, art objects by local artists (www.esartleague.info)
Egret Moon Artworks, 4044 Main Street, Chincoteague (336-5775)
Paintings and prints of local artist Zebie Hursh
Elizabeth Hunt Pottery, 6 College Avenue (Room 116), Onancock (709-1288)
Hand-thrown carved stoneware for home and garden
ESO Art Center, 15293 King Street, Belle Haven (442-3226)
Local artists' studio; occasional exhibits
Folk House, 35044 Lankford Highway, Painter (442-2224)
American primitive paintings by award-winning local artist Danny Doughty
Gallery at Eastville, 16310 Courthouse Road, Eastville (678-7532)
Design studio and workshop; glass, jewelry, knitwear, original art
Glass Expressions, 6 College Avenue (Room 106), Onancock (787-4410)
Stained glass commission work, repairs, supplies, classes
Island Arts, 6196 Maddox Boulevard, Chincoteague (336-5856)
Paintings by local artist Nancy Richards West; sculpture, ceramics, fabrics
Linda Nerine Gallery, 6519 Church Street, Chincoteague (336-5322)
Photographs by local photographer Linda Nerine; innovative jewelry, toys
Main Street Shop & Coffeehouse, 4288 Main St., Chincoteague (336-6782)
Gallery room exhibiting artists from on and off the Shore
Next Door Gallery, 9 North Street, Onancock (787-9417)
Paintings & botanicals of local artist Charlotte Heath; art pottery
Osprey Nest Art Gallery, 4096 Main Street, Chincoteague (336-6042)
Paintings by local artist Kevin McBride; decoys, sculpture, jewelry, rugs

Painter Gallery, 33412 Lankford Highway, Painter (442-9537)
  Studio and gallery of local artist Joseph Adams ("Adamo")
Quilt Studio, 6 College Avenue (Room 104), Onancock (710-1816)
  Art quilts and textiles by local artist Lois Sprague
Pink Room Abstracts, 6 College Avenue (Room 115), Onancock (442-4116)
  Mixed media by local artists John Alan Nyberg and Eric Nyberg
Print Gallery, 6 College Avenue (Room 108), Onancock
  Watercolors, photographs, textiles by local artist Roberta Dean
Red Queen Gallery Onancock, 8 North Street, Onancock (787-4040)
  Celebrating local and regional artists; something for every price range
Richardson Studio/Gallery, 24 King Street, Onancock (789-3220)
  Paintings by local artist Jack Richardson
Ron Hugo Gallery, 4067 Main Street, Chincoteague (709-0493)
  Photography by local photographer Ron Hugo, fine art, antiques
Seaside Gallery, 3 Marina Village Circle, Cape Charles (331-8680)
  Paintings by local artist Thelma Peterson and others; sculpture
Smiling Dolphin, 10237 Rogers Drive, Nassawadox (442-2112)
  Local artists of the Eastern Shore Art League
Stage Door Gallery, 301 Mason Avenue, Cape Charles (331-3669)
  Paintings, sculpture, and other media, changing exhibits by local artists
Turner Sculpture Ltd., Route 13 between Onley and Melfa (787-2818)
  Gallery and foundry of wildlife bronzes by renowned local sculptors William and David Turner
Wooden Fish, 555 Mason Avenue, Cape Charles (331-3474)
  Carved fish and other whimsical creations by Ryan Dockiewicz

The old Onancock School at 6 College Avenue, Onancock, houses a number of galleries and studios, including some of those listed above. The best time to visit them all is during the town's Second Friday Art Walk, 5:00-8:00 p.m. on the second Friday of the month.

There are a number of local art associations on the Eastern Shore of Virginia, including the Art League and the Artisans Guild; watch for notices of exhibits and shows, or call the Smiling Dolphin (442-2112).

The Artisans Guild of the Eastern Shore sponsors an annual Open Studio and Vineyard Tour every Thanksgiving weekend. In 2009 thirty artisans exhibited at 12 studios, workshops, and galleries. The tour is self-guided, and includes a tasting tour of two local wineries. (www.esartisansguild.org).

There is also an annual spring Sneak Peek Studio Tour offering day-trippers a visit to several artists' studios in the lower part of the peninsula. (www.sneakpeek-studiotour.com).

Art Studios
A number of local artists exhibit from studios in their homes, rather than from public galleries; visits are by appointment only - you must call ahead!
Burton, Bill, 15509 Smith's Beach, Eastville (678-7708)
  Woodcarvings; butterflies and moths a specialty
Carpenter, William, 11 Parker Street, Onancock (787-7261)
  Watercolor portraits
Clarke, Mary Ann, 304 Fig Street, Cape Charles (331-2409)
  Watercolors, "shorescapes," Gyotaku (fish printing)
Creger, Larry, 37316 Tide Court, Greenbackville (824-0554)
  Handcarved decoys and shorebirds
Crockett, Billy, 21417 Hopkins Road, Parksley (665-4806)
  Handcarved decoys and shorebirds

Doughty, Albert "Buck," 15336 Seaside Road, Cape Charles (678-7540)
Welded metal creations
Drew, Don & Donna, 19202 Birch Tree Lane, Melfa (787-3797)
Three-dimensional works of whimsy in copper, brass, wrought iron
Hoover, Bruce & Janet, 17252 Big Road, Bloxom (665-4597)
Vessels from turned wood
Layton, D. Brooke, 23586 Holly Cove Road, Onancock (787-7282)
Watercolors of the East Coast from Canada to Florida
Lentz, Robert, 13477 Evans Farm Road, Pungoteague (492-4295)
Turned vessels and wood sculpture; appointment only
Lewis, Robbie, 100 Market Street, Onancock (787-7588)
Decoys carved in the traditional manner
Mama Girl, 13554 Shellbridge Road, Painter (442-3255)
Paper sculptures and paintings by local folk artist Mary "Mama Girl" Onley
Meyers, Carol, 4443 Shady Lane, Chincoteague (336-1546)
Wheel-thrown and handcrafted whimsical teapots and cookie jars
Pierson, Carole Boggemann, 29155 Harmony Road, Townsend (678-3340)
Plein-air and studio paintings in oils
Platt, Ken, 30389 Bobtown Road, Pungoteague (442-7155)
Functional and ornamental glassware
Spector, Maurice, 29279 Harborton Road, Pungoteague (442-5595)
Sculpture in wood and stone, drawings
Taylor, Rose, 6326 Occohannock Neck Road, Exmore (442-9672)
Painting and photography, pet portraits a specialty
Zidovec, Vesna, 30 Kerr Street, Onancock (787-7797)
Ceramics, masks, framed tiles, mirrors

Automobile Repair
Complete Car Center, Route 13, Nelsonia (665-4013)
Dave's Quality Service Center, 3213 Main Street, Exmore (442-4952)
Straight Line Automotive Service, 401 Mason Ave., Cape Charles (331-1303)
Woody's Auto Service, 161 Market Street, Onancock (787-8630)
   This by no means exhausts the list of reputable shops on Virginia's Eastern Shore. In addition to these and other service stations and repair shops there is a Ford/Lincoln/Mercury dealership, with service department, in Keller (787-1209). At Pocomoke City, Maryland, seven miles above the state line, there are dealerships servicing GM, Chrysler/Plymouth/Dodge, Ford/Lincoln/Mercury, Subaru, and Jeep/Eagle.

Bookstores
Book Bin, 25304 Lankford Highway, Onley (787-7866)
15,000 titles, including complete collection of Eastern Shore books; special orders, stationery, fine toys; coffee bar
Book Hounds, 4031 Main Street, Chincoteague (336-5850)
Used and antiquarian books; signed books and collectibles
Kite Koop Discount Book Store, 4019 Main Street, Chincoteague (336-3300)
Hardbacks, paperbacks, local books
Sundial Books, 4065 Main Street, Chincoteague (336-5825)
New, used, antiquarian books, music, local art, gifts, special orders, coffee
Vineyard Bookstore, 6 North Street, Onancock (301-0322)
Religious books, gifts and supplies

Fishing: Small Boat Rental, Supplies, Bait & Tackle
Bailey's Bait & Tackle, 327 Mason Avenue, Cape Charles (331-1982)
Barnacle Bill's, 3691 Main Street, Chincoteague (336-5920)
Cape Charles Marine, Route 13 at #641, Cape Charles (331-2414)

Capt. Bob's Marina, 2477 Main Street, Chincoteague (336-6654)
Capt. Steve's Bait & Tackle, 6527 Maddox Blvd., Chincoteague (336-0569)
Captain Zed's Tackle Shop, 17 Atlantic Avenue, Wachapreague (789-3222)
Chris' Bait & Tackle, 28316 Lankford Highway, Townsend (331-3632)
Clammee Hands, 2118 Harbor Drive, Greenbackville (824-0771)
Don's Tackle Shop, 20247 Wachapreague Road, Keller (787-7451)
East Side Rentals, 7462 East Side Drive, Chincoteague (336-5555)
Eastern Shore Outfitters, 4306 Main Street, Exmore (442-4009)
Snug Harbor Marina, 7536 East Side Drive, Chincoteague (336-6176)

Fishing: Charter Boats

Cape Charles
360 Degree Charters, Captain Tom (410-6420
Beverly Elizabeth, Capt. Dale Ballard (678-7717)
Cape Charles Fishing Center (442-7376)
Carolyn D II Charters (410-742-7762)
Charter Eggs to Sea (678-7385)
Lt. Bay Charters (678-3718)
Teachers Pet Charters (410-326-6254)
Top Dog Charters, Capt. Neil Lessard (647-3017)
Cherrystone
Miss Jennifer, Capt. Ray Cardone (678-5257)
Chincoteague
Bay Breeze, Capt. Doug Cunningham (336-5271)
Bucktail, Capt. Dave Seaman (336-1534)
Chincoteague Cruises, Capt. Charlie Birch (336-5731)
Chincoteague View, Curtis Merritt Harbor #52 (336-6861)
Driftaway Charters, Capt. Brett (336-6959)
Fish Tales, Capt. Pete Wallace (336-3474)
Fishawn Charters, Curtis Merritt Harbor #71 (336-1953)
Island Queen Inland Charters, Curtis Merritt Harbor #16 (336-3528)
Islander Charters, Capt. Mac McDowell (336-5191)
Light Tackle Charters, Capt. Walt (410-957-1664)
Little Duck, Capt. Jimm Whealton (336-3254)
Miz Liz Charters, Capt. Joe Yontz (894-5086)
Proud Mary, Capt. George Garner (336-5931)
Reel Time, Capt. Fred Gilman (336-2236)
Reelriot Charters, Capt. Bill Lertora (888-389-5603)
Shammy, Capt. Glenn Clawson (703-407-1882)
Tools of the Trade, Capt. Kevin Merritt (336-3565)
Two Aces, Capt. John Henry (336-3565)
West Wind Charters, Capt. Jordan West (894-2834)
White Lightning, Capt. Frank Murphy (703-407-2700)
Wonderful 1, Capt. Wayne Lewis (336-6835)
Greenbackville
Topless, Capt. Perry Romig (824-5580)
Onancock
James Gang, Capt. B. W. James (787-1226)
Oyster
Two Keys, Capt. Charles Donnell (609-259-1461)
Quinby
Ron-Jo, Capt. Royce Parks (442-9324)
Wachapreague
Almost Persuaded, Capt. Lindsay Paul (787-4598)
American Maid, Capt. Bill Gingell (787-2731)
Bonnie Sue, Capt. Bob Turner (787-2467)

Canyon Lady, Capt. Jimmy Wallace (787-3272)
Class Act, Capt. Bobby Marshall (789-3357)
Foxy Lady, Capt. Nat Atkinson (787-7978)
Hobo, Capt. Ray Parker (787-1040)
Lucky Dawg, Capt. Mike Parker (787-3786)
Lyn B, Capt. Bill Bowen (787-1074)
Marlin Magic, Capt Bill Tyson (787-1908)
Miyot, Capt. Dave marsh (710-8289)
Nita Dream, Capt. Frank Large (540-297-2307)
Scorpio, Capt. Sam Parker (787-3070)
    Willis Wharf
Safari, Capt. Monty Webb (442-7915)

Golf
Bay Creek Resort & Club, 1 Clubhouse Way, Cape Charles (331-8620)
Captain's Cove Golf & Yacht Club, 5370 Captain's Corridor, Greenbackville (824-5478)

Hunting Guides
Andy's Guide Service, Chincoteague (336-1253)
Assawoman Outfitters, Mappsville (824-5438)
Chincoteague Hunting & Fishing Center, 6751 Maddox Blvd, Chincoteague (1-888-231-4868)
Chincoteague Waterfowl Hunting, 7361 Whealton Court, Chincoteague (336-3254) .
Eastern Shore Safaris, 6276 Sturgis House Drive, Jamesville (442-7684)
Fishmaker Angling Info Services, 26267 Shoreman Dr., Bloxom (665-5163)
Fisherman's Lodge, 20210 Harbor Point Road, Quinby (442-7109)
Holden Creek Gun Club, Sanford (824-9666)
Hooks & Feathers, 7271 Jones Lane, Chincoteague (336-6812)
Little Duck Charters, Curtis Merritt Harbor #80, Chincoteague (336-3254)
Marshall, Teddy, Tangier (891-2576)
Pruitt, Jeff, Tangier (891-2561)
Pruitt, Ken, Tangier (891-2561)
Thomas, Donald, Tangier (891-2251)
Wachapreague Motel, 17 Atlantic Avenue, Wachapreague (787-2105)

Kayaking
Assateague Explorer, 6352 Burton Avenue, Chincoteague (336-5956)
Broadwater Bay Ecotours, 6035 Killmon Point Road, Exmore (442-4363)
    Exploring the Barrier Islands by kayak
Capt. Bob's Marina, 2477 Main Street, Chincoteague (336-6654)
    Kayak rentals and tours
Kiptopeake State Park, Route 13, 3 miles north of Bridge Tunnel (331-2267)
    Kayak rentals
Southeast Expeditions, 32218 Lankford Highway, Cape Charles (331-2680)
    Guided sea kayaking Seaside and Bayside; rentals and instruction; for kayaking on Onancock Creek call 787-2933
Tangier Museum & Interpretive Cultural Center, 16215 Main Ridge, Tangier
    Check in here for use of free Public Kayak Dock behind the museum
Up a Creek With a Paddle, 27369 Phillips Drive, Melfa (693-1200)
    Guided kayak tours, Chincoteague, Seaside, and Bayside
Wachapreague Outfitters, 15 Main Street, Wachapreague (787-2490)
    Kayak rentals

Museums
Barrier Islands Center, 7295 Young Street, Machipongo (678-5550)

Exhibits preserving and celebrating life on the Barrier Islands of the
Eastern Shore, located in the handsomely restored Almshouse (1803) of
Northampton County

Beebe Ranch, 3062 Ridge Road, Chincoteague (336-6520)
A little museum of Misty of Chincoteague in the house and stables of the
Beebe family; Misty herself preserved here; admission charged

Cape Charles Museum, 814 Randolph Avenue, Cape Charles (331-1008)
Housed in an electric generating plant of 1947; frequently changing
exhibits about Cape Charles and surrounding area

Eastern Shore Railway Museum, 18468 Dunn Avenue, Parksley (665-7245)
Restored railroad station, railroad cars, memorabilia and relics. Admission
by donation.

Eastern Shore of Virginia National Wildlife Refuge Visitor Center, Route
13 at the Bridge-Tunnel, Kiptopeake (331-2760)
Antique and working decoys, audio-visuals, natural history displays

Eastville Historic District, Eastville (678-5126)
Old courthouse, clerk's office and debtor's prison maintained by
Association for the Preservation of Virginia Antiquities. For free admission
inquire at Clerk's Office

Exmore Railroad Museum, Bank & Front Streets, Exmore (442-4546)
Railroad exhibits and memorabilia, including a caboose (1949). Open
Saturdays and Sundays. Admission by donation

Ker Place, 69 Market Street, Onancock (787-8012)
Elegant, restored mansion (1799) housing museum of the Eastern Shore
Historical Society. 10:00-4:00 except Sundays, Mondays, and holidays;
closed January and February. Admission charged

Locustville Academy, 28055 Drummondtown Road, Locustville (787-2460)
Ante-bellum country schoolhouse maintained as a local museum. Open by
chance, or call ahead. Free

Oyster & Maritime Museum, 7125 Maddox Blvd., Chincoteague (336-6117)
History of Chincoteague and its surroundings. Weekends only Labor Day
thru Memorial Day. No admission charged

Refuge Waterfowl Museum, 7059 Maddox Blvd., Chincoteague (336-5800)
Decoys, boats, wood-carving exhibits, etc. Daily 10:00-5:00 in season.
Admission charged

Tangier Museum, 16215 Main Ridge Road, Tangier (891-1660)
An old store houses the islands new museum and interpretative Cultural
Center, "a homey collection of all things Tangier" and a must for visitors
to the island; no admission charged

Wallop's Flight Facility Visitor Center, Route 175, Wallops Island (824-2298)
History of manned space era includes displays, films, demonstrations, and
a piece of moon rock. Open 10:00-4:00 Thursday thru Monday, every day
July 4th thru Labor Day; closed December-February. Free

Recreation

Bike Depot, 7058 Maddox Boulevard, Chincoteague (336-5511)
Bike Rentals, 44 King Street, Onancock (787-8818)
Birdie's Bayside Mini-Golf, 111 Mason Avenue, Cape Charles (331-3099)
Boulevard Beach Surf & Skate, 6290 Maddox Blvd., Chincoteague (336-3271)
Bullfeathers Videorama, Four Corner Plaza, Onley (787-1887)
Chincoteague Watersports, 6176 Landmark Plaza, Chincoteague (336-1754)
Chincoteague Pony Center, 6417 Carriage Lane, Chincoteague (336-6313)
Pony shows, pony rides and lessons
Corner Videos, 6491 Lankford Highway, T's Corner (824-5935)
Dream Roller Rink, 32438 Chincoteague Road, Wattsville (824-4515)
Eastern Shore Family YMCA, 26164 Lankford Highway, Onley (787-5601)

Eagle's Nest Lounge & Billiards, 18497 Dunne Avenue, Parksley (665-7822)
Eastern Shore Hang Gliding, 9114 Bayford Road, Weirwood (442-7519)
Jus' Bikes, 6527 Maddox Boulevard, Chincoteague (336-6700)
Libertino Bowling Lanes, 3649 Willow Street, Chincoteague (336-1575)
Midtown Bike Store, 6332 Maddox Boulevard, Chincoteague (336-2700)
Movie Gallery, 22491 Lankford Highway, Cape Charles (331-4742)
Movie Gallery, 25116 Lankford Highway, Onley (302-1222)
Queen Hive Farm, Atlantic Road, Assawoman (854-1320)
   Trail riding and riding lessons
Refuge Golf & Bumper Boats, 6528 Maddox Boulevard, Chincoteague (335-5420)
Steve's Videos, 6691 Maddox Boulevard Road, Chincoteague (336-1958)
Surfside Golf, 6557 Maddox Boulevard, Chincoteague (336-4543)

Seafood (Retail Dealers)

Alisa's Market, 7304 Lankford Highway, Oak Hall (824-6482)
Charles F. Charnock & Son, Tangier (891-2525)
Chincoteague Shellfish Farms, 7564 East Side Rd., Chincoteague (336-1985)
Creek Point Seafood, 19353 Saxis Road, Saxis (824-3644)
Dockside Seafood, 19565 Quinby Bridge Road, Quinby (442-7904)
Don's Seafood Market, 4113 Main Street, Chincoteague (336-5715)
East Side Seafood Market, East Side Road, Chincoteague (336-1843)
Edwards' Seafood, 26177 Lankford Highway, Onley (787-2224)
Fish House, 9 King Street, Onancock (787-3700)
Gary Howard Seafood, 5315 Deep Hole Road, Chincoteague (336-5178)
Great Machipongo Clam Shack, 6468 Lankford Hwy., Nassawadox (442-3800)
H. M. Terry Inc., 5039 Willis Wharf Road, Exmore (442-6251)
His & Hers Seafood, 6382 Maddox Boulevard, Chincoteague (336-1151)
John H. West Seafood Inc., 4150 Townsend Drive, Townsend (331-3545)
Martin's Crab House, 19377 Saxis Road, Saxis (824-4796)
Metompkin Seafood & Produce, Route 13, Mappsville (824-0503)
Nandua Seafood Co., 30460 Back Creek Road, Hacks Neck (442-6884)
Ricky's Seafood, 7432 Beebe Road, Chincoteague (336-6867)
Robin Hood Bay Seafood, 20819 Saxis Road, Saxis (824-4600)
Seafood Lobsters, 32120 Nock's Landing Road, Atlantic (854-1955)
Susan's Seafood, Route 13, New Church (824-5545)
Tom's Cove Aquafarms, 7466 Lighthouse Lane, Chincoteague (336-1945)
Williams Seafood, 9262 Starling Creek Road, Saxis (824-5846)

Shopping

Bad Girlz Collective, 233 Mason Avenue, Cape Charles (331-2293)
   Funky, "artsy-fartsy" gifts, antiques
Best Nest Interiors, 115 Mason Avenue, Cape Charles (331-4437)
   Upscale furnishings and accessories on a coastal theme
Blue Crab Bay Co., 29368 Atlantic Drive, Melfa (787-7799)
   Home of this well-known local brand; seafoods, seasonings, gifts, parcels
Blue Crab Gallery, 4076 Main Street, Chincoteague (336-5507)
   Unique and unusual gifts
Bonnie's Bounty, 6213 lankford Highway, T's Corner (824-4211)
   Virginia hams, decoys, souvenirs, "Cat's Meow"
Brant, 6572 Maddox Boulevard, Chincoteague (336-5531)
   Gifts, Christmas shop
Brush Stroke, 6448B Maddox Boulevard, Chincoteague (336-6750)
   Paint-your-own-pottery studio
C. D. Marsh Jewelers, 45 Market Street, Onancock (787-3333)
   Chesapeake Bay bracelets, gifts

Cape Charles Christmas, 16 Strawberry Street, Cape Charles (331-2956)
Ornaments, jewelry, decor — not just for Christmas
Cape Charles Emporium, 316 Mason Avenue, Cape Charles (331-1880)
Art and photography, jewelry, gifts, golf cart rentals
Chincoteague Bear Factory, 6237 Maddox Blvd., Chincoteague (336-5653)
Make, buy, clothe your own stuffed animal
Clay Werks Ltd., 4253 Lankford Highway, Exmore (442-0567)
Imported and domestic tiles, mosaics
Complete Angler, 1 Marina Village Circle, Cape Charles (331-8640)
Fishing and boating equipment, "meeting the angler's needs"
Crab Shack, 16240 Main Ridge Road, Tangier
Gifts, books, souvenirs, artifacts of Tangier
Dawn, 63 Market Street, Onancock (7899-7700)
"A unique shop for women and home"
Dora's Sea Glass, 109 Mason Avenue, Cape Charles (331-3180)
Jewelry and decor items made from sea glass; local books
Eastern Shore Pottery, Route 13, Capeville (331-4341)
Planters, pots, lawn figures, baskets, etc.
Enchanted Island Boutique, 6219 Maddox Blvd., Chincoteague (336-6443)
"A casual chic beach boutique;" paintings by Nancy Hogan Armour
Flying Fish Gallery, 4086 Main Street, Chincoteague (336-1731)
Unique handmade items by artisans from all over the country
GardenArt, 44 King Street, Onancock (787-8818)
Flowers, shrubs, pots, statuary, accents and decor for inside and outside
Great Space Etc., 61 Market Street, Onancock (789-7744)
Home accessories, antiques, interior design services
Guinevere's Enchanted Treasures, 4044 Main St., Chincoteague (336-5477)
Original art and accessories
Gull Hummock Gourmet Market, 213 Mason Ave., Cape Charles (331-1500)
Gourmet foods, wine, cheese, gifts, paintings, mosaics
Gull Watch Basketry, 3632 Main Street, Chincoteague (336-3754)
Distinctive handwoven and traditional baskets
H & H Pharmacy, 6300 Maddox Boulevard, Chincoteague (336-3115)
Full pharmacy plus local gifts and books
Hard Times Thrift Shoppe, 125 Market Street, Onancock (709-9150)
Items by "starving artists" and other neat stuff, some antiques
Herb Daisy's Decoys, 3498 Ridge Road, Chincoteague (336-6806)
Decoys by local carver Herb Daisy, souvenirs
Herbal Instincts, 141 Market Street, Onancock (787-7071)
Organic and natural foods, coffees and teas, cheeses
Hidden Treasures Craft Gallery, 18463 County Road, Parksley (665-1128)
Unique handmade jewelry, homemade soaps, lotions, fabrics, art, prints
Hospice Thrift Stores, 165 Market Street, Onancock (789-3302) and
3306 Lankford Highway, Exmore (442-3777)
You never know what you'll find!
Hot Stuff, 6273 Cropper Street, Chincoteague (336-3118)
Over 500 different hot sauces and marinades
House of Deals, 20 Market Street, Onancock (787-8213)
Hardware and much more; "you name it, we've got it"
Island Butterfly, 4107 Main Street, Chincoteague (336-6990)
"Extraordinary finds" in decor, jewelry, clothing
Island Cottage Collection, 6361 & 6208 Maddox Blvd., Chincoteague (336-5636)
Gifts on a nautical theme
Island Decoys, 6136 Maddox Boulevard, Chincoteague
Decoys and carvings
Island Style, 4809 Main Street, Chincoteague (336-3010)

"Totally out of the ordinary gifts for home and person"
Jaxon's, 18509 Dunne Avenue, Parksley (665-5967)
Old-fashioned variety store, a local favorite
Jim's Gift Shop, 16165 Main Ridge Road, Tangier (891-2580)
Gifts, souvenirs
Kite Koop & Bookstore, 4019 Main Street, Chincoteague (336-3399)
Kites, games, toys, souvenirs, and books
Lotts' Arts & Things, 4281 Main Street, Chincoteague (336-5773)
Posters and prints, jewelry, glass, unusual gifts
Marsha Carter Gifts, 6351 Cropper Street, Chincoteague (336-3404)
Distinctive handcrafted gifts
New Ravenna, 3268 Broad Street, Exmore (442-3379)
Factory outlet for local creators of fine mosaics and tiles
North Street Market, 5 North Street, Onancock (787-8805)
Gourmet food and kitchen shop, wine and cheese, espresso bar, wine bar
Payne's Sea Treasures, 3376 Ridge Road, Chincoteague
Shells, driftwood, "gifts from the sea"
Pony Tales, 7011 Maddox Boulevard, Chincoteague (336-6688)
Salt-water taffy, candy, souvenirs, books
Psychotronic, 4102 Main Street, Chincoteague (336-0048)
Hollywood collectibles, posters, LPs
Purple Pony Shirt Company, 4116 Main Street, Chincoteague (336-6336)
Screen-printed and embroidered Tees, sweats, bags, flags
Quail Cove Farms, Machipongo Lane, Machipongo (678-5622)
Outlet for locally grown natural and organic foods
Rayfield's Pharmacy, 2 Fig Street, Cape Charles (331-1212) and
9502 Hospital Avenue, Nassawadox (442-6159)
Full pharmacy plus local gifts, books, artworks
Rookery at the Refuge, 7058 Maddox Boulevard, Chincoteague (336-5511)
Gifts of distinction
Saffron, 321 Mason Avenue, Cape Charles (331-1919)
Stationery, fine linens, perfumes, potpourri, consignment boutique
St. Francis Thrift Shop, 18477 Dunne Avenue, Parksley
You never know what you'll find!
Sandy's Place, 16233 Main Ridge Road, Tangier (891-2367)
Gifts, souvenirs, books
Seaside Garden Art Emporium, 4098 Main Street, Chincoteague
Antiques and collectibles
Thomas Gardens, Route 13, T's Corner (824-3610)
Flowers, plants, rare plants
Threadgoodes, 4211 Main Street, Chincoteague (336-6858)
Unique decor items, gourmet foods, gifts, accessories
Tracinda's Country Treasures, 28040 Locustville Road, Locustville (787-4611)
Country crafts and furniture, jewelry
Veranda / Purple Pelican, 3 Marina Village Circle, Cape Charles (331-8680)
Original art works, whimsical and unique gifts, clothing
Virginia Hospitality Shop, 4098 Main Street, Chincoteague (336-3606)
Gifts and special products with a Virginia theme
Visions of Color, 6207 Maddox Boulevard, Chincoteague
Paintings, hand-crafted jewelry, gifts
Walter & Walton's Emporium, 23 Market Street, Onancock (787-1995)
Upscale accessories and accents for the home; imported furniture
Wanda's Gift Shop, 16139 Main Ridge Road, Tangier (891-2230)
Souvenirs, gifts, T-shirts
Weirwood Station, 9335 Red Bank Road, Weirwood (442-9007)
Quilts, fabrics, yarns, gifts, local pottery, patterns

What's Your Fancy, 24266 Bennett Street, Parksley (665-5127)
Gourmet kitchen shop, Yankee candles, gifts
White's Copperworks, 6373 Maddox Boulevard, Chincoteague (336-1448)
Folk art
Wine, Cheese, & More, 4103 Main Street, Chincoteague (336-2610)
Imported and domestic wines and cheeses, coffee, tea, gift baskets

For general shopping (food, medicines, clothes, etc.) there are five main areas on the Eastern Shore of Virginia: Cape Charles/Cheriton, Exmore, Onley, Parksley, and Chincoteague. This list focuses on the specialty shops more likely to be enjoyed by the traveler.

Theatres, Performing Arts
Movies
Idle Hour, 36008 Belle Haven Road, Belle Haven (442-9951)
Island Roxy, 4074 Main Street, Chincoteague (336-6301)
Roseland, 48 Market Street, Onancock (787-2010)
Live Theatre, Music, Performing Arts
Arts Enter Palace Theatre, 305 Mason Avenue, Cape Charles (331-2787)
Cape Charles' largest movie house (1941) is now used for drama, ballet, live performances by professionals and locals, community performances
Eastern Shore's Own Art Center, 15293 King Street, Belle Haven (442-3226)
Stages two dramatic productions each year; ballet, music, drama classes and performances
North Street Playhouse, 34 Market Street, Onancock (787-2358)
Local not-for-profit theatre group (1966) stages plays, readings, and concerts year-round in 99-seat theatre originally built as a movie house in 1914)

Classical music and dance are brought to the peninsula by the Arts Council of the Eastern Shore (A.C.E.S.); watch for notices of upcoming events, or call 442-4614.

The Madrigal Singers present two concerts each year, for Christmas on the first weekend in December, for spring on the first weekend in April; tickets are usually sold out; watch for notices, or call The Book Bin at 787-7866.

Tours, Cruises, Sailing, Eco-Tourism
Assateague Explorer, 6352 Burton Avenue, Chincoteague (336-5956)
Pony watching, wildlife cruises
Broadwater Bay Ecotours, 6035 Killmon Point Road, Exmore (442-4363)
Tours of the Barrier Islands by vessel or kayak; sunset wine and cheese cruises; year-round
Capt. Barry's Back Bay Cruises, 8157 Sea Gull Dr., Chincoteague (336-6508)
Tours and lore aboard a pontoon boat seating 6
Capt. Hook Charters, 2477 Main Street, Chincoteague (990-1217)
Cruising and fishing aboard a 26-foot pontoon boat
Capt. Clark's Seaside Tours, 5335 Poplar Grove Ln, Cape Charles (331-4016)
Customized tours of the Barrier Islands and Seaside from pontoon boat
Capt. Dan's Island Tours, 4175 Main Street, Chincoteague (894-0103)
Tours of Chincoteague Island waters
Chincoteague Cruises, Capt Charlie Birch, Chincoteague (336-5731)
Ponies, dolphins, birds, wildlife nature tours
Chincoteague Wildlife Refuge Visitors Center, Assateague Island (336-3696)
Land and boat tours of Chincoteague National Wildlife Refuge
Day Sail Charters, 3801 Main Street, Chincoteague (336-5271)

Sailing Chincoteague and Assateague aboard the 22-ft sloop Bay Breeze
Eastern Shore Adventures, Eyrehall Drive, Cape Charles (615-2598)
Custom eco-tours of the Barrier Islands, depart Oyster and Willis Wharf
Eastern Shore Canoe & Kayak, 15256 Hinman Street, Bloxom (665-5606)
Guided tours, rentals, anywhere on the Eastern Shore of Virginia
Eastern Shore of Virginia National Wildlife Refuge, Kiptopeake (331-2760)
Field trips, float trips, canoeing with refuge interpreters
Full Moon, Capt. Russell Fish, Chincoteague (336-6451)
Scenic and nature cruises
Island Queen Inland Charters, 7535 Doe Bay Lane, Chincoteague (336-3528)
Nature and sunset cruises aboard a 24-foot pontoon boat
Linda J Charters, Curtis Merritt Harbor #38, Chincoteague (336-6214)
Nature and sunset cruises aboard the 24-foot pontoon Linda J
Oyster Bay Outfitters, 6332 Maddox Boulevard, Chincoteague (336-0070)
Kayak tours of Chincoteague and Assateague, rentals
Sail Cape Charles, Capt. Dave, Cape Charles (973-479-3346)
Sailing on the 29-foot sloop StewardShip
Schooner Serenity, Bay Creek Marina, Cape Charles (710-1233)
Daily sunset tours of the Chesapeake Bay aboard a sailing vessel
Seaside Tours, 5335 Poplar Grove Lane, Cape Charles (331-4016)
SouthEast Expeditions, 32218 Lankford Highway, Cape Charles (331-2660)
Guided sea kayaking Seaside and Bayside, rentals, retail, and instruction
Spider's Explorer, 3801 Main Street, Chincoteague (990-4242)
Pontoon cruises
Tangier-Onancock Ferry, 2 Market Street, Onancock (891-2505)
*Daily boats to Tangier Island, Memorial Day thru October 15; boat departs
from Onancock Wharf. Cruises also available from Crisfield, Md (410-968-
2338) and Reedville, Va. (804-453-2628)*
Tangier Waterman's Tour, Tangier (891-2331; 891-2900)
Island watermen offer tours of Tangier; check also at the Tangier Museum
Tidewater Expeditions, 7729 East Side Drive, Chincoteague (336-3159)
Sunrise and sunset eco-tours by canoe and kayak, rentals

Vineyards, Wineries
Bloxom Vineyard & Winery, 26130 Mason Road, Bloxom (665-5670)
Free wine tasting, fresh baked goods; Wednesdays-Sundays, 1:00-6:00 p.m.
Chatham Vineyards and Winery, 9232 Chatham Rd., Machipongo (678-5588)
Tasting room
Holly Grove Vineyards, 6404 Holly Bluff Drive, Franktown (442-2844)
Tours and tasting; by reservation

The Eastern Shore
of Virginia

(Maryland to Painter)

Assateague Island

Greenbackville

Signpost

Sinnickson

Horntown

Wagram

New Church

CHINCOTEAGUE

Miona

T's Corner

Wattsville

Pitts Wharf

Oak Hall

Bullbegger

Atlantic

Wallops Island

Jenkins Bridge

Temperanceville

Sanford

Grotons

Assawoman

Crisfield

Saxis

Hallwood

Assawoman Island

Mearsville

Nelsonia

Guard Shore

Bloxom

Modest Town

Guilford

PARKSLEY

Metompkin

Hunting Creek

Lee Mont

13

Metompkin Island

Watts Island

Deep Creek

Tasley

ACCOMAC

Chesconessex

Daugherty

TANGIER

ONANCOCK

Onley

Cedar Island

Cashville

Locustville

Melfa

Locust Mount

Bobtown

Harborton

Keller

WACHAPREAGUE

Hacks Neck

Pungoteague

Parramore Island

Painter

Quinby

13

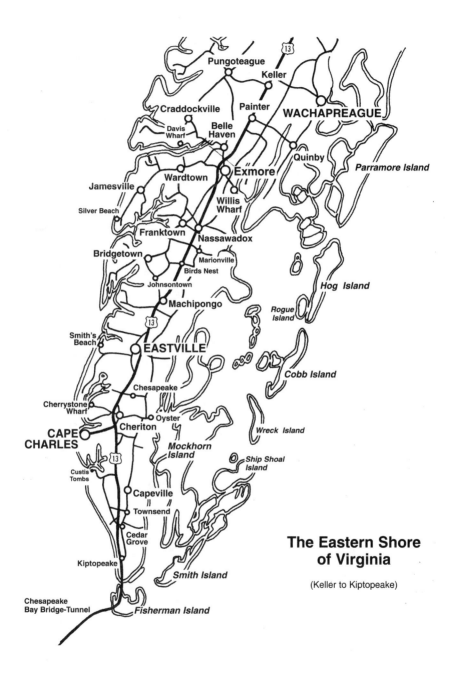

The Eastern Shore
of Virginia

(Keller to Kiptopeake)

INDEX

Accomac, 74-80
antiques, 188
apartments, 187
Arbuckle Place, 133,
   illus. 7
architecture, 5-11
Arlington, 24, 30
art galleries, 189
art studios, 190
Assateague, 53-56
Assateague Lighthouse,
   54, *illus.* 41
Assawoman, 134
Assawoman Island, 73
Atlantic, 135
auto repairs, 191

Bacon Hill, 124
Baily's Neck, 156
Baker, Elijah, 24, 32, 79,
   122
Ballard House, 123
Barrier Islands, 67-73
Barrier Islands Center, 21,
   35, 69, 194
Battle of the Barges, 96,
   99
Battle of the Chesa-
   peake Capes, 28
Bay Creek Railway, 83,
   180
Bay Creek Resort, 83, 87
Bay View B&B, 184
Bay Watch B&B, 140, 184
Bayford, 174
Bayly Memorial Hall, 79
"Bayside," 5
Bayside (village), 153
Bayview Inn, 184
Baywood B&B, 184
Beebe Ranch, 50, 194
Belinda, 147
Belle Haven, 167
Bell's Neck, 124
Bennett, Henry, 105, 109
Big Mill Pond, 140

"birding," 12, 57
Birding Festival, 12, 117
Birdsnest, 21, 35
Birdsnest Tavern, 122
Birth of a Nation, 85
Bizzotto's Caffe, 179
Blackbeard, 69, 72
boat rental, 191
Bobtown, 159
Bogue's Bay, 134
bookstores,191
Boston, 166
Box Tree Creek, 120
Bradford's Neck, 125
Bridgetown, 175
Brownsville, 68, 122
Bullbegger, 143
Burton's Shore, 129
bus service, 14

campgrounds, 188
Canton, 60, 61, 65
Cape Charles, 81-87
Cape Charles Hotel, 84,
   183
Cape Charles House
   B&B, 184
Cape   Charles
Lighthouse,
   27, 30, 69, 119
Cape Charles Museum,
   83, 194
Capeville, 119
Captain's Cove, 139
carnivals, 13, 49, 56, 112
Cashville, 156
Cassatt, Alexander, J.,
   85,106
Cat's Bridge, 124
Cattail Neck, 149
Cedar Gables B&B, 184
Cedar Grove, 119
Cedar Island, 72, 115,
   129
Cedar View Beach, 166
Channel Bass Inn, 48,
   183, 184
Charlotte Hotel, 98, 179,
   184
charter boats, 192
Chatham, 176, 199
Cheriton, 23, 32
Cheriton House B&B, 184
Cherrystone Wharf, 23,
33
Chesapeake, 23, 33
Chesapeake Bay Bridge
   Tunnel, 27-30

Chesapeake   Charm
B&B,
   86, 184
Chesapeake House, 64,
   180, 184
Chesconessex, 153, *illus.*,
   142
Chincoteague, 41-57
Christ Episcopal Church,
   92
Church Neck, 176
Civil War, 17, 24, 33, 40,
   43, 61, 75, 92, 96, 129,
   143, 166
Clam, 150
Cleveland, Grover, 71
Cobb Island, 70, 120
coffee shops, 183
Cokesbury, 103
Cokesbury Chapel, 99
Colonial Manor Inn, 102,
   184
Confederate Monument
   (Eastville), 91
   (Parksley), 105, 108
Corbin Hall, 138
cottages, 187
Craddockville, 166
Creekside B&B, 184
Cropper, John, 96
Crudup, Arthur, 172
cruises, 198
Crystal Beach, 154
Crystal Palace, 173
Cushman's Landing, 119
Custis Tombs, 24, 30

Daugherty, 129
Davis Wharf, 166
Debtor's Prison
   (Accomac), 76
   (Eastville), 91, 193
decoys, 13, 53, 57, 70,
   114
Deep Creek, 153
Deep Hole, 51
delis, 182
Delmarva Peninsula, 1
Dixon, Thomas, 85
Drummond's Mill, 152
Drummond's Mill Farm,
   152, *illus.* 8

East Point, 157
Easter Decoy Festival, 57
Eastern Shore Commun-
   ity College, 19, 38
Eastern Shore Wildlife

Refuge, 117, 194
Eastern Shore Yacht &
    Country Club, 159
Eastville, 88-94. 194
Eastville Inn, 91, 179
Emmanuel Episcopal
    Church, 85, 144
Evans Wharf, 158
Exmore, 19, 36
Eyre Hall, 22, 34

fast food, 182
"Father of Rock and
Roll,"
    172
Ferber, Edna, 163
festivals, 13, 56-57
Finney's Wharf, 156
Fisherman Island, 27, 69
Fisherman's Lodge B&B,
    124, 184
Fisher's Corner, 18, 38
fishing boats, 191
Fitzhugh, William B., 177
Flag Pond, 145
Folly Creek, 79, 129
Folly Creek Landing, 129
Foxcroft, 175
Franklin City, 139
Franktown, 172
Freeschool Marsh, 146

Garden and the Sea Inn,
    16, 40, 184
Garden Week, 6
Gargatha Neck, 73, 131
Garrison B&B, 124, 184
Gladstone House B&B,
    185
golf, 193
Greenbackville, 139
Greenbush, 80
Griffith, D. W., 85
Guard Shore, 149
Guilford, 149

Hacks Neck, 165
Hadlock, 20, 36
Hammocks, The, 146
Happy Union, 171
Harborton, 162
Harborton House B&B,
    163, 185
Harvest Festival, 13
Haven, The, 79
Henry, Marguerite, 44,
45,
    50, 185

Helltown, 17, 39, 133
Hills Farm, 151
Hillsborough, 167
Hog Island, 71, 119, 123
Holly Brook Plantation,
    21, 35, illus. 15
Hopkins & Brothers Store,
    101
Horntown, 137
hospital, 20, 36
Hungars Creek, 177
Hungars Episcopal
    Church, 175, illus., 169
Hungars Glebe, 176
Hunting Creek, 150
hunting guides, 193

ice cream, 183
Indiantown Neck, 120
Inn & Garden B&B, 179,
    185
Inn at Onancock, 103,
    185
inns, 184
Island Manor House, 45,
    185

Jackson, Mrs. Andrew,
    134
Jamesville, 170
Jenkins Bridge, 144
Johnson's Cove, 170
Johnson's Wharf, 151
Johnsontown, 176
Justisville, 150

kayaking, 193
Keller, 19, 37
Kellogg House, 85, 185
Ker Place, 97, 194
Killick Shoals Lighthouse,
    52
King, Martin Luther, 24, 32
Kiptopeake, 117
Kiptopeake State Park,
    26, 30

Lankford, Charles M., 173
"Laughing King," 23, 33,
    91, 94
Lee Mont, 151
Little Hell, 158
Little Hog Island, 123
Little House, 79, illus. 9
Locust Mount, 115
Locustville, 127-129
Locustville Academy,
    128,

194, illus. 116

Machipongo, 21, 35
Makemie, Francis, 78, 99,
    102, 145, 146
Makemie Monument, 78,
    145
Mappsburg, 124
Mappsville, 17, 39
Margaret Academy, 159
Marina Village, 87
Marionville, 122
Marrying Tree, 143
Marsh Market, 148
Marshall, Peter, 23, 32
Mason House, 149
Mearsville, 149
Melfa, 19, 37
Metompkin, 131
Metompkin Island, 73
Mifflin, Warner, 139
migrant labor, 4, 17, 39
Migratory Bird
    Celebration, 12, 57
Miona, 143
Miss Molly's Inn, 45, 185
Misty of Chincoteague,
    44, 46
Modest Town, 133
Montrose House B&B,
    185
Morley's Wharf, 170
motels, 186
Mount Airy, 164
Mount Prospect, 101
Mount Wharton, 134, illus.
    8
movies, 198
Muddy Creek, 149
museums, 194

Nancock Gardens, 103
Nassawadox, 20, 36, 122
Nassawadox Creek, 170,
    172, 174
Nature Conservancy, 68,
    122
Nelsonia, 17, 39
New Church, 16, 39
North Chesconessex, 153
North Street Playhouse,
    88, 198
Nottingham Ridge B&B,
    185

Oak Grove Methodist
    Church, 126, illus. title
    page

Oak Hall, 17, 39
Occohannock Creek, 166, 167, 170
Occohannock Neck, 170
Old Mercantile Building, 79
Old NASA Dock, 134
Old Plantation Lighthouse, 87
Old Town Neck, 94
Onancock, 95-104
Onancock School, 102, 190
Onley, 18, 38
Oyster, 119
Oyster Bay, 52
Oyster Festival, 57
Oyster & Maritime Museum, 53, 194

Painter, 19, 37
Palace Theatre, 84, 198
Parks, Benjamin, 105, 107
Parksley, 105-109
Parramore Island, 72, 113, *illus.* 67
Pavilion, The, 84, *illus.*, 81
Pear Valley, 177, *illus.* 7
performing arts, 198
Pickett's Harbor, 26, 30, 185
Piney Island, 53
Pitt's Wharf, 143
Pony Penning, 51, 56
Poplar Cove, 154
Pretty Byrd Cottage, 165, 185
Pungoteague, 159
Pyle, Howard, 44

Quinby, 124

railroad stations, 19, 20, 21, 26, 30, 35, 94, 107, 140, 194
Railway Museum
(Exmore), 20, 194
(Parksley), 107, 194
recreation, 194
Red Bank, 122
Refuge Waterfowl Museum, 53, 194
rental houses, 187
restaurants, 179
Route 13, 15-40
Rural Felicity, 129

sailing, 198
St. Charles Catholic Church, 85
St. George's Episcopal Church, 160, *illus.*, 155
St. James Episcopal Church, 76
Salt Works, 170
Sandford, Samuel, 146
Sanford, 145
Savage Neck, 93
Savage, Thomas, 92, 93, 94
Savage's Mill, 131
Saxis, 146
Scarburgh Neck, 166
Schooner Bay, 153
seafood dealers, 195
Seafood Festival, 56
Seagate B&B, 86, 185
Sears & Roebuck houses, 85, 86, 101, 168
"Seaside," 5
Seymour House, 76, *illus.* 9
Shad Landing, 145
Shadyside, 21, 35
Shield's Bridge, 167
shopping, 195
Shore Memorial Hospital, 20, 36
Show Boat, 163
Signpost, 138
Silver Beach, 170
Sinnickson, 138
Slutkill Neck, 157
Smith, Capt. John, 59, 69
Smith Island, 17, 69
Smith's Beach, 94
Spinning Wheel B&B, 103, 185
Still Pond, 167
Stran Place, 152
Sunset Inn B&B, 185
Swan's Gut Creek, 138, 139, 140
Sylvan Scene, 176

T's Corner, 16, 40
Tangier Island, 58-66
Tangier Museum, 64, 194
Tasley, 18, 38
Temperanceville, 17, 39
theatres, 198
Thomas, Joshua, 60, 65
Tom's Cove, 55, 56
tours, 198

Townsend, 26, 30, 119
Trower, 126

Upshur, Abel Parker, 176

Vaucluse, 176
vineyards, 199
Virginia Coast Reserve, 68, 69, 122
Virginia Information Center, 16, 40
Virginia Institute of Marine Science, 112

Wachapreague, 110-115
Wagram, 143
Wallops Island, 135-137, 194, *illus.* 130
Wallops Park, 137
War of 1812, 60, 111
Wardtown, 170
Warwick, 124
Washington, Booker T., 166
Waterfowl Open House, 57
Watson House B&B, 45, 185
Wattsville, 137
Webb's Island, 120
Weirwood, 21, 35
Welcome Center, 26, 30
Wessels Root Cellar, 148
Whaley, Zedekiah, 96, 99
Wharton Place, 134
White Rabbit, 153
Willis Wharf, 122, *illus.* 178
Wilson, Woodrow, 62
Windrush Farm B&B, 93, 185
wineries, 199
Wise, Henry A., 18, 38, 75, 76, 156, 159, 173
Wise, John S., 27, 30, 117
Wise Point, 27, 30, 117
Wishart's Point, 135
Wood, Leonora W., 23, 32
Woodbourne, 79
Wynne Tref, 127

Ye Beare & Ye Cubb, 160, 183

Zion Baptist Church, 17, 39, 131